STUKA
SQUADRON

Stukagruppe 77 — the Luftwaffe's 'Fire Brigade'

PETER C. SMITH

Patrick Stephens Limited

First published in 1990

British Library Cataloguing in Publication Data
Smith, Peter C. (Peter Charles), *1940–*
Stuka Squadron: Stukagruppen 77—the Luftwaffe's 'fire brigade'
1. World War 2. Air operations by Germany. Luftwaffe. Junkers stuka aeroplanes
I. Title
940.544943

ISBN 1–85260–286–4

Patrick Stephens Limited, part of Thorsons, a division of the Collins Publishing
Group, has published authoritative, quality books for enthusiasts for more than
twenty years. During that time the company has established a reputation as one of the
world's leading publishers of book on aviation, maritime, military, model-making,
motor cycling, motoring, motor racing, railway and railway modelling subjects.
Readers or authors with suggestions for books they would like to see published are
invited to write to: The Editorial Director, Patricks Stephens Limited, Thorsons
Publishing Group, Wellingborough, Northants, NN8 2RQ.

Patrick Stephens Limited is part of the Thorsons Publishing Group, Wellingborough,
Northamptonshire NN8 2RQ, England.

Typeset by Burns & Smith Ltd., Derby

Printed by Butler & Tanner Limited, Frome, Somerset

1 3 5 7 9 10 8 6 4 2

Contents

Author's Note

This book tells the full story of a German Junkers Ju87 'Stuka' dive bomber Geschwader, or wing, from its formation in peacetime to its final actions in combat towards the end of World War II. Although the work of the whole wing is recorded, its actions are mainly viewed though the eyes of I./St.G.77's officers and men whose work represents that of them all.

I
The Sturzkampfflugzeug Concept

The story of Sturzkampfgruppe 77, from its formation to its demise, is the remarkable tale of a German dive bomber unit from birth to death. Created just a few weeks before the outbreak of World War II in September 1939, this crack Luftwaffe unit spearheaded the German military conquests of almost the whole of Europe. In collaboration with other dive bomber units, St.G.77 showed the world again and again what could be achieved by the remarkable combination of Junkers Ju87 dive bombers and fast-moving Panzer groups against the old ideas and old formations of the other major powers. The *Blitzkrieg*, or lightning war, transformed the situation and nations were conquered in campaigns lasting days or weeks rather than years.

The story of St.G.77 is the history of the first really successful application of close air support. CAS is now a recognised and well-proven part of all the world's fighting forces, but between 1939 and 1942 it was St.G.77 that pioneered both the method and the application in actual combat. Moreover, it carried out CAS with a breathtaking efficiency that took the forces of Germany from the North Cape to the Spanish border and from the Pas-de-Calais to the banks of the Volga.

The remarkable achievements of St.G.77 were based on firm foundations, which were laid down long before the first bombs dropped on Poland on 1 September 1939. The firm rocks on which the Luftwaffe's CAS policy were built can be identified as three major factors: firstly, the suitability of the Junkers Ju87 dive-bomber (forever to be known as the Stuka, the abbreviation of the German word for *all* dive bomber aircraft) for the task assigned to it. Secondly, the fact that the majority of Hitler's new Luftwaffe leaders had Army backgrounds and were therefore both keen and eager to help the land forces rather than remain aloof from them. Thirdly, the conviction and total belief in the application of dive bombers in close support of tanks by one such outstanding Luftwaffe leader, Günter Schwartzkopff. Let us examine each factor in turn.

The concept of the *Sturzkampfflugzeug* goes back much further than the establishment of the Lufwaffe in the mid-1930's. The oft-repeated claims that the introduction of the dive bomber into the German air force was solely due to Generaloberst Ernst Udet, Director of its Technical Department and his influence by the American 'Helldivers', do not bear close examination. Certainly this was *one* factor, but it was far from the only, or even the most decisive one. Dive bombers and dive bombing had been part-and-parcel of German military application experiments long before that event. Nor did dive bombing originate with the Junkers K-47 experiments in the 1920s; nor indeed with the United States Marine Corps applications in Nicaragua in 1919 or Haiti 1927.

It is an established fact (if one that is usually ignored) that the invention, and also the first combat usage, of dive bombing, (the delivery of bombs on enemy targets in a vertical, or near-vertical, dive) was by the British Royal Flying Corps in 1917. Second Lieutenant Harry Brown of No.84 Squadron made the first true dive bombing attack on the Western Front, when he sank a German ammunition barge by this method. Post-war exhaustive trials, painstakingly documented, took place in 1918 by the fledgeling Royal Air Force at their proving ground of Orfordness, Suffolk, using Sopwith Camel and SE5a aircraft.

After this the RAF abandoned dive bombing, both as a method of attack itself and also as part of the general rejection of the role of close support for the aeroplane, which took place when Lord Trenchard led it up the blind ally of 'victory by air power alone' and they embraced strategic bomber concept. Dedicated to the myopic vision of four-engined bombers laying waste enemy cities unaided by such impediments as armies or navies, any hint that the RAF might assist the troops on the ground by precision dive bombing attacks on tactical objectives was scorned as smacking of 'subservience'. Limited British experiments took place in the late 1920's and spasmodically up to 1939, but there was wholesale vested opposition to any adaptation of the dive bomber by the RAF leaders.

A similar tale was evident in the air forces of France, Italy and the United States Army Air Corps. Although the Royal Navy sought dive bombers the RAF blocked and hindered their development at every turn. The United States Navy and Marine Corps alone of the victorious powers embraced and adopted dive bombing, later to be followed by the Japanese. In Europe, Germany, banned from having any military aircraft of her own under the terms of the Versailles Treaty's *Begriffsbestimmungen* clauses of 1922, conducted clandestine experiments in Sweden and in the Soviet Union, which gradually led them to realise just how potent a weapon dive bombing could be.

The first stirrings of this discovery had as its origins in a design for a monoplane fighter aircraft by Dipl-Ings Karl Plauth and Hermann Pohlmann, two of the Junkers aircraft firm's team of designers. Plauth himself was killed in an accident on 1 November 1927, but his brain-child continued to be developed as a 'training and sports aircraft', the A-48. Its real purpose was as a two-seater fighter aircraft with the speed and agility of a single-seater interceptor, and this was secretly to be developed as the K-47. As such, the A-48 was first flown by test pilot Wilhelm Zimmermann on 20 October 1928 at Dessau. Flying trials continued for the rest of that year without any registration marks.

For its day the K-47 was an advanced machine. It was built with an oval fuselage section form to give strength and used duraluminium to save weight. It was fitted with a Bristol Jupiter VII engine, which gave a maximum speed of 180 mph at just under 10,000 feet. To evade the restrictions of the Treaty, in January 1925 Junkers set up a subsidiary company in Sweden, located at Limhamn, near Malmo. It was here that the prototype K-47 was assembled and first flown in January 1929, with Swedish markings, as the S-80. As a fighter the K-47 was limited, although some were sold to China, but in 1930 a new and significant role began to be planned for this machine: dive bombing.

The strength and ruggedness of the K-47, along with its ease of handling, made it an ideal vehicle for such trials, which were initiated following enquiries from Japan. Junkers designer Ernst Zindel oversaw the fitting of primitive bomb racks for ten 110 lb and four 55 lb bombs, an experimental two-ring eye sight for vertical bombing (the much earlier British experiments had utilised the Aldis telescopic sight), a direction gyro, altimeter and recording camera, air brakes and automatic recovery devices, all to be associated with dive bombing aircraft of the late 1930's.

The first of 26 actual dive bombing runs were conducted by test pilot Willi Neuenhofen in 1933. They continued throughout the following year as a triple participation operation between Junkerswerke, which provided the K-47's, the Flygvapnet (the Swedish air arm), which provided equipment and facilities, and the Finnish air force and manufacturers, which provided the actual bombs and the modified bomb racks. The trials were carried out at the Bofors works site and dummy bombs were also dropped at sea near Limhamn.

Dives were conducted in excess of 70 degrees even then, with airspeed building up to about 300 mph. Both Neuenhofen and the K-47 stood up to such stresses well; both the bomb-release gear and the primitive sight gave excellent results. Dives were made from about 11,500 feet down to 6,500 for actual bomb release. The trials were pronounced a success, and further modification was carried out on the on-board equipment. Underwing dive brakes were added in Germany, a telescopic sight was fitted as was an inclination meter to determine the exact diving angle. A barograph, an aerial log and a thermometer were emplaced and a BMW Hornett engine was fitted. Then a second series of tests was held at Rinkaby, Sweden, between August and September 1933.

In this series of 12 test bombings, dives were made at 45 degrees to more than 70 degrees from a height of around 6,500 feet with bomb release at 2,625 feet and 19 bombs, from 28 lb up to 111 lb, were dropped against a simulated warship target some 722 ft long by 98 ft wide. Average distance from centre was 98 ft, which gave a 60 per cent hit rate, far in excess of anything horizontal bombing was achieving, or would achieve for more than a decade.

A third series of experiments took place in secret at a German location, but meanwhile great interest had been shown by the other participating powers. Accuracy allowing for comparatively small forces of aircraft to achieve a decisive number of strikes on important targets was an attractive cost-effective method, as ideal for small powers like Sweden with limited resources as it was for Germany trying to build up a striking force quickly now that Adolf Hitler had come to power.

With much German interest, the Swedes had set up a special experimental dive bombing flight under Captain Bjorn Bjuggren at Froson equipped with three Hawker Hart S-7 biplanes. The Harts were fitted with dive bombing sights set at the fixed diving angles of 60, 70 and 80 degrees. The trials were conducted in August and September 1934 and featured the effect of wind on dive bombing accuracy, the testing of an automatic dive bombing sight. This was built by the German firm Askania and connected to a gyro and altimeter to give a signal when the optimum release height was reached in the dive, and the use of bombs boosted to their targets by rockets after launch to achieve greater armour penetration. Such weapons were also to be later employed against Allied warships by the Germans in World War II, but it was accuracy of the dive bombing that made the most immediate impact.

In all, 50 bombs were dropped by Neuenhofen and the Swedish pilot Captain Svensen, with an average error of 23 ft. So accurate was the new bomb sight that, with modifications and improvements, it was copied by the Swedish company Aga-Baltic, who at one time were trying to sell it to Britain, much to the concern of Askania. They need not have worried: the British had *no* interest in dive bombing sights however accurate!

The evaluation of these four tests coincided with the arrival on the scene of Junkers Ju87 V-1, which first flew on 1 September 1935, with four more prototypes following in 1936. That the work with the K-47 in Sweden had given Junkers the edge in dive bomber development quickly became apparent.

It will be remembered that there had been a third dive bomber trial outside Sweden. This had been conducted by the Reichswehr as at that time the existence of the Luftwaffe had not been revealed. The trials were conducted at the test centre at Lipezk. Here it was not so much the techniques of dive-bombing that concerned the Army, as the practical aspects of the vertical diving aircraft as a close support tactical weapon to aid the ground troops. The experts were in full agreement that such CAS was valueless unless accurately delivered. It was equally obvious to all that such precision bombing could only be attained from an aircraft which aimed itself and its bomb load directly at the target in a steep dive.

The head of the development section of the supply department of the Reichswehr was a certain Major Dr Ing Freiherr von Richthofen. Later to achieve everlasting fame as the man who used the Stuka most effectively in World War II, at this stage of proceedings he was far from an eager convert. He gave vent to many misgivings with regard to the dive bomber. The development of anti-aircraft gunnery in Germany was far in advance of that of other nations and many felt that present the gunners with a nil-deflection shoot by attacking aircraft diving low into gun muzzles was almost suicidal.

Despite these feelings, tenders were put out to selected aircraft builders to come up with designs to meet a dive bomber development project. This was the *Sofort-Programm* produced by the C-Amt of the Luftfahrtkommissariat. These tenders resulted in the two original and specialised German dive bomber design prototypes, the Henschel Hs123 and the Fieseler Fi98. The establishment of the first German dive bomber group had been initiated as early as October 1933 and the fighter unit Jagdgeschwader 132 was thereupon assigned the additional job of providing dive bomber training in addition to its normal duties. Following its lead, two more fighter units had followed suit by 1 April 1934. They utilised the standard German fighter aircraft of the period, Arado Ar65 and Heinkel He51 biplanes. These were to serve as dive bombing trainers until newer types under development had come to full fruition. But work was already well in hand to replace these with the first specially built dive bomber aircraft, the Heinkel He50.

The He50 had sprung from Japanese Navy interest in dive bombers, for which the German firm of Heinkel had put in a bid with a compact and sturdy little biplane. The original Japanese specification was for a single-engined, two-seater aircraft capable of operating from carriers or on floats, which is why Heinkel, who specialised in seaplanes, were favoured. The aircraft had to be stressed for catapult launching and for carrying a single external 550 lb bomb into combat in a vertical dive.

Heinkel produced the first float-plane prototype in the summer of 1931 and the second, which was a land-based version, appeared as the He50 aL soon after. Dive bombing tests followed at Breitling near Warnemünde with 1,000 lb blocks of concrete being dropped in power dives at moored floating targets in the bay. Further development followed and the He50 formed the basis of future Japanese Navy dive bomber expansion.

Back in Germany Heinkel had received orders for three modified He50s for evaluation by the Fliegstab of the Reichsverkehrsministerium at the proving grounds of Rechlin. These were designed as single-seaters, fitted with the 600 hp SAM 22B engine and capable of carrying one external 1,102 lb bomb. The machine did not measure up to all expectations for the Heinkel He50 biplane, since it was incapable of attaining a speed of more than 185 mph in a power dive, which experts considered too slow for dive bombing. However, lacking anything more immediately suitable and with the formation of the first ever dive bomber unit ordered, it was put into limited production. It was planned to have an operational establishment strength of He50's by 30 September 1935. Orders were placed for 25 in 1933 and for a further 51 on 1 January 1934. Owing to the urgent need for such aircraft, an export batch of 12 machines, the He66 bCH, destined for the Chinese Air Force, was retained for six months' German use as the He50 B.

The first dive bomber unit came into official being on 1 October 1935, and dive bomber Gruppe I./162 was subsequently (1 April 1936) assigned the unit name *Schwerin*. It had a mixed aircraft complement of Arado Ar65 and He51 fighters. At 28 March 1935, I./162 lay at Schwerin as part of Luftkreis II.

Two more dive bomber units were formed at this time, II./St.G.162 at Lübeck-Blankensee and I./St.G.165 at Kitzingen, each with three Staffeln and each being allocated three He50s to supplement their original aircraft. In 1936/37 Stab 162 lay at Schwerin, with I./162. The Stab and II./162 were based at Lübeck as the 'Immelmann' Geschwader. The Stab and I./165 were located at Kitzingen under Luftkreis V. Later the II./165 dive bomber unit was added, based at Wertheim.

Meanwhile, the second generation of German dive bombers was under evaluation. Of the two main contenders, the Hs123 from the Henschel Flugzeugwerke proved itself superior to the Fi98 from the Fieseler Flugzeugbau. Both were single-seater biplanes, equipped with the 650 hp BMW 132A-3 radial engine, and capable of carrying a single 551 lb bomb in a swing-out crutch below the main fuselage. This crutch was designed to swing the bomb out and clear of the propeller arc in a vertical dive attack and was widely adopted worldwide. But whereas the Fi98 was a more conventional fabric-covered machine, Henschel went for an oval-section metal monocoque fuselage with a divided undercarriage enclosed in a streamlined fairing.

Development of both types had commenced in 1934 and the prototypes took to the air early the following year. One thing had been deemed essential for a successful dive bomber: strength. The Hs123 was the stronger of the two, whereas the fabric-covered Fieseler suffered in comparison during dive bombing trials conducted that same year. In fact the Henschel proved itself superior to the Fieseler in every respect, and was thus selected to re-equip the Luftwaffe's dive-bomber formations. Ernst Udet himself put the machine through its paces at Johannisthal on 8 May 1935, giving a stunning display.

The main entrance to the Luftwaffe induction centre at Gustrow where Heinz Sellhorn 'joined up' on 6 April 1937. In fact it was the Compulsory Labour Service Camp run by the Nazi party, through which most of the nation's youth was introduced to service life. (Sellhorn Archiv)

Fresh-faced young recruits to the Luftwaffe look suitably dazed as they are marshalled for kitting out at the snow-bound barracks at Gustrow, early in 1937. (Sellhorn Archiv)

Swearing the oath. All new recruits had to swear allegiance on the swastika national flag to Hitler personally, not just to the German nation. (Sellhorn Archiv)

Sellhorn's class, already far more presentable and dignified after a few months in the camp, is pictured here with its instructor at summer camp on 1 May 1937. (Sellhorn Archiv)

Military exercises for the young recruits at Gelande-ausbildung near Quedliburg on 17 March 1938. Learning basic military skills was an essential part of Luftwaffe training. (Sellhorn Archiv)

Midday lunch hand inspection for cadets at the 1. Fbk. of I./St.G.165 at Kitzingen dive bomber base in 1937. (Sellhorn Archiv)

Although replaced in front line dive bomber service before the outbreak of the Second World War, the Henschel Hs123 saw much action as a ground attack weapon in Poland, France and Russia between 1939 and 1942. This pre-war photograph shows the very clean, simplified lines of this last biplane, the standard 'splinter' camouflage scheme and the national markings of that period. (Schwartzkopff Archiv)

Two further prototypes followed the latter with a variable-pitch airscrew. Not everything went smoothly, for two of these machines crashed under testing at Rechlin, both losing their upper wings during power dives. Yet further stressing was built into the fourth prototype along with re-designs of the undercarriage fairings, tailplane bracing struts and junctions of the wings struts. Full-scale production was ordered in 1936 from Henschel's Schönefeld and Johannisthal factories as the Hs123 A-1. They had a maximum speed of 214 mph and could also carry four 110 lb bombs under the wings.

Hs123s first joined the Luftwaffe with St.Gr.I./162 'Immelmann', and later joined other units; several were sent to Spain to be evaluated in combat conditions with the Legion Kondor under Wolfram von Richthofen, Chief-of-Staff and an Air Force Commander. Here the Hs123 proved itself more suitable as ground attack aircraft (*Schlachtflieger*) than as true dive bombers and subsequent models were aborted. It was already being replaced by the third generation of German dive bombers in serving units back home.

It was only now, at this late stage, that Ernst Udet looms large on the dive bomber scene in Germany. An ex-First World War ace and crony of Hermann Göring, he had led a freebooting life as a test and stunt pilot around the world. While in the United States he had fallen under the spell of the American 'Helldiver' dive bombing display teams, so much so that Göring bought him a couple of Curtiss Hawks as part of his efforts to lure him into joining the Luftwaffe.

Although fully convinced on the concept of dive bombing, Udet had hitherto made no contribution to German development, as he had no official connections. That all changed when he first joined the GAF and then had replaced von Richthofen in charge of the technical supply department (Technisches Amt). Only now was he able to champion the dive bomber fully, replacing the lukewarm attitude of other senior officers with a much more positive outlook.

Already three new designs were on the drawing boards to compete with Junkers Ju87, which had been steadily developed in the interim. Although the Ju87 was the firm favourite, a competition was held to evaluate all four of the third generation Stukas prior to equipping the rapidly expanding dive bomber arm to back up Hitler's increasingly risky gambles in the field of foreign policy and expansionism.

As well as Junkers Ju87, the contenders were the Arado Ar81, the Blohm and Voss Ha137 and the Ernst Heinkel's sleek He118. The Arado and the Blohm and Voss were both composite biplanes, small and obviously outclassed. They soon fell by the wayside and the real competition came down to a straight choice between the Heinkel and the Junkers dive bombers.

The Heinkel was a lovely machine, a sleek mid-wing monoplane designed by Walter and Siegfried Gunter and based largely on their He112 fighter design. It had an oval-section all-metal fuselage with an internal bomb bay for aerodynamic

Below One of the I./St. G.165's new Antons gets its engine stripped down at Kitzingen dive bomber base, 1938. Ease of maintenance made the Junkers Ju87 series popular with mechanics in the field when war arrived. This early model Ju87 A features the four-colour camouflage scheme standard at that time, dark brown, green with a green-grey 'splinter' and a light blue under-surface. Note the huge 'trousered' undercarriage. (Sellhorn Archiv)

Bottom Three of the new Junkers Ju87 A–1s of the newly re-equipped Kit-zingen Stuka unit lift off from their home base on a training mission in the summer of 1937. The propeller spinners were red, blue, yellow and green according to the Staffel allocation. (Schwartzkopff Archiv)

cleanness which could carry a 1,100 lb bomb (as a single-seater) or a 551 lb bomb with both crew members. It was powered by the new Daimler-Benz DB600 12-cylinder liquid-cooled engine and had a top speed of 245 mph. Compared with the crank-winged Junkers with its fixed-trousered undercarriage, the He118 looked like a racehorse next to a carthorse! But what was wanted was a warhorse not a showhorse. The Heinkel could only dive at angles of 50 degrees, and its retractable undercarriage was flimsy, and with nothing like the powerful shock-absorbing gear of the Junkers. Hitler's vision of his armies thrusting east to establish a new German empire in the Russian steppes required aircraft that would stand up to rugged pounding, constant moves forward and primitive operating conditions. The He118 would be ideal when operating from tarmac-coated home bases but would not be able to live in the harsh terrain of the pro-jected battlefields of Poland and Beloyrussia.

Favourites or not, all were tested against each other in the summer of 1936 at the Rechlin proving ground. As predicted, although the He118 was visually pleasing and apparently superior to the others, it was eliminated along with the Ar81 and the Ha137. The fact that Udet carried out a trial flight and crashed the He118 might have been one factor against it. The fact that Junkers had a far greater research and experimental time behind his design was more likely.

Whatever the reason, the winner was the sturdy little monoplane with the characteristic inverted-gull wings and the 'trouser' spats, the Ju87. In 1938, therefore the Junkers Ju87 A was adopted as standard equipment for the dive bomber formations, while the Hs123, which had served as second-string equip-

A Kette of Antons belonging to I./162 passes overhead with immaculate spacing in a 1937 fly-past at Kitzingen. The Junkers Ju87 dive bomber began to replace the biplanes in the Stuka units in 1937. They first saw real combat in February 1938, with the Kampfgruppe K.88 during the Legion Kondor intervention in the Spanish Civil War. (Schwartzkopff Archiv)

The top men of the Reich visit the IV Sturz-kampflehrgeschwader (Dive Bombing Training School) at Barth in Pommern, commanded by Oberstleut-nant Günter Schwartzkopff, in 1938. Left to right: General Wilhelm Keitel, Chief of the Armed Forces High Command; Adolf Hitler; Hermann Göring, head of the Luftwaffe; General Ernst Udet, a long-time protagonist of the dive bomber. (Frau Schwartz-kopff)

ment for the 'Immelmann' 162 dive bomber group, was utilised as ground attack aircraft and used for combat testing the lessons of Spain by personnel of the experimental squadron.

In the years since the war the Luftwaffe has been much criticised for adopting the dive bomber instead of the long-range heavy bomber. But looking at things from the German point of view in the 1930s, the choice was perfectly logical. The adoption of the dive bomber was strictly in accordance to the then current policy of the Luftwaffe, to be the versatile and mobile flying arm of the Wehrmacht, and to give the latter direct and close support in its land operations.

The Luftwaffe had hardly emerged from secrecy before Hitler began his step-by-step programme to restore German power and pride over her dismembered territories. Remilitarisation of the Rhineland commenced on 7 March 1936. On that day 165 Dive Bomber Group, operating from Kitzingen, moved two Staffeln to Frankfurt-am-Main airport and the third Staffel to Mannheim. Both groups had only been in existence for a relatively short time and their fighting qualities were 'basic'. They would no doubt have shaken up the French had they been called into action, but they were not.

If no combat experience had resulted from that audacious move then a Kette (flight) of the new Junkers Ju87s was to gain plenty. They were sent to join the Hs123s of the Legion Kondor in Spain. The Spanish Civil War had broken out in the summer of 1936. German intervention on behalf of the Nationalist forces under General Franco enabled the operational testing of both the Ju87 A-1, three of which arrived in Spain in September of that year, and the new dive bomber aircrew. Fresh crews were rotated in Spain to gain experience.

Valuable lessons were immediately learnt, not from combat but from the problems associated with getting machines ready for action and keeping them operational, no matter how bad the conditions. This lesson was to be as valuable to the Luftwaffe as any actual combat. A report from the Rugen evaluation staff read: 'The operational dive-bombing trials that have been in progress since September 1936, with three Junkers Ju87 A-1s, have remained at an elementary

Stuka dive bomber aircrew await the call for action during the Sudetenland crisis of September 1938. The Ju87 A in the background is painted in the 'splinter' camouflage of the period and carries the old-type Luftwaffe fuselage codes, 52+A11. The Anton's individual pilot cockpit cover is open ready for a unit scramble as the hours to Hitler's deadline tick away. The location is the German airfield of Jena-Rodingen to the south-west of Leipzig, just across the mountain border from Prague. (Sellhorn Archiv)

Ju87A ready for action during the Sudetenland crisis of September 1938. The message on the 551 lb bomb is addressed to Eduard Benes, the Czech president. In the event, after the Munich conference, the Stukas were able to move into the Czech airfields unopposed. (Sellhorn Archiv)

stage owing to difficulties encountered in connection with the equipment.'

Meanwhile the type continued to be improved. In October 1938 dive bombing trials were resumed with Bomber Group K/88, flight-testing the new Junkers B-1. This latter model featured an improved engine, aerodynamic cleaning of the undercarriage ('spats' instead of 'trousers' being the most obvious point visually) and other improvements. Almost immediately better results were obtained.

By December 1938 the Legion Kondor had three Ju87 B-1s at its disposal. At home by 1938 the number of operational dive bomber Gruppen had reached a total of nine, and all the Henschel Hs123s had been replaced by Ju87s.

More moves followed on the diplomatic front to which the newly expanded dive bomber arm was expected to lend its growing clout. Between 1 and 10 October 1938, following the Munich Conference the Sudetenland area of Czechoslovakia, which had been ceded to Germany, was formally occupied. As part of the military movements, all 200 dive bombers were placed on alert, and units moved into Czechoslovakian airfields.

Generalfeldmarschall Hermann Göring (centre), chief of the Luftwaffe, inspects the Guard of Honour at the Dive Bomber Training School at Barth during the visit of the Italian Air Chief Marshal Balbo in October 1938. Oberstleutnant Günter Schwarzkopff acts as his escort on the right of this photo. (Schwartzkopff Archiv)

Generalfeldmarschall Hermann Göring explains a point to Air Chief Marshal Balbo at Barth in 1938. The two men struck a firm friendship during this visit, and Göring invited Balbo for a cruise on his yacht. In return Balbo presented Hermann with a star fashioned from black and white diamonds. Balbo was impressed with the Stukas and initiated ideas for Italy to build her own dive bombers. The resulting aircraft, the Savoia-Marchetti SMB5, was a flop, and Italy used Ju87s during the war with some success. (Siehe via Sellhorn Archiv)

From 7 November 1938 the growing momentum to expand the Luftwaffe further was provided for in the 'Concentrated Aircraft Procurement Programme'. Drawn up by the Chief of the Operations Staff, Oberst Jeschonnek, there were now to be eight Sturzkampfgeschwader ready for action by the autumn of 1942. These were to be equipped by the planned fourth generation of dive bombers, the new, twin-engined Messerschmitt Me210, a dive bomber version loosely based on the 'Destroyer' type of long-range fighter. This was under development and was ultimately destined to replace the Ju87. (Due to a number of design problems and prolonged teething problems, it never did.) Later even this schedule was changed and for a further increase in the number of Sturzkampfgeschwader to twelve.

So much for the plans. The facts were impressive enough for by 1 July 1939 the Luftwaffe had no less than 27 dive bomber squadrons on strength. All were fully equipped with the Junkers Ju87 B-1s (including some experimental naval carrier-borne squadrons), in total 366 machines.

II
Günter Schwartzkopff
Father of the Dive Bomber

With the rapid expansion of the dive bomber arm, and the development of the three generations of dive bombing aircraft, the progress of this type of air warfare seemed assured. Behind the scenes in the Luftwaffe the story was not so smooth or certain. The concept had aroused factions both for and against. Although the mercurial Udet gave his weight to the pro-faction it was to remain the task of a more practical and responsible man to analyse methodically and diligently, and to prove and advance the system, stage-by-stage, into a workable and feasible programme. That man was Günter Schwartzkopff.

Schwartzkopff was one of the many former army men who transferred to the flying branch during and after World War I but who retained his army roots in his new profession. He sought out and brought in other like-minded individuals, both of his generation and a later one, and together these men, known collectively as the 'Old Stuka Hands', worked throughout the 1930s to make the Stuka concept feasible. For his work in this field Günter Schwartzkopff was to become affectionately known throughout the Luftwaffe as 'The Father of the Stuka'.

Günter Schwartzkopff was born on 5 August 1898, at Forbach-bei-Posen. His elder brother remembers the event well and described it thus in a letter to Günter's son, Peter, written in January 1959:

When your father was born in 1898 he was not a healthy child. A professor who came to live there told our mother that the child would not live. But a vet who came to the yard told her to feed it with oranges. And this apparently gave the child good health. My brother grew up sturdy and strong.

In October 1914 when your father was 16 years old he joined the Army. After being wounded several times with the infantry he came in 1916 for training in the air branch. There were many bad air crashes. After being in action on the Russian front in 1918 he was transferred to the Western front and finally was presented with the Iron Cross by Kaiser Wilhelm II.

In fact Günter Schwartzkopff, the son of a minor government official, was only eleven years old when he first became an officer cadet. At the outbreak of war he was a 16-year-old officer cadet wearing the uniform of the Infantry Regiment 47 and it was with this unit that he first saw action in 1914 in the carnage of the First World War. He was later badly wounded at Verdun. In the summer of 1915 he went as Leutnant to the Fliegertruppe, flying missions on both the eastern and western fronts. He was based at Wicklow in Poland where the technical officer was Oberleutnant Ruppert, who became a firm friend. Günter himself became an outstanding young pilot and was awarded the Iron Cross 1st Class and the

Order of Hohenzollern with Swords by the Kaiser for his aerial exploits.

After the Armistice, Günter was discharged from the army and briefly settled in the small Schlesien town of Hirschberg. But in 1920 he was taken back into the new State Army and resumed his military career once more as an infantry officer (as military flying was banned), with the Reichswehr. He fought on the frontiers for his own homeland as a member of the Reichswehr 6th Infantry Regiment, garrisoned at Mecklenburg (Schwerin). It was here that he met, courted and married his wife.

Again his brother gives us a clear insight of the man at this period, a picture which was to remain for the rest of his life:

To understand your father's character you must know that, iron energy, solidarity and comradeship were his mainstays. His comrades soon recognised the soldier and leader in him. From 32 officers who took part in the highly selective interview for re-enlistment into the tiny peacetime army, only seven were chosen. Your father was not allowed to fly but, from time to time, he was able to conduct civil flying to refresh and update his knowledge. The holidays, time and money for this were paid from the Army secret 'Black fund'!

Günter not only worked hard, but he played hard also, as his brother recalled to his second son:

Many lovely hours I spent with your father going hunting. For me it was the greatest pleasure to be with him in the woods. His passion for the sport was even greater than mine. His main interest were the deer and he was an excellent shot! Despite his dedication to his work you should know that, like many others, that through the terrible inflation of those Weimar days your parents were in financial trouble. They only had your father's income. He was economical – going many weeks without beer and cigarettes. All his friends and family were pleased to give him whatever they could, but they had to make sure they did this without him knowing! My mother-in-law prepared the family a meal at that time few could afford.

'The three Schwartzkopffe.' All three of the Schwartzkopff family were serving in the Luftwaffe on the outbreak of war in 1939, two of them in the same unit. Left to right they are Günter, Franz and Rudolf, seen together for the last time at Celle air base. (Schwartzkopff Archiv)

The new Kommandeur of the I./St.G.165 at Kitzingen, Major Oskar Dinort, who took over command from Schwartzkopff on 31 August 1937. (Zachmann via Sellhorn Archiv)

Your own temperament and interests for your surroundings put you in a hostile position towards school and its work. I remember in Kitzingen when your father and I came home one day late. Your father asked you to show him your school work. 'I have not done it and I do not wish to discuss it!' was your reply. You father was very much like his second son! I am sure your father loved you all. His only wish was your future and livelihood.

I hear that you do not have a good picture of your father. Today you can recognise what conditioned him and his attitude as you have a family yourself. You will understand when I say that a man – like your father – who has built up two air bases (Celle and Kitzingen), and who was an outstanding commander could, on top of all that, be concerned with feeding and keeping his wife and children. Who can wonder he welcomed the political changes that came? Very often I warned him about that rascal Hitler – but mostly Günter thought differently. His attitude often cost us soldiers the friendship of neighbours.

With the arrival of Hitler in power in 1933 (while the Luftwaffe was still a clandestine unit), Günter transferred to the RLM (air ministry). He was called into the War Ministry at Berlin and here he drew up a list of all those who had served with him as volunteer flyers so they could once again join him. Many experienced aviators were to rejoin the colours this way, thus giving the fledgeling Luftwaffe a hard kernel of highly talented and experienced officers on which to base its expansion. Goering's apparent 'miracle' of creating an air force out of nothing really rested on such hard, but unobtrusive, work.

In June 1935, with the rank of Major, Günter became Kommandeur of the Fliegerschule at Celle (Sale), and was promoted to Oberstleutnant of St.G.165. at Kitzingen in 1936.

Under his inspired leadership, Stuka development was in good hands. Moreover Schwartzkopff was fortunate to gather around him a fine team of skilled pilots and aircrew who became fired with his own enthusiasm. There was a good blend of the old and the new in this team which helped make the I./165 Kitzingen unit (having been renumbered from 1./162) supreme from June 1936 onward.

The man who was to be Schwartzkopff's second-in-command and right-hand man was the aristocratic Clemens, Graff von Schönborn-Weissentheid. He was to become one of the best-known Stuka leaders. His career was the opposite of most of his contemporaries for he flew first before learning soldiering. Born in Munich in 1905, he had spent the years between 1928 and 1934 at the Deutsche Verkehrsfliegerschule at Schleissheim and Brunswick. In April 1934 he commenced military training when he joined the 10 (Saxon) Infantry Regiment and went to the Dresden Infantry School.

His refresher army training done, in 1935 he transferred to the Luftwaffe as an Oberstleutnant (using commander). In 1936 he was appointed as Staffelkapitän to the Jagdgeschwader 'Richthofen' (the former Fliegergruppe 'Damm' and II./JG.132, 4.Staffel) based at Jüterbog-Damm. Here he mastered the dive bomb-

Below *After military training, recruits had to specialise before being sent to dive bomber groups. Those like Heinz Sellhorn who were selected as radio operators went to specialised schools to learn their new trade. In the centre of this photo is Oberleutnant Kraft, in command of the 4. Bordfunker (radio operator) training company, at Halle, Saale airfield, 1939.* (Sellhorn Archiv)

Bottom *Training for radio operators included flights in the flying classrooms provided by specially equipped Junkers Ju52 transport aircraft. This trainee is at work aboard one such flight from Welzow airfield near Cottbus, south-east of Berlin.* (Sellhorn Archiv)

ing techniques and, in September 1937, he became Gruppenkommandeur of the II./St.G.165 at Schweinfurt.

Destined to become another of the great leaders of the St.G.77 was Helmut Bruck, a native of Kittlitztreben/Bunzlau, born there in February 1913. He commenced his notable career as an ordinary Stuka pilot and was to go on to become firstly the unit's Kommodore and finally General der Schlachtflieger.

Helmut first joined Luftwaffe as an officer cadet on 1 August 1935. His basic pilot training was taken at the Magdeburg Fliegerschule between October and March 1936 and he joined the Fliegergruppe 'Kitzingen' (later I./St.G.165) as a newly appointed Hauptmann on 1 April 1936. Such were his skill and expertise that by 1 November 1938 he had been promoted to Staffelkapitän in the 1./St.G.165 (which subsequently became the I./St.G.51, and then finally, the I./St.G.77).

Another of the Stuka 'Old Guard' with strong military background was Alfons Orthofer. Born in December 1909, at Neustadt/Donau, and known to all as 'Ali', he was to become one of the best-known members of the St.G.77.

He had served in the Bavarian 20th Infantry Regiment from April 1931, but, on 18 May 1834, Ali transferred to the Luftwaffe as Leutnant. He trained as a fighter pilot initially and served with the JG.134 but, on 1 October 1935 he was promoted to Oberleutnant with the I./St.G.165 in Kitzingen.

With the Stukas his progress was rapid and on 1 March 1937 he was appointed as Staffelführer of the II./St.G.165 in Schweinfurt. From 1 January to 30 April 1939, Ali carried out the same duty with the I./St.G.162 at Jever, having been promoted to Hauptmann. However, the Stuka arm temporarily, lost this fine officer on 1 May when he left to take up a position as special duties officer with the RLM in Berlin. But Ali was no 'desk officer' and vowed to return to his beloved Stukas should there be any prospect of combat flying.

Destined to become another famous Stuka leader, Karl Henze did not join the Luftwaffe until the spring of 1936, at the age of 20. From Holzminden/Weser he entered as an officer cadet. In the following two years he learnt the dive bomber pilot trade as a trainee pilot with 1./St.G.165. Upon qualifying he joined 2./St.G.77 as Leutnant in 1938.

A man with similar wide experience was Waldemar Plewig, who was born in Ostrowo Poland in January 1911. He entered the army in April 1931 as a *Jager* in the 7th Infantry Regiment, being promoted to Leutnant in March 1935. Later that same year he changed over to Luftwaffe and became a military instructor at the Gotho pilots' school.

By 1936 Waldemar was the adjutant and Oberleutnant at the Perleberg Gliding school. His switch to the Stukas followed and in July 1937 when he was appointed Staffelführer III./St.G.162, later doing the same job with the I./St.G.163 at Langensalza. On 1 January 1939 he was promoted to Hauptmann when that unit became the III./St.G.2 'Immelmann', but by outbreak of war in September Plewig was again a Staffelkapitän in the II./St.G.77.

With such a rapid expansion of the arm, promotion through the ranks was always open to men with the obvious talent and feel for dive bombing. One such was Josef 'Sepp' Huber. Born in July 1915 at Kempten/Allgau, he enlisted in the Luftwaffe in October 1935 and joined I./St.G.165 at Kitzingen the following April. Between November 1936 and August 1937 Sepp served in Spain with the

Legion Kondor as an aircraft mechanic of a fighter Staffel. He returned home and rejoined the I./St.G.165, volunteering for Stuka pilot training. This was duly granted, and he underwent a series of courses between March 1938 and September 1940 to achieve this ambition.

Kurt Huhn, born on 1 August 1912 at Paaren/Osthavell, was one of Göring's young protégés, having entered the state police service in April 1933 as a recruit. He soon expressed a yearning to fly and, like so many of his young companions, he transferred to the Luftwaffe in August 1935. He was promoted to Leutnant that October, and, after training, he joined I./St.G.165 at Schweinfurt on 1 January 1938.

Two other stalwarts of this period should be mentioned. Arnulf Blasig, a 23-year-old Berliner nicknamed 'Blasmich', was a young Leutnant with St.G.162 'Immelmann' from October 1936 to February 1937. From then until October 1938, he served with the III./St.G.165.

Alexander 'Alex' Gläser was born in January 1914, at Budingen/Hessen and was to become one of the best pilots and unit commanders of the St.G.77. By the end of May 1939 he was serving with that unit also as a newly-promoted Leutnant.

In 1938 Schwartzkopff was made Gruppenkommandeur in time for the July 1938 Sudetenland operations. It was in this post that Günter had now become chiefly instrumental in bringing the Ju87 to its top operational status and to the legendary fame that was to come in World War II. This fact is confirmed by the

The outgoing chief of the IV Dive Bomber Training School at Barth, Pommern. Oberstleutnant Schwartzkopff (centre, in helmet) parades the Guard of Honour for his successor, Oberst Dr Knauss (right) in 1939. Taking the salute is the Kommandeur of all the Luftwaffe training schools, Oberst Forster. (Schwartzkopff Archiv)

Senior dive bomber officers enjoy recorded music at an open air meal at Neudorf-bei-Oppeln on the eve of war, August 1939. Left to right: Gruppenkommandeur II./St.G.77, Clemens Graf von Schönborn-Wiesentheid; unknown; Hauptmann Walter Enneccerus; Gruppenkommandeur of I.St.G.77, Hauptmann Freiherr Friedrich Karl von Dalwigk zu Lichtenfels; the Geschwaderkommodore of St.G.77, Oberstleutnant Günter Schwartzkopff (Sellhorn Archiv)

The 2. FBK enjoy a sing-song around the swimming pool at Kitzingen barracks in 1939. The officer playing the accordion is Leutnant Lau. (Karl Schubert via Sellhorn Archiv)

Personnel of 2./St.G.77 at their peacetime base of Neuberg, north of Augsburg in south-west Germany, on 25 August 1939. With a message chalked up on the SC 250 bomb, technicians and flying personnel await the move to wartime stations. Left to right: Rosenhauer; Franz Grun, armourer; Wilbert; Dengler, armourer; Zeilinger; two unknown radio men. (Schierie via Sellhorn Archiv)

wording on his official epitaph (which is on a plaque at Kaserne near Hamburg).

His main work was to create the correctly worked-out dive bombing techniques for the Junkers Ju87 Stuka. He soon found the great possibilities which were hidden in this new kind of bombing approach. Once he was sure, he gave his whole work to develop the Ju87. Energy and determination helped him and also his ability to lead. There were lots of difficulties in the beginning. Many of the new Luftwaffe leaders – whom he had to enlighten – were not from his former World War comrades. His squadrons were initially fighter units and thus were mostly educated in the role of the hunter and not the ground attacker, especially when it involved new and unproven technical problems. For those experienced fighter pilots it seemed like going backwards for, by the outbreak of war, all the fighter planes in Europe were advancing their speed and climbing rates almost daily. Schwartzkopff did not demand a higher standard of work on technical and industrial aspects than that which he could himself contribute. He understood perfectly the need to instil into his crews his own enthusiasm by example. It was with love and affection that he personally christened the Ju87 'Jolanthe' after the pig in a Berlin musical comedy.

Diving skill and accuracy were of the paramount importance and under his personal leadership were continually improved and bettered. Releasing bombs when diving was scientifically and practically examined and lessons were painstakingly learned from their dedicated experiments.

Stern and dedicated to his chosen mission as he was, Günter nonetheless had a good sense of humour, as the adoption of 'Jolanthe' showed. A letter from Dr Georg Dotterweich, at that time a young Hauptmann in his squadron, also illustrated this side of his nature, but naturally Günter used his humour to drive home a lesson.

Your father was very popular with his men and officers. He always saw to it that nobody went short and that all were well cared for equally. I remember that once, while we were all in a casino in Cologne Butzweilerhof, he publically rebuked a Staffelkapitän because the officer insisted on being driven, instead of himself walking to a dinner. This meant his driver had to wait outside for him without food.

Meanwhile, as the establishment strength of the group expanded, fresh faces joined the veterans around Schwartzkopff. Again it was a mix of fresh-faced young hopefuls and veterans. Among the former was Günter Hitz from Kohlfurt-bei-Görlitz/Schl., where he was born in 1916. Although only 23, he was to be known in the war years, when life was brief and hectic, as one of the 'old' Stuka airmen. He joined I./St.G.165 (later I./St.G.77) from the Stukaschule Kitzingen in August 1939 and commenced his service with the 1. Staffel.

One of the many former glider pilots who joined the Stukas was Georg Jakob. A native of Furth/Bayern and born in March 1915, Georg was only 19 when he enlisted with an infantry regiment garrisoned at Augsburg in November 1934. But he was already an avid glider pilot and within a few months he had officially transferred to the Luftwaffe.

He spent the period 1936–37 at the war College then, as a newly-promoted Hauptmann, undertook a course at the pilot/observer school. On qualifying on 1 July 1938, Georg specialised in dive bombing and served with the I./St.G.165 at Kitzingen until 14 May 1939 when it became I./St.G.77. Georg was to stay with this unit until 1942 seeing much hard action.

One of the first of the new young volunteers to be trained as a Stuka pilot was Rudolf Weigel, from Ludwigshafen/Rhein. On his nineteenth birthday he had volunteered for the Luftwaffe. After undergoing pilot training and dive bomber conversion he made rapid progress and by the eve of the war was established as Kettenführer (flight commander) of the 5./St.G.77.

Gliding proved the sport that unlocked the door to flying for many of that generation of young German men. Lothar Lau from Königsberg in East Prussia was another such. Born in 1913 and already an established and skilled glider pilot, he volunteered for the Luftwaffe while serving as an officer cadet in an infantry regiment. He was immediately taken by the Luftwaffe and sent for pilot training. He qualified on 29 April 1936, was promoted to Leutnant, and transferred to the Stukas the following year. By 1939 Lother was an Oberleutnant with the St.G.77.

Yet another ex-police cadet, Franz Kieslich, a 20 year old from Bochum, had been trained by the Bonn police school before joining the Cologne police force. He then transferred to state police. But, on 1 April 1935, Franz transferred to the Luftwaffe as corporal. He volunteered for pilot training and, on completion of this, joined St.G.168 at Lübeck and then at Graz after the Anschluss was carried out and Austria became the Ostmark of the Reich.

From the spring of 1938 to the summer of 1940 Franz performed valuable service as a dive bomber instructor at Kitzinger school. Denied action at the start of the war, he was to more than make up for it later on.

A former fighter pilot who found his true metier with the Stukas was Paul Langkopf. Born in July 1915, at Sarstedt-bei-Hildesheim, Paul had joined the KG 157 Boelcke as a qualified pilot in April 1937. It was not until 1939 that he switched over to the Stukas, joining St.G.77's strength on 1 August.

Of similar background was Walter Stimpel. Born at Oelsen/Pirna, he joined the Luftwaffe on 1 April 1936 at the age of nineteen. By 1 January 1938 he was a Hauptmann and both fighter and bomber pilot training followed before he decided to specialise in the élite dive bomber arm. He joined Stuka Geschwader 165 in Schweinfurt on 1 July of that year.

Hermann Ruppert had been born in Russia on 8 August 1915 at Irbit in Siberia, but had been raised in Germany. He was another keen young volunteer to join the newly announced Luftwaffe as soon as he was able, for he had earlier, in May 1935, joined 1. Fahr-Abteilung at Lübeck.

On 15 September this was 'Officially' changed over to Luftwaffe as Fliegerstaffel 1 based at Kassel. Herman became an officer cadet in March 1936 moving to the Aufklarungsstaffel 2/124, also at Kassel. Between October 1936 and February he was at Dresden and, as a Hauptmann, by 1 July 1938, transferred to the Stukaschule and the St.G.165 in Wertheim/Main. By 15 May 1939 he was serving with the II./St.G.77.

Another youthful pilot destined to achieve fame with the Stukas was Helmut Leicht, born in November 1916 at Ludwigsburg in Württemberg. Aged 20, Helmut entered the Luftkriegsschule 4 at Berlin-Gatow and by 1 July 1938 had come to I./St.G.165 as a Leutnant.

Deserving of mention also is Alois Wosnitza. Born on 17 November 1914 at Gleiwitz/Oberschlesien, he was once described as 'A typical example of the Stuka experts who on the basis of skill and experience survived the five war years.'

Not all the famous Stuka men were pilots. Many of the rear-seat men were to

Camouflaged Stukas of I./St.G.77 await the final command to attack their targets in Poland at Neudorf on the river Oder (now Opele, Poland), August 1939. Their targets lay over the border to the north-east: Wielun and the Polish defence lines. (Schwartzkopff Archiv)

A graphically-enhanced 550 lb bomb on the arms of the swing rack of a Junkers Ju87 B–2 of Stab I./St.G.77 in Poland on 1 September 1939. The tip of both adjustable arms were secured to bolts on the bomb itself. In the dive the arms were swung down and out of the machine's belly, allowing the released bomb to clear the large propeller arc while in a vertical dive. (Schwartzkopff Archiv)

Armourers fit a pair of SC 50 110 lb bombs to the underwing racks of a Stuka. Such weapons often had whistles fitted to their tail fins to enhance the Stuka's own screaming dive. (Schwartzkopff Archiv)

The differences in potential Stuka bomb loads at the beginning of the war. The large single 500 kg bomb could either be armour-piercing or high explosive, and was carried on the swinging crutch below the fuselage; however, the rear-seat man had to be dropped to take it, so more normally the SC 250 was carried. The bombs' locking pins and location points are clearly visible in this photograph. (Schwartzkopff Archiv)

'With love' is the sarcastic message on this 250 lb bomb for delivery to the defenders of Warsaw by the victorious Stukageschwader 77 late in September 1939. (Schwartzkopff Archiv)

achieve equally legendary fame for the number of combat missions they were to fly. Franz Hettinger from Stuttgart was to become one of the greatest of these radio operators and rear gunners. He was a professional soldier initially but joined the 1./St.G.165 on 1 November 1938, becoming Helmut Bruck's partner from the first day, flying with him in hundreds of subsequent operations.

It was on 1 May 1939 that I./165 was again renumbered as the I./St.G.77 with Hauptmann Friedrich-Karl Freiherr von Dalwigk zu Lichtenfels as CO. Freidrich-Karl Freiherr von Dalwigk zu Lichtenfels, despite his awesome title, had the nickname 'Kuken' (chicken). Of the older generation of flyers he had been born in April 1907 at Torgau on the river Elbe. He was truly one of the 'Old Guard' that built the Stuka arm during the 1930s.

He joined Luftwaffe as Leutnant on 1 October 1933 and soon became established with the 11./St.G.162 Geschwaderstab as an Oberleutnant. Dalwigk was promoted to Hauptmann in March 1937 and in the interim his unit had been renamed as I./St.G.167 and he became Staffelkapitän of the 2. Staffel. When in April 1938 it had again been renamed as 2./St.G.168 and had moved to Graz, 'Chicken' went with it and he stayed when it became the 1.St.G.76 in May 1939. On the eve of the war however, Dalwigk transferred to I.St.G.77 to assume command in readiness for the forthcoming Polish campaign.

Meanwhile the II./165 at Schweinfurt became the 11./St.G.77, with Hauptmann Graf Clemens von Schönborn-Wiesentheid as CO. Now a group captain, Günter Schwarzkopff was overall Kommodore of the reconstituted St.G.77. His brother recalled:

He was enormously happy when he received his greatly merited promotion to Oberst. He arranged a journey by Rhine steamer with his officers to celebrate. We all dressed in civil clothes and we addressed him as major-general. He even put a bet for three bottles of champagne if I could fully dressed walk into the Rhine. I did and I won! But sadly the champagne never did arrive because your father's death came soon after.

He was also quite humorous. I once told him that the young men believed they could only drive heavy cars around – whereas I maintained, they should be sporting and use bikes. The following day I had the order to go to the Stab Richthofen based near München-Gladbach and a bike stood by the door as my transport. I duly started out, trying to put on a pleasant face with a 35-kilometre journey ahead of me! I eventually made it and was then told to return with two large parcels of secrets which they tied with wires to my bike. On my way back a group commander overtook me in his staff car and I begged him to take my parcels, which he duly did – to my great relief.

Later that evening on my weary return your father received me at the Casino, which we were using as our headquarters, and, with a stern face, he asked me for a receipt for the parcels I had given away! Of course I had none. So your father shouted at me and informed me I was totally unreliable etc. I was struck quite speechless at the enormity of my crime. But as soon as your father saw I was full of remorse he laughed out loud. It turned out it was all a put-up joke. They had telephoned München-Gladbach and asked them to prepare a 'Secrets' parcel of builder's bricks for me. From that time on I was more careful in my outspoken opinions of my brother officers!

One last anecdote on Günter is worthy of inclusion.

His strength was great and he knew no boundaries. His real genius was shown there as commander. He was hard towards everyone – but he was much harder to himself. He stood right at the front and shoulder-to-shoulder with his young airmen.

III
Blitzkrieg on Poland

On 1 September the ultimatum to Poland ran out and World War II commenced. In the front line, where it was to remain for the next six years, lay the hunched shapes of the Stuka dive bombers of St.G.77. All the years of training, experiment and the honing to perfection of their diving and attack techniques were now to come to final fruition. There was still much doubt about the effectiveness of the short-range dive bombers. Close air support was not one of their prime functions even now; back-area bombing of strategic targets in the immediate rear of the enemy armies, bridges, ammunition dumps, rail centres and yards, radio stations, these were the principal Stuka targets. But, as with the rest of the bomber arm, it was to the destruction of the Polish Air Force that all other objectives were seconded until vital air superiority had been won. Only then would the Stukas be turned loose to show what they could do.

From 25 August 1939, both I, and II./St.G.77 had been deployed and at instant readiness for the move to the Polish frontier. To prevent the enemy detecting their presence prematurely, Günter Schwartzkopff had got his units into place. The Stukas flew in to Neudorf, an airfield west of Oppeln, on the afternoon before the attack.

The whole group was to work in the southern sector of the front under the overall control of Luftflotte 4. They were to operate in close conjunction with Major-General Hoepner's XVI Army Corps. This force, built around the tanks of 1 and 4 Armoured Divisions, was to act as the spearhead for 10 Armee. The whole operation was planned to roll at 0430 on 1 September. The objective of the Panzers was to make a wide sweep to out-flank the strong Polish defence works which ran from Wielun, in the north, to Lublinitz, in the south. A successful breakthrough here would cut off and encompass the whole of the valuable Polish industrial area around Tschenstochau. Once this had been achieved the tanks were to proceed at best speed towards the river Warte and establish a bridgehead there around Radamsko.

For St.G.77 immediate control was exercised by Generalleutnant Freiherr von Richthofen, who set up his command base at Schönwald Castle in Silesia. But the first day of combat almost turned into a disaster due to the weather. For dawn on 1 September showed the target area to be wreathed in ground mist and the sky itself was overcast and gloomy.

Just the month before, during a mass training exercise at Neuhammer, similar conditions had led to a serious accident. A film of low-flying mist had covered the bombing range just before a mass diving attack with smoke bombs had been led in by Walter Sigel and I./St.G.76. This had not been reported to the airborne Stukas with the result that 13 of the aircraft had plunged full-tilt into the ground wiping out their crews. It was precisely to avoid such another tragedy that Hans Seidemann, Richthofen's chief-of-staff, issued a warning against launching the planned attacks. Richthofen had been ordered to send his Stukas initially against Polish airfields at Krakow in the south. But the foggy conditions resulted in a 'holding' order being sent to all units. This suggestion was *not* well received! As Schwartzkopff's brother was to tell his son Peter:

Stuka aircrew and machines were not much used to blind flying in those days. So when the day loomed overcast and cloudy and the time came to fly the first combat missions none of the weathermen and higher officers could explain to Schwartzkopff how to attack without expecting heavy losses. To comply was impossible and the mission was therefore cancelled.

Your father thought that the orders not to fly reflected against his personal honour and ordered Stuka No. 108, his own personal machine, to be made ready anyway. He climbed aboard and with him went his loyal Feldwebel [Sergeant] radioman. All his comrades begged him not to fly. His second-in-command, Graf Schönborn-Wiesentheid, came over to me begged me to ensure that *no one* should fly, but they ignored this and they took off.

The target attacked, and attacked successfully, was a line of concrete bunkers and gun emplacements immediately in front of the German advance, identified as Lublinitz 23.

After 35 minutes we heard gunfire. His plane re-landed. He had been in radio contact with Luftflotte HQ and he had been ordered by them that the planned-for attacks '...will *not* take place'. So he impatiently awaited a new fresh decision from the Luftflotte.

Afterwards General von Richthofen excused himself that the order was not meant like that, that it was in no way a personal reflection at all. Remember that your father was not only a Gruppen commander but also well-known at the same time as *the* acknowledged expert on the Stuka weapon. As such he was personally responsible as such directly to the

Günter Schwartzkopff (right) examining a lubricating oil installation filter prior to its being fitted to a Stuka engine. Günter always maintained a keen interest in every aspect of his men and their aircraft's workings. (Schwartzkopff Archiv)

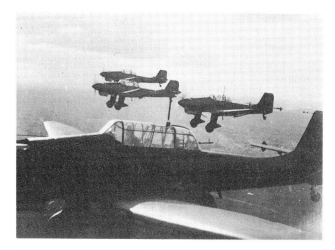

The Stab Staffel of St.G.77 returns to base after a sortie over Poland in September 1939. Note the empty bomb release forks and the fact that no rear gunner/radio men are flying, which indicates that either heavy bombs were carried or that it was a long-range sortie. (Author's collection via Peter Schwartzkopff Archiv)

Being a strongly built aircraft of all-metal construction, the Stuka, although a slow and relatively poorly defended aircraft, often survived a scale of damage that would have incapacitated more sophisticated types. Here is the tail of a Junkers Ju87 B-2 of Stab I./St.G.77 on its return from an attack over Warsaw. (Schwartzkopff Archiv)

Air Ministry. All questions and orders to group commanders and all questions about these very specialised machines were answered by him. His influence was therefore very great, he was called to all meetings.

But he had cause to thank me that day for the enemy attacked in the direction of Rutuo with seven divisions from the south and in support had an air fleet comprising nearly 100 aircraft, both bombers and fighters. He had proceeded with his lone mission and run into this mass alone and been confronted by them all – that's why he *had* to land again, despite his personal feelings. In appreciation for his lone stance he much later received the highest praises from the Polish Oberst and commander concerned.

After the campaign, when Goering arrived in person with praises and Gunter's medals, your father gave him all the names of his men, and there was quite a dispute. Your father refused the medals – he said that he had enough from the first World War. He said his men deserved them more. He also declined the offer to take over another squadron, he told Goering he did not want to leave his comrades.

Richthofen himself was airborne in a Stork scout plane at 1100, strayed over the front line and was hit by ground fire from Polish troops. This resulted in a further order to the effect that no aircraft were to fly low unless strictly necessary! The

Back safely, but only just! A Junkers Ju87 B–1 of Stab I./St.G.77 after the collapse of the undercarriage during a crash-landing back at base following heavy flak damage over the target in the Polish campaign. Ground personnel (known as 'Blackmen' from their distinctive coveralls) look on in pensive mood. (Schwartzkopff Archiv)

Seen from the rear gunner's seat of a 3./St.G.77 Stuka, over the barrel of the gunner's MG15 machine-gun, a sister aircraft in close formation. (Sellhorn Archiv)

Stukas again ignored the man who had always opposed their existence and who now led them in battle. Air reconnaissance reports brought in reports of heavy concentrations of Polish cavalry moving up on Wielun on the northern flanks of the German XVI Army Corps. These were initially engaged by the I./St.G.2 around 1300 and then, in the mid-afternoon, it was the turn of I./St.G.77.

They taxied out and took off en masse, with the 'Black men' of the ground staff shouting the traditional farewell to pilots about to go into action, *'Hals und Beinbruch!'* (Break your neck and leg!).

During the earlier dive bomber attacks, what appeared to be the Polish brigade headquarters at a farmhouse to the north of the town had been attacked by Oscar Dinort's flyers to good effect. This same location was given to Schwartzkopff and his main target and all 60 of his Ju87s concentrated their dives on this area, causing the complete annihilation of the enemy staff and control and the resulting disintegration of the whole brigade. Scattered to the four winds by bombs and machine-gun bullets, it ceased to be a threat and Wielun fell to the advancing German land forces that same night.

The influence of the Stukas was even more marked the following day, 2 September. Von Richthofen had agreed with General von Reichenau that every available Stuka would be thrown in to blast a path for the tanks of 1 Panzer division under Generalleutnant Schmidt. This unit was way out ahead of XVI Army Corps in its drive to gain the Warte crossing. Pushing ahead in this manner left the division's right-hand flank open to counter-attack from the direction of Tschenstochau which it had bypassed. Therefore Günter Schwartzkopff's main task was to suppress any enemy moves against this exposed flank and to nip in the bud all Polish attempts at re-grouping before they could begin.

In pursuance of this policy, both I. and II.St.G.77 made continual dive bombing attacks on Polish troop columns and concentrations, mainly in the Radomsko area. An interested observer of the German *Blitzkrieg* in full cry was the French air force General Armengaud. He gave his superiors in Paris a very detailed report on just how the Polish army was broken by the Stuka/Panzer combination, a report, incidentally, by which the complaisant Allies fatally failed to profit.

The German system consists essentially of making a breach in the front with armour and aircraft, then to throw mechanised and motorised columns into the breach, to beat down its shoulders to right and left in order to keep on enlarging it, at the same time as armoured detachments, guided, protected and reinforced by aircraft, advance in front of the supporting divisions in such a way that the defence's manoeuvrability is reduced to impotence. It would be madness not to draw an exact lesson from this pattern and not to pay heed to this warning.

By 3 September the Germans were across the Warte and, although Britain and France solemnly declared war that day, there was absolutely nothing at all practical that they could do to help their stricken ally. St.G.77 hit hastily prepared Polish positions protecting the River Pilica, and IV Panzer thrust on eastward to the north of the Ilza Gora hills toward Kamienna.

The psychological effect of the dive bomber in a power dive was enormous, even to battle-hardened troops. To reinforce the already unmistakable Vulture-

The aftermath of St.G.77's attack on Radom railway station in September 1939. The cutting of vital communications and transport links was one of the 'back area' tasks of the Junkers Ju87 dive bomber. (Author's collection via Sellhorn Archiv)

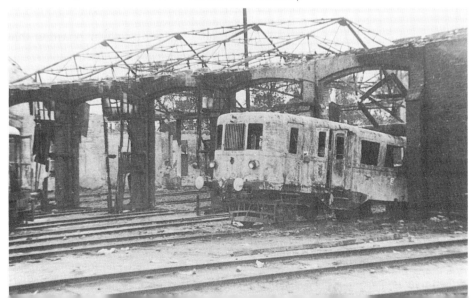

A discussion at a forward airstrip near Radom, hastily set up in the wake of the Panzers, between Staffelkapitän Oberleutnant Sayer, 2.Staffel St.G.77 (left) and Gruppenkommandeur I./St.G.77, Hauptmann von Dalwigk and his adjutant Oberleutnant Ulitz. (Rosenhauer via Sellhorn Archiv)

like silhouette of the Junkers Ju87 and the screaming sound of its engine attacking vertically, small propeller-driven sirens were attached to the undercarriage struts which gave them an unholy and eerie howling sound. The Stuka crews christened them 'The Trombones of Jerico'. In France whole battalions of green or reservist troops were to surrender after a few doses of this treatment alone.

'A planned withdrawal to previously prepared positions,' became the main announcement from the Poles, repeated for day after day in the British newspapers. It was repeated on bus and tube with heavy irony by the British public who could read between the lines better than their masters gave them credit for. In truth, the planned withdrawal was little more than the rout of the whole Polish army once the 'hard-skin' of the prepared frontier positions had been pierced or by-passed. Gradually the Stukas turned the route into an on-rush towards the Vistula river but before they got there the Poles hoped to stage a decisive ambush.

One of the most important elements of the *Blitzkrieg* effect was the degree of aerial observation conducted by the GAF ahead of the advance. Strongpoints and troop concentrations which would normally have given many nasty surprises to the advancing Germans were never free of the all pervading 'eye-in-sky'. Accurate Stuka strikes to aid the army were dependent on early and accurate notification of their potential targets. Despite post-war boasting that the Polish air force was preserved almost intact, it did little to prevent the slow and vulnerable German observation aircraft and Stukas having the skies almost totally to themselves.

This fact alone engendered an almost hopeless feeling among the defending troops. The knowledge that they could scheme and burrow and lie in wait but were always bound to be observed and subsequently 'Stukaed' out of existence took the heart of them long before actual clashes. The Polish troops were brave and hardy, but endless retreat and endless bombing without respite eventually break even the most resilient of soldiers.

Thus it was that, on 7 September, strong Polish forces were observed on the southern side of the advancing German 10 Armee in the thickly-wooded hills around the town of Ilza. They were pulling back towards the safety of the Vistula river and General von Reichenau immediately put in hand steps to head them off. This was achieved after some fierce ground fighting as the desperate Poles tried to break out and, by 9 September, the German Panzers had encircled and trapped some six Polish divisions south of Radom. It only remained now for the Stukas to finish them off. Von Richthofen now sent in all available Stukas, more than 150 in all, including both Gruppen of St.G.77.

St.G.77 had moved up to keep pace with the army and by 8 September they had occupied forward bases at Tschenstochau and Kruszyna. They had also been reinforced by III./St.G.51. This gave Schwartzkopff some 140 Stukas immediately available. Before they could strike against the Ilza pocket however, they had been assigned the task of eliminating batteries of Polish heavy artillery located in the suburb of Praga, which were shelling the German forces advancing into western Warsaw itself.

This attack was launched on 8 September. The day dawned fair with perfect ground visibility and a maximum strike was put up by all available Stukas. Hand-held maps had already been marked in red with the locations of the heavy guns. The bridges across the river were used as sighting points to help the Junkers align themselves before going into their attack dives. Despite heavy flak all the dives were well pressed home and good targeting achieved. Nonetheless Polish resistance continued to be strong in the western suburbs and the Germans were forced to fall back.

The Stukas were needed everywhere and St.G.77 was next day switched to the south to clean up the Ilza pocket in close support of the Panzers. One of Schwartzkopff's Staffelkapitäns recorded how:

With their white crosses on their backs the tanks showed us the way. Wherever they went, we came across throngs of Polish troops, against which our 100 lb fragmentation bombs were deadly. After that we went almost down to the deck firing our machine-guns. The confusion was indescribable.

Strike after strike was made against this unhappy Polish force. It finally surrendered on 13 September. But well before this event St.G.77 had their targets hastily switched back again to the north-west of the Polish capital. Here an almost intact force, the Army of Posen under General Kutrzeba, had, on the night of 9/10 September, struck unexpectedly across the Bzura from the north around Kutno and moved towards Lodz. This threatened to annihilate the screening German 8 Armee and cut off the advancing 10 Armee.

An emergency appeal was issued by Polish Army Group South calling for every available aircraft to be thrown in to avert this dangerous movement. Accurate attacks by the dive bombers cut the bridges across which the Poles had advanced, thus cutting them off from their supplies. Stopped in their tracks they were then subjected to non-stop bombing and were cut to pieces.

This danger at an end, on 25 September the Luftwaffe resumed its attacks on Warsaw, Operation 'Seaside'. As the bulk of the twin-engined bombers had been withdrawn to watch the hitherto neglected Western Front, the bulk of these attacks were carried out by 240 Stuka dive bombers and over 100 Junkers Ju52 transport planes, both operating as horizontal bombers, the former bombing, the latter dropping incendiaries. By an all-out effort, with the aircraft of St.G.77

Towards the end of the Polish campaign, the Ju87s attacked strategic targets in the city of Warsaw itself. Here the gas works were picked out by St.G.77 from the surrounding area and totally demolished. (Schwartzkopff Archiv)

flying three sorties each day, this totally unsuitable force for the job achieved decisive results, dropping 500 tons of bombs and 72 tons of incendiary devices on the Polish fortifications in the city. The brave stand in the Polish capital was all the more poignant by its uselessness. In fact the Polish Commander-in-Chief, Marshal Edward Smigly-Rydz, who had promised his people he would 'sign a victorious peace in Berlin', had, as early as 19 September, sought refuge in Rumania.

The St.G.76 reverted to its proper precision role once more for the final acts of the Polish campaign when the strong fortress of Modlin was subjected to prolonged attacks on both 26 and 27 September. Meanwhile Soviet Russia had invaded from the east and at midnight the Poles laid down their arms.

There can be no doubt that the work of the dive bomber in this quick and conclusive campaign had been decisive. The laurels earned by St.G.77 in leading the attack were well-merited and indeed the *whole* campaign had cost a total of only 31 Junkers Ju87s lost in combat. It was a stunning début. Even the official British verdict, so often deeply biased against dive bombing, was forced to concede that:

The outstanding success of the campaign was the successful use of the Ju87 dive bomber. With little or no opposition to hamper them the units equipped with this aircraft were able to exploit the accuracy of bomb aiming inherent in the steep dive, as well as the demoralising effect on personnel exposed to dive-bombing attacks.

For Günter Schwartzkopff and his team the results were no more than they had been predicting for some time and the results of their own dedicated training and hard work. Even the most vociferous opponents of the Stuka within the Luftwaffe were silenced. More, as General Albert Kesselring was himself to point out, 'In this campaign the Luftwaffe learned many lessons…and prepared itself for a second, more strenuous and decisive clash of arms.'

While the St.G.77 was earning its spurs in Poland, fresh young pilots and radio operators were undergoing their detailed training in readiness to join their ranks and take the place of those that had fallen. Typical among these was a young

radio operator/rear gunner, Heinz Sellhorn. He had volunteered for the Luftwaffe on leaving school and, at the age of 17 was sent to a Flieger Ausbildungs
Regiment (the recruit depot). Here he underwent the usual 12 month basic training, which included the normal physical training and military disciplines of drill
and weapon training, with map-reading and principles of wireless operation
given in lectures. These were interspersed with route marches and army-type
discipline under canvas and in barracks. After passing out of the recruit depot,
the young men joined the Fluganwärterkompanie, a pool of such recruits
awaiting their deployment either to flying training or radio operator postings.
Two months were spent in the study of general aeronautical subjects in preparation for this, during which they could be studied to see which job they were most
suitable for. At the end of this period Heinz had commenced his basic radio training skills.

Those young men selected for dive bomber pilots while at normal pilot schools,
went on to a further specialised dive bomber school. Here they spent an additional four months during which, after 15 dives with an instructor, they would go
solo. There was a limit during training of 15 dives per day as the strain was intense. Training dives were usually conducted from 12,000 feet to bomb-release
and pull-out at 3,000 feet. While tactics and navigation were stressed, the main
emphasis on these courses was, as one would expect, on achieving accuracy.

The Stuka was an easy aircraft to fly. All-round vision, so essential in dive
bombing, was excellent and the aircraft was so designed and built that it reached
its most 'natural' flying position when heading straight down vertically in a
power dive. Most other specialised dive bombers were dived at angles of 70
degrees, adapted fighters at 50 degrees or less, but the Junkers Ju87 was *the* true
dive bomber, and heading down towards the target at 90 degrees found it at its
very best.

The sequences for warm-up, take-off, flight to the target, dive and landing
were listed in detail in an St.G.77 pilots' handbook for the Ju87D.

1.   Set the throttle quadrant to '1'.
2.   Set the petrol fuel cock to 'Both'.
3.   Handpump the primer.
4.   Switch on fuel booster pumps.
5.   Push the self-start handle on the left-hand side for ten seconds to energise the inertia
     starter and booster coil. Then pull the handle out to fire the engine.
6.   Set magnetos at 'M1 + M2' to energise.
7.   Open fuel cock a little.
8.   Boost fuel pump to the 4–5 mark.
9.   Move the self-start handle as the engine fires, at the same time further depressing the
     booster switch. Once the engine is running smoothly release the self-start handle.
10. With under 1,000 U/min allow the engine to turn over gently until the oil
     temperature is at 40 degrees and the water temperature is at 60 degrees.
11. The engine will then be 'running up'.

If starting by hand cranking then the procedure would be the same for the first
three operations and then:

4.   Set the crank to 'Swing energy start' on the engine, and insert the crank at the rear,
left-hand side. The two ground crew required to provide the motive power would then
turn the crank to Point 5, then apply their muscles! With the tailplane held the brakes

off revs could be made up to 1,600 rpm. Above this a maximum rpm of 2,200 could be achieved with the boost but the tailplane needed to be held down as the nose-heavy dive bomber would tilt over.

Warming-up procedure was as follows:

1. Allow the temperature to reach Point 1.0 on the *Atas* booster scale.
2. Slowly open the throttle to 'full'.
3. Change ignition setting to 'M1', and then to 'M2', revving at 'M1' being 100 max, and to 'M27' being 150 U/min per min for magneto checks.
4. Turn fuel cock first to 'left-' and then 'right-hand' fuel tanks.
5. Taxi out with tailwheel in 'free' position.

Take-off procedure was as follows:

1: Tailwheel locked into position.
2: Fuel pumps checked switched 'on'.
3: Airscrew pitch handle set to 'start'.
4: Trimming tabs set to 'zero'.
5: Flaps set to 'take-off' position.
6: At 116 km/h (72 mph) lift-off speed is reached after a distance of approx 450 metres.
7: Power is achieved 1.15 *Atas* boost and 2,300 rpm.
8: Flaps automatically retract and signal lamps for both sets as indicated when in 'zero' (Rest) positions. For normal flight.
9: The speed is increased to 215 km/h for initial climb.
10: For each 1,000 metres of climb speed can be dropped back 10 km/h.
11: On attaining a height of 3,500 metres (11,480 feet) move supercharger from 'low' to 'auto'.

Once over the required target the Stuka went into its dive sequence. The cockpit procedures for this were as follows:

1: Set flaps to 'cruise' position.
2: Set elevator trims to 'cruise' position.
3: Set rudder trim to 'cruise' position.
4: Set airscrew pitch at 'cruise' position.
5: Switch on contact altimeter.
6: Set contact altimeter to required release altitude mark.
7: Set supercharger to 'auto'.
8: Throttle back the engine.
9: Close cooler flaps.
10: Open dive brakes.

Actuating the dive brakes at the end of this sequence automatically set in train the pull-out mechanism and the safety pilot system as well as making the Ju87 nose over. Red indicators on the top wing surfaces indicated to the pilot that his powerful dive brakes had correctly extended. Simultaneously the dive recovery mechanism and safety pilot control were activated. The latter was a unique hydraulic device which restricted the movement of the control column to within 5 degrees either side of neutral. The object of this was to limit high G loading on pull-out.

The Askania dive recovery mechanism was activated by the bomb release and automatically returned the elevator trimmer flaps to 'normal' which there initiated the aircraft's pull-out. It could be overidden by the pilot if necessary.

Above *Ground personnel place 110 lb bombs on the underwing racks of a Ju87 B–1 in the field during exercises carried out in the spring of 1940 prior to the offensive in the west.* (Schwartzkopff Archiv)

Left *Schwartzkopff in his Storch aircraft.* (Schwartz-kopff Archiv)

The actual angle of the dive was calculated by the pilot with the aid of inclination marks etched on the front screen of the starboard side of the cockpit. They were calibrated from 30 degrees in tens through to 90 degrees and highlighted in red.

Once vertical (the normal angle for the Stuka) speed built up rapidly to 335 mph within 1,370 metres where it could be held. Maximum permitted speed in a dive was well over 600 km/h (to 404 mph) and the pilot sighted the target up over the aircraft's nose. A Revi C-12-C bombing and gun-aiming reflector sight had

Above *I./St.G.77 re-equipped with the Junkers Ju87B in 1939. Here 1. Staffel is seen coming in to land at Celle airfield.* (Sellhorn Archiv)

Right *A stepped-up echelon of Ju87s from the I./St.G.77 peeling off into the dive attack.* (Maahs via Sellhorn Archiv)

replaced the *Sturvi* sight used on the *Antons*. As mentioned, so perfectly balanced was the Ju87 that the aircraft could be kept turned easily and simply using the ailerons to keep the machine on the target.

Neither the rudder nor the elevator trimmers were used in the dive sequence. As the height rapidly reeled off the altimeter, a signal light lit up. On this signal the pilot depressed the control column to initiate the Askania automatic pull-out device which worked at a height of 450 metres (1,475 feet). A force of some 6G was exercised on the crew at this point. Should this device fail, the pilot could manually override on the stick and elevator trimmers.

Once the nose had come up again with bomb load gone, the pilot retracted the dive brakes, re-set the airscrew pitch to its setting and opened the throttle to 1.35 *Atas* of boost before closing the radiator flaps.

Landing procedure was as follows:

1: Reduce speed to 200 km/h (125 mph).
2: At 180 km/h (112 mph) lower flaps.
3: The tailwheel is then locked. [The Stuka, being nose-heavy for diving purposes, had a penchant for making nose-down landings unless a three-point landing could be achieved each time.]
4: Set airscrew pitch to 'fine'.
5: Reduce speed to 120 km/h (75 mph) for final approach.

To switch off the engine the procedure was:

1. Turn off all coolers.
2. Allow the motor to cold run at 1,000 rpm to cool the engine temperature to below 95 degrees.
3. Close cooler valves.
4. Give little fuel.
5. Turn ignition to 'finish'.
6. Turn fuel cock to 'quickstop'.
7. With airscrew stopped, lock brakes.

Those like Heinz Sellhorn who were selected for radio operators went to their own specialised schools before moving on to join their units. The training of W/T operators for the Luftwaffe took about a year and involved basic wireless-telegraphy and signals work as well as basic navigation techniques. Stuka radio equipment was basic anyway; since the aircraft was specifically designed for short-range and close support operations, the more complex direction-finding and navigation equipment was not deemed necessary.

Heinz was assigned for radio training, which was conducted at the school set up at Halle/Saale airfield. Much of the wireless operator training was done actually in the air. Several of ubiquitous Junkers Ju52/3m's were fitted out as flying classrooms and lessons learned on the ground were transferred to the sky as much as possible.

Heinz was first airborne in Ju52 AGOX to conduct his training (described as 'tactical work') at 1440 on 24 September 1939. This flight lasted for 184 min and the distance covered was 605 km. This was to set the pattern for the rest of the course. Between 25 September and 23 November a further 25 such flights took place with various Ju52's teaching aircraft (mainly AGOX but also G6+FU, G6+Es, S3+F32, S3+F33 and so on) and with pilots Uffz Debesky, Minier, Kopp, Thieme, Gefr Messerschmidt, Fw. Ittner, Fw Wobst, Uffz Forbst, etc.

A Stuka rear-man's job combined the working of the main FuG VIIa cockpit radio which was positioned directly behind the pilot's seat and for defence work he had a MG15 machine gun which was mounted in a rotating rear gun mount with a pivotal ball-and-socket attachment.

It was not until December that, all qualifications achieved, Heinz was assigned to his Stuka unit, 1.Stuka 77. The first flight in a Junkers Ju87 took place on the 4th. With Leutnant Jacob as his pilot instructor aboard Ju87 S2+GH, Heinz took part in a Staffel exercise from Celle airfield. They took off at 1417 and the exercise lasted for 91 min, with distance covered being 380 km.

Heinz's diary gives a picture of the slow but increasing tempo of practice and more practice, as expertise was carefully built up during that long hard winter. Hitler's eager plans to get on with smashing the West had to take a back-seat to his advisors' caution and the bitterness of the weather. This gave new recruits to the Stuka units time to perfect their skills and the already blooded veterans a chance to bring in lessons of the Polish campaign.

28. Uffz Papenheim: Ju87 S2+GF, Ketten exercise, Celle, 5-12-39, 0905–Celle, 5-12-39, 1030: 85 mins, 350 km.
29. Uffz Papenheim: Ju87 S2+GF, Staffel exercise, Celle, 6-12-39, 0904–Celle, 6-12-39, 1006: 62 mins, 260 km.
30. Uffz Papenheim: Ju87 S2+GF, Staffel exercise, Celle, 7-12-39, 1502–1542: 40 mins, 165 km.
31. Uffz Papenheim: Ju87, Ketten exercise, Celle, 27-12-39, 0942–1058: 76 mins, 320 km.
32. Uffz Papenheim: Ju87 S2+GM, Ketten exercise, Celle, 28-12-39, 0915–1024: 69 mins, 290 km.
33. Lt Jacob: Ju87 S2+GH, Ketten exercise, Celle, 28-12-39, 1350–1500: 70 mins, 290 km.
34. Uffz Papenheim: Ju87 S2+GJ, Ketten exercise, Celle, 29-12-39, 0858–1014: 76 mins, 320 km.
35. Uffz Schuh: Ju87 S2+GO, Staffel exercise, 10-1-40, 1343, Celle: 93 mins, 390 km (killed in Russia 1941).
36. Uffz Schuh: Ju87 S2+GO, Staffel exercise, Celle, 12-1-40, 1343–1509: 96 mins, 400 km.
37. Lt Hitz: Ju87 S2+GH, Staffel exercise, Celle, 18-1-40, 1323–1428: 65 mins, 270 km.
38. Uffz Papenheim: Ju87 S2+GF, Bombing work, Celle, 19-1-40, 1006–1030: 24 mins, 100 km.
39. Uffz Papenheim: Ju87 S2+GF, Bombing work, Celle, 19-1-39, 1040–1100: 20 mins, 85 km.
40. Lt. Leicht: Ju87 S2+GF, Targeting flight, Celle, 2-2-40, 1004–1020: 16 mins, 65 km.
41. Uffz Knauer: Ju87 S2+GF, Targeting flight, Celle, 2-2-40, 1026–1037: 11 mins, 45 km.
42. Uffz Papenheim: Ju87 S2+GF, Targeting flight, Celle, 2-2-40, 1043–1115: 32 mins, 130 km.
43. Uffz Weniger: Ju87 S2+GG, Targeting flight, Celle, 2-2-40, 1120–1133: 13 mins, 55 km (killed on 18-8-40 over the Channel).
44. Lt. Leicht: Ju87 S2+GG, Bombing work, Celle, 9-2-40, 1345–1415: 30 mins, 125 km.
45. Lt. Leicht: Ju87 S2+GG, Bombing work, Celle, 9-2-40, 1423–1442: 19 mins, 80 km.
46. Lt. Leicht: Ju87 S2+GG, Bombing work, Celle, 9-2-40, 1453–1510: 17 mins, 70 km.
47. Lt. Leicht: Ju87 S2+GG, Bombing work, Celle, 9-2-40, 1517–1541: 24 mins, 100 km.
48. Lt. Leicht: Ju87 S2+GG, Bombing work, Celle, 9-2-40, 1615–1652: 37 mins, 155 km.
49. Uffz Knauer: Ju87 S2+JH, High flying, Lippstadt, 19-2-40, 0920–1037: 77 mins, 320 km (7000 m).
50. Uffz Knauer: Ju87 S2+JH, Ketten exercise, Lippenstadt, 7-3-40, 0840–0850: 10 mins, 40 km.

Spring was coming, and with it a new urgency for the Stuka units. The movement to German airfields near the French and Dutch border areas only gave confirmation that this period of 'Phoney War' would not last very much longer.

IV
Across the Maas and the Meuse

As the tension grew from the beginning of the new year so did the pace and urgency of the Stuka training. Major Waldemar Plewig gave me this description of the build-up of St.G.77's momentum in readiness for the spring operations in the west:

After various moves in the wake of the Polish campaign, after we returned home we were eventually based at Cologne. Here the Group intensified its preparation and, in April, I was made Kommandeur of the II./St.G.77 which was at its peacetime base of Schweinfurt. We were soon involved in detailed planning with the paratroops who had been assigned to storm the Belgian fortress of Eben Emael.

From January 1940 both these units were placed under the strictest security blanket and it was not until 0200 on the morning of 10 May that I was allowed to give my men details of their operational orders. The day before, 9 May, my commander, Günter Schwartzkopff, and I were still at Lippstadt, where our training school existed. We were actually involved in taking examinations for corporals when we received the command to set the much rehearsed operation in train.

The operation against a pinpoint target in the very limited area of Fort Eben Emael, where we had to bomb right next to the previously landed gliders and paratroops, not only called for the highest accuracy, but placed great responsibility on my young aircrew.

We exercised as in peacetime, and nobody except myself knew which target was next. When the Luftwaffe High Command proposed that we should use live bombs in these training sessions with our troops on the ground, I declined, and pointed out that an accidentally misplaced bomb during training could ruin both forces' morale and thus adversely influence the real operation's efficiency when it came.

They eventually agreed with me and so we practised with cement training bombs with similar weights and properties but no explosives. My wing was also supplied with the so-called sirens, the 'Trombones of Jericho'. Trials with the 'Organ Pipes' on the undercarriages of the Ju87B did not have the required success as they 'somersaulted' when we were in the dive which made them useless. My very clever maintenance engineer proposed a solution filling the ventilators with ball bearings. This worked fine and before the opening of the French campaign we were fitted with these. They were a big morale booster. For example, at the training camp of Köln-Wahn before 10 May 1940, we attacked a bunker. A lot of Wehrmacht generals had come to watch. When our chain of Stukas dived on the target bunker with the sirens at full cry it had a quite unnerving effect on most of the onlookers – save one. Never have I seen so many red-striped pants bending for cover in front of one lieutenant and two sergeants. After they recovered and saw the accuracy of our shooting combined with that morale effect they quickly changed their bias against the Luftwaffe and afterward the Army was only too glad of our support!

For Heinz Sellhorn still learning his trade, it was fairly obvious from the increased tempo of operations at Lippstadt that something big was brewing, even if he was not privy to the exact details. Again entries from the diary reflect this in both types of targets and the numbers of missions conducted:

51. Uffz Palisek: Ju87 S2+LH, Staffel exercise, Lippstadt, 26-3-40, 1415–1541: 86 mins, 360 km.
52. Lt Hitz: Ju87 S2+HH, Staffel exercise, Lippstadt, 29-3-40, 1425–1552: 87 mins, 360 km (Bombing work and low-level attack).
53. Fw Knauer: Ju87 S2+JH, Bombing work, Lippstadt, 1-4-40, 0826–0854: 28 mins, 115 km.
54. Fw Knauer: Ju87 S2+JH, Bombing work, Lippstadt, 1-4-40, 0905–0954: 49 mins, 205 km.
55. Fw Knauer: Ju87 S2+DH, Bombing work, Lippstadt, 1-4-40, 1405–1429: 24 mins, 100 km.
56. Fw Knauer: Ju87 S2+DH, Bombing work, Lippstadt, 1-4-40, 1436–1452: 16 mins, 65 km.
57. Fw Knauer: Ju87 S2+DH, Bombing work, Lippstadt, 1-4-40, 1505–1524: 16 mins, 65 km.
58. Fw Knauer: Ju87 S2+DH, Bombing work, Lippstadt, 1-4-40, 1605–1632: 27 mins, 110 km.

Of course there were many new faces as the build-up increased. Flying his first war sorties with the St.G.77 was Oberleutnant Hans-Karl Sattler, born at Herbstein/Oberhessen in 1917. He had volunteered for the Luftwaffe, and was initially assigned to a Flak unit but at the age of twenty he had begun his Stuka training and was with his unit, the III./St.G.77, as the hours to zero ticked away.

Helmut Leicht was among Plewig's team waiting to support the paratroops at Maastricht and Eben Emael before assisting the Panzer units in the thrust from Sedan.

Major Heinz-Günter Amelung, from Magdeburg, had served as a pilot with 6./St.G.77 in Poland. Hauptmann Gerhard Bauhaus, born in 1908 at Brunen-bei-Wesel, had also fought in Poland with the IV./LG.1, but transferred to the Stukas in February 1940 as a pilot with the Stabstaffel of the St.G.77. Similarly, Hauptmann Karl Fitzner from Düsseldorf had joined the Luftwaffe in 1935 and received pilot training. He had then served with the Legion Kondor in Spain as an Unteroffizier, first with 5./J.88 and then with K/88 with the Stuka-Staffel between mid-1938 and March 1939. He served as one of the instructors at the Stukaschule and then in Poland with the 1./St.G.77 with which unit he awaited the 'Go' against France.

Major Helmuth Bode, a 33-year-old from Metz/Lothringen, had been a reservist as flying instructor at the Deutsche Verkehrsfliegerschule in 1936 but in June 1938 became active with the rank of Oberleutnant as pilot with Kustenaufklarungsstaffel 2/506 Dievenow. He volunteered for the dive bombers and, between June and August 1939, attended the Stukaschule at Kitzingen. By 1939 he had become Staffelkapitän 1.(Stuka)/186 at Kiel/Holtenau. He was to fly his first combat missions as the Gruppenkommandeur of III./St.G.77.

Leutnant Werner Haugk, age 28, from Gelsenkirchen, was also to cut his teeth in the French Campaign with St.G.77. He had entered the Wehrmacht in October 1934 before transferring, like so many others, to become a Stuka pilot in August 1939.

Others already had plenty of combat flying experience under their belts. The very popular Hauptmann Georg 'Jonny' Jauernik, born at Leiswitz/Oberschlesien in November 1915, had served in Poland and was waiting with his fellow pilots of II./St.G.77 to settle accounts with the main enemy.

Oberfeldwebel Hans Meier from Hamburg-Wandsbeck was the same age but already one of the most experienced pilots of the St.G.77 for he had flown with the 7. Staffel of III. Gruppe, for a considerable time in Poland.

A former Hamburg policeman, Oberstleutnant Gustav Pressler had transferred to the Luftwaffe as officer cadet in April 1934. By the following October he was a Leutnant at the Magdeburg flying school. Dive bomber and fighter training with the Geschwader 'Immelmann' in Schwerin-Gorries followed in March 1936 and in May 1937 he was serving with III. Stuka/Lehrgeschwader in Barth (Pomerania), as head of the I. Flugbetriebskompanie. By the spring of 1939 Gustav had become Staffelkapitän of the 4./St.G.77 both at Schweinfurt and in Breslau-Schöngarten prior to combat missions in Poland.

Serving with III./St.G.77 in May 1940 was Oberleutnant Johann Waldhauser from Freising/Obb who had joined the army as long ago as March 1931. He had switched to the Luftwaffe as an Unteroffizier in 1935 and then received Stuka training. He had fought as an Oberfeldwebel in the Polish campaign and was actually one of the first Stuka men to be awarded the Iron Cross, Second Class as a result.

Hauptmann Otto Schmidt, born February 1917 at Bruhlhof/Gemeinde Wehbach/Sieg, had also fought in Poland with the I./St.G.76 and was to fly Stukas in France with the same unit, which only later became the third group of St.G.77. Werner 'Piepel' Weihrauch was to fly his first war sortie with the 3. Staffel.

A few newcomers were not destined to get into action yet. Oberfeldwebel Adolf Weiss from Munich was one. He had commenced Stuka pilot training at Insterburg in 1939, but did not join the 4./St.G.77 until the French campaign was over. He had to wait until August to make his début during the difficult days of the Battle of Britain. Franz Kieslich transferred to 7./St.G.77 in France but saw no action. Their time was yet to come.

The bulk of those waiting on their forward airfields in those hot late spring days we have met already. Herbert Dawedeit was with the 8. Staffel, and so was Gerhardt Bauer. Friedrich-Karl Freiherr von Dalwigk zu Lichtenfels was destined to take part in almost every one of the attacks in the west, where his decisive leadership frequently proved the turning point on difficult missions. After combat in Poland Kurt Huhn was a Staffelkapitän, and Oberstleutnant Georg Jakob was to fly a record 38 combat missions in France in the weeks ahead.

'Alex' Gläser was with the 2. Staffel, Karl Henze continued as the popular Gruppenadjutant of the I./St.G.77 where he was to remain until mid-1941. Günter Hitz who had served in Poland with I./St.G.77 was still with that unit. Franz Hettinger was ready, as was Helmut Bruck, already famous, and earning his reputation for luck after being shot down on his second mission on the first day of the Polish campaign and being rescued by German Panzer forces. That experience had far from dampened his ardour for the fray ahead.

Alois Wosnitza was to be flying with 2./St.G.77 in France. Hermann Ruppert, Rudolf Weigel, Paul Langkopf and Walter Stimpel were all ready.

St.G.77, however, lost some of its more experienced men to other commands just prior to the *Blitzkrieg* in the west. Arnulf Blasig, who had served as Oberleutnant and Kompaniechef with I./St.G.77 in Polish campaign had been transferred to IV/LG 1. Similarly, after serving with St.G.77 Lothar Lau was made Staffelkapitän of 8.St.G.2 in March 1940 and continued his career with that outfit. Clemens Graf von Schönborn-Wiesentheid had become Kommandeur of the III./St.G.2 'Immelmann' in France in February 1940. But on the whole the team was as strong as ever if not more so. And now, for better or worse, at first light on 10 May 1940, the die was cast.

The German plans called for heavy attacks into Holland and Belgium to quickly force and overrun the traditional maze of forts, river and canal lines, and strong defensive positions that dominated this triangle of border defences. Not only would it speed the advance of German forces into the Low Countries, but it would have the desired effect of pulling the main Allied armies up into Belgium and stretching their necks in readiness for the decisive 'Sickle' cut which would sever the head from the administrative body. The plan worked perfectly and the Allies, alarmed at the speed and intensity of the German attacks, duly complied, keeping their eyes fixed firmly on this battlefield while the huge German build-up in the Ardennes went unhindered.

The well-planned attack by Plewig's Stukas and the paratroops on the Belgian fortress of Eban Emael went off almost exactly as planned. A garrison of 1,200 men surrendered to 70 German paras, the latter losing only six men dead in the battle, St.G.1 had accurately bombed the Belgian support positions in close support of airborne troops and, with no relief forthcoming, the garrison commander had given in.

In the initial German push into the Netherlands one of the most crucial operations was the securing in good condition of three important bridges over the Maas which would open the way to the very heart of Rotterdam. One bridge was at Moerdijk and two at Dordrecht, and St.G.77 played an essential part in their capture. As usual Günter Schwartzkopff led from the front. As his brother related:

Silhouetted against early morning sunlight reflecting from the clouds, a Rotte of Berthas heads west towards the Belgian frontier from its German base in May 1940. (Schwartzkopff Archiv)

On 10 May, very early in the morning, the Geschwader flew over the Kölner Platz in battle formation. It was still dark, and only the Stukas' exhaust valves showed any light. Your father had earlier gone from squadron to squadron and begged officers and men to keep highest discipline for this vital battle then commencing. Then all the aircraft took off. Your father was first and led the way. After one and a half hours the first 'planes started to come back from their mission; last back your father. He stayed over the target because he wanted to see what damage was done by the bombs. Some of his 'planes were shot down but did their jobs well.

The first combat mission of the *Blitzkrieg* against the West to be noted in the Sellhorn logbooks took off from Cologne (Köln) airfield at 0555. With Unteroffizier Palisek piloting Stuka S2+HK, the target was positioned at the village of Dreimgstadt, some nine kilometres west of Maastricht. This was conducted without incident and, after a hasty landing, re-arming and re-fuelling 1./St.G.77 was airborne again at 0815. This time the Stukas hit positions at Cygenbilsen, nine kilometres north-west of Maastricht.

Now was set the pattern of St.G.77's operations: non-stop missions were the norm, several a day, the dive bombers picking out fortifications, bunkers, command headquarters and defence works all along the border and operating an intensive shuttle to and from the most crucial points of the battle front. At the beginning they were working from their own main peacetime bases on German soil, but soon they were being hurried forward, on an almost daily basis, as the advance began to penetrate and roll forward towards the coast.

They changed aircraft for the third sortie and, with Sellhorn in S2+MH, took off at 1100 from Köln to conduct ground-strafing attacks on Dutch forces offering resistance at the hamlet of Vroenhofer, some five kilometres south-west of Maastricht again. Here, while the Stukas kept the defenders' heads well down, one of the vital bridges over the Albert Canal was taken at the rush by the German 'Storm-Group Iron' and captured intact.

St.G.77 followed up this success an hour later by a dive bombing attack on enemy-fortified positions by Kesselt, four kilometres south-west of Maastricht. The final mission of an epic day was a longer-range dive bombing sortie directed against shipping, docks and harbour installations at the port of Antwerp.

Next day the pressure was maintained in the north with an early attack against Oitschaft Poppel, a village 15 kilometres from Tinschoirt. They then transferred to Aachen airfield to prepare for the next moves.

Although the Dutch army counter-attacked at Dordrecht, the 120 paratroops of 11 Company, 16th Infantry Regiment held on to their gains. Similar sacrifice reaped benefits at Moerdijk. These holding operations were given almost continuous Stuka support. Yet further sorties preluded the deep armoured thrusts made by the Germans on either side of the fortress town of Liège. On 12 May, St.G.77 combined with St.G.2 in attacks on enemy armoured columns to the west of Liège.

Following this, on 15 May, with Sellhorn once more flying Ju87 S2+BH, they flew from Aachen early in the morning and delivered precision attacks on enemy positions close by Gembloux, some 17 kilometres north-west of Namur.

It was now time for the 'Sickle' to be swung. By the evening of 12 May, the spearheads of 20 mile long Panzer and motorised infantry divisions had reached the river Meuse near Sedan. The task of the Stukas was, as always, to crush any

Ju87 aircraft of a Staffel from the I./St.G.77 seen over Köln/Aachen airfield on 13 May 1940, during the opening days of the campaign in France and Belgium. (Schobert via Sellhorn Archiv)

resistance at this northern extension of the Maginot Line. Therefore VII Fliegerkorps was transferred in readiness.

For the operations in France, I. and II./St.G.77, which were controlled by Fliegerkorps VIII, led by Generalleutnant Wolfram Freiherr von Richthofen, were sent south to work as a part of under Luftflotte 2. The Stukageschwader were assigned to the direct support of both General von Reichenau's 6th Army and General Hoepner's 16th Panzerkorps. Their first tasks in this respect were concentrated attacks on Allied columns pushing up into Belgium in the Liège area on 11 and 12 May.

Waldemar Plewig recalled to me:

After the concentrated operations at Eben Emael they transferred our whole wing. The further operations asked of us as we crossed the Maginot Line required great precision from our pilots as we had to drop the bombs just in front of our own troops amongst the guns.

In order to assist the German 19 and 21 Armies in their crossing of the Meuse near Sedan on 13 May, St.G.77's Stukas were fully armed and fuelled on their new home airfields. Then they were ready. Daring advance units had already found unguarded ways across the river but they needed reinforcing and back-up. Thus, at 1600 that afternoon a very effective precision attack was delivered by St.G.77 on defending French artillery emplacements and anti-aircraft positions on the west bank of the river. They tipped over and dived low through thick flak. The results were remarkable. According to one account:

The noise was terrifying; the wailing of engines and sirens pierced by the shriek and crash of falling bombs totally demoralised the defenders. After five hours, during which more than 200 Stukas sorties were flown, the German Army crossed the Meuse to find the French soldiers too stunned to fight back.

St.G.77 had opened the door to an incredible victory. But it had paid a high cost. Not in numbers, very few Stukas had been lost, but the highest price of all, their leader. Oberst Günter Schwartzkopff died on 15 May leading as always, while making a dive-bombing attack at Le Chesne near Sedan. For his outstanding

15 May 1940. In the sunlit fields of Le Chesne in northern France lies the shattered and almost unrecognisable wreckage of Schwartzkopff's Stuka. Hit by French AA gunners during an attack, he was leading his dive bombers in the vital strike which broke the enemy and allowed the full flood of the Blitzkrieg to sweep west. (Schwartz-kopff Archiv)

The tailplane of Schwartz-kopff's wrecked Stuka. Both Günter and his rear-seat man died instantly. Contrary to Göring's orders, the Kommodore was once more personally leading St.G.77 into action. (Schwartzkopff Archiv)

work and his personal success he was posthumously distinguished with the Ritterkreuz and promoted to Generalmajor. How did it happen? Günter Schwartzkopff's brother was to tell his son Peter this story:

I was in Aachen with my formation – the telephone rang. It was your father to tell me that he would be with me after the mission at 1700. At 1615 a formation of dive bombers came over Aachen at 2–3,000 metres' height. I sat on the grass and waited. First came two wounded crew, both men were in a bad state. At 1800 I was finally told that your father had not returned. But there was contradictory news; your father was first up and after being shot down was supposed to have gone up again and fought against the enemy.

Another story had it that he had used his parachute to escape from his damaged aircraft. They added that more than 1,000 planes from both sides were in the air and 100 planes at least on both sides were shot down. There will never be a full explanation. His papers, all personal belongings – diary, medals, rings, sign of ranks were taken away. A general who landed at Aachen told me that the loss of your father was the greatest loss. On May 12 Goering had promulgated an order ordering that your father relinquish command and return to Berlin to work as an inspector. His great knowledge and skill were deemed too valuable to risk on the field of battle. That order arrived at Luftflotte HQ on the 14 May.

Whether after some two or three years had passed your father would have been the scapegoat for failures by the politicians, like Udet, I don't know, but it would have been possible. His straight character and love for his Fatherland may have provided reasons enough to get rid of him. All were convinced better he should die in battle.

Dr Bamberg also wrote to Peter Schwartzkopff many years later:

I was at that time Lieutenant but never kept a War diary – it was the duty of the captain. As I remember, he thought that your father's aircraft had been hit by French flak while leading the dive attack. It is tragic that your father, who was at all times correct, in this case had not listened to an order to remain grounded. It cost him his life. He was known as 'Father of the Stukas' for he had both created and led this force. His knowledge of the Stuka was vital and for that reason he should not have flown any more. But he did not like to sit back when others had to fly against the enemy.

His name is commemorated on a plaque at the General Schwartzkopff Barracks in Hamburg. His posthumous promotion to Generalmajor was retrospective as of 1 May 1940, the posthumous award of the Ritterkreuz following on 24 November. His place as Kommodore of St.G.77 was taken by Graff von Shönborn-Wiesentheid.

Apart from this tragic loss the river crossing had been won, the French outer crust of defence was pierced in several places and the Panzers rolled through. To their surprise they found that behind that outer shield lay very little. Against reserve troops already demoralised by the effect of Stuka or scared-stiff by tales of the screaming dive bombers and German tanks running wild in their rear, the Germans found little opposition to their advance. Cautiously at first, then with increasing confidence, they pushed on.

Waldemar Plewig recalled this period thus:

We followed the flood of the battle moving constantly to various advanced airfields. Thanks to the really excellent organisation of General Pflugbeil and the ever-readiness of the two airfield service squadrons, which had been strengthened by the Workers Battalion of young men of under normal active service age but who had high technical 'know-how', we could in quick succession give our advancing Panzer formations badly-needed and required air support. During this intensive period St.G.77 was set aside to concentrate solely on support of protection of army units and was held exclusively for such work under the Richthofen Fliegerkorps.

The other key, apart from mobility and accuracy, was knowledge of the enemy. St.G.77 was well served by spotting aircraft who reported every Allied move and counter-move in advance. Using a wide variety of aircraft, camera-equipped Dorniers for long-range work and the little Hs126s over the immediate battle-front, each French attempt at a stand was smashed before it got started. Where the spotter planes were seen the Stukas would quickly follow.

During the advance through France [Plewig continued to me] on one of our rare periods of 'rest' without operations we set out to search for one of our aircraft which had crash-landed. On our way we bumped into a large group of French POWs milling around. We could not see any German guards so our interpreter, Captain Psalter, asked where they were off to. Despite their unenviable position one of the Frenchmen still had the spirit to shout back defiantly 'Berlin'!

I have always found such humour. The French then asked us to which unit or 'planes we belonged and our interpreter shouted back 'Stukas'. At this moment there was an ear-bursting noise and in loud and excited French they were all shouting, 'Attention Stuka'

Armourers and 'Blackmen' fusing and preparing a SC500 heavy bomb load on a forward airstrip in France in 1940. Note the protective ring around the nose cap used during transportation and for crated storage.
(Schwartzkopff Archiv)

Straight down! When the Stukas dived, they did so vertically, unlike most other dive bombers. This is the rear-seat man's view over the pilot's shoulders. The target is a French airfield, May 1940. (Sellhorn Archiv)

I./St.G.77 Stuka above the bomb explosions exactly placed on target in France, 1940. (Scheffel via Sellhorn Archiv)

The Battle of France 1940. The charred corpse and burnt-out remnants of a French field artillery gun after a column of the enemy had been caught by the Stukas moving up into position near the Dutch town of Maas early in the campaign. (Sellhorn Archiv)

A dive bombing attack by the I./St.G.77 on a French troop column in a village during the initial German advance to the coast, May 1940. (Sellhorn Archiv)

up and down the column. In no time at all the whole column, they were part of an infantry division, to left and to right were in full cover in the ditches. It was not easy to persuade the confused *poilus* to get up, they were still waiting for the oncoming 'planes. Their instant reaction to just one word proved to us the value of our contribution to the victory.

During the attack around the Belgian fortress town of Namur, we got orders to attack a large bunker with bombs. For this mission I fetched our reserve squadron from Lippstadt so that the pilots who had not yet been in combat could have a try. After about twenty bombs had hit we observed a white flag appear above the target. It ended in a verbal exchange between the 'Top Brass' and the German corps commander gave permission for the Belgian captain to be allowed to retain his sword. The latter gave the reason for his surrender as that his garrison company could not stand the high-pressure waves generated by our bombs inside his bunkers.

Very few effective French counter-attacks with tanks took place, even though the Allies actually had *more* tanks than the Germans (despite all the wartime and post-war myths to the contrary!) The French 4th Cuirasse Division, led by one Colonel Charles de Gaulle, tried, but was badly savaged by Stukas during their attempted counter-attack at Montcornet on 18 May. French tanks from this force were later found in ambush positions by the German reconnaissance aircraft, as Plewig relates:

One special task we were given, when we could not see any targets and we had to take responsibility, was to attack some French tanks which were well hidden in farmyards. With the newly-developed fragmentation bomb we achieved great success in our task. The French tanks were all ready to attack but we managed to disable them all by damaging their tracks.

Young Sellhorn was in the thick of it with various pilots. Flying with Feldwebel Mier in S2+HH from St Trond airfield, midway between Liège and Brussels, into which 1./St.G.77 had already moved such was the pace of the advance, he took off at 1925 on the evening of 16 May. One hundred kilometres distant, the dive bombers' target was Fort Sinarle six kilometres west-north-west of Namur. Next morning Urberoffizier Palisek piloting S2+LH, was his partner. They took off from St Trond at 0745 and attacked a column of retreating Allied infantry located in a small village 14 kilometres west of Rethel.

But already St Trond was far behind the advancing Panzers and, on the afternoon of 19 May, the Geschwader shifted base again, flying into Rocroi airfield in northern France, between Philippeville to the north and Charleville Mézières to the south. They were well inside that fateful corridor that the Germans were rapidly expanding as they reached for the sea. On 21 May they took time out to conduct a Ketten exercise from their new base with a 350 kilometre round flight that morning before re-commencing their work in earnest.

At 1935 the following evening they took off from Rocroi to strike at the British positions and the airfield at Merville, just 12 kilometres north of Béthune. Already the German spearheads had reached the Channel coast at Abbeville and a British armoured counter-attack south from Arras to sever the German corridor had been beaten off by Rommel and the 7th Panzers. The BEF was now fighting a rearguard action as it pulled back into an increasingly small perimeter with its back to the sea at Dunkirk and La Panne, while the ports of Boulogne and Calais were beleaguered. The garrison and trainloads of refugees were hastily evacuated at the former, the troops ordered to fight to the last at the latter.

The main British GHQ at Arras was soon invested on three sides and a French advance on 23 May was heavily counter-attacked by the Stukas near Cambrai and brought to a bloody halt. 1.St.G.77 itself launched an attack that morning, lifting off from Rocroi and hitting concentration of British troops discovered in some woodland 12 kilometres north of Arras. That afternoon they made a second attack, at 1430, this time dive bombing gun batteries at Ly, eight kilometres south of Le Chesne. The third attack made that day by the dive bombers was against destroyers and transports off the port of Boulogne itself. They took off from Rocroi for a 250 kilometre flight at the edge of their range, and reached the coast at 1925 to find the costal waters full of shipping.

This was the first time St.G.77 had attacked the high-speed targets of British destroyers and they found them difficult targets to pin down. Nonetheless, the impact of the Stukas on the warships was instant. Twenty-four Ju87s from 1./St.G.77 concentrated on the destroyer flotilla and followed their skidding evasive weaving by aileron turns. Bomb release was a low height in a determination to pin the ships down. The French destroyer *Orage* was hit and set on fire,

Cockpit detail of the Junkers Ju87B. (Sellhorn Archiv)

and sank after her survivors had been taken off. A second French destroyer, *Frondeur*, was badly damaged. The British destroyer *Whitshed* was near-missed and damaged, with casualties aboard, but carried on with the evacuation. The Germans lost no bombers either to the ships' fire or nine RAF Spitfires which arrived as the attacks were ending.

The Stukagruppen had brought to the battlefield an extreme concentration of air striking power. They had devastated rear areas and had been instrumental in opening the path to the Channel coast. All this was done with minimal loss, despite exaggerated Allied claims, for although a few Stukas were lost, in addition to their leader, overall casualties were very light. On 25 May, St.G.77 flew a series of counter-artillery operations near St Quentin. Boulogne had fallen on 25 May and next day the first attack was made by St.G.77 on the town of Calais itself. Wave after wave of Stukas pounded the British positions non-stop for an hour between 0900 and 1000.

The Germans were now having problems in reaching the coast and another shift forward of bases was urgently required. The supply parties and transport was now at full stretch trying to keep up with the dive bombers and it was still from Rocroi that Stab St.G.77 was operating on the evening of 25 May when their targets were this time French troop concentrations located in some woods between Flers-sur-Noye and Jumei, 15 kilometres to the south of Amiens. The split between the French, now mainly south of the river Somme and the rest of the Allies hemmed in on the Channel coast, was complete.

Two days later on 27 May, Fliegerkorps VIII was unleashed against Dunkirk. Stab St.G.77 was still working from Rocroi and another long-range strike was made against troop concentrations and ammunition columns in the village of Poperinge, to the west of Ypres and on the extreme edge of the Dunkirk perimeter. For the first time Sellhorn's aircraft, the faithful S2+MH piloted by Palisek, was hit from the ground fire in return, a solitary machine-gun bullet hole being taken in the rear fuselage without effect.

On 29 May all three Stuka Geschwader attacked beaches and shipping at Dunkirk around about 1500. The RAF and Royal Navy claimed 11 out of 180 Ju87s had been destroyed, but this was not the case. The figures were wildly exaggerated and RAF claimed 78 German planes shot down (later reduced to 43), the Royal Navy claimed 13, French pilots claimed 10. In truth, total Luftwaffe losses of *all* types that day were only 29 machines. As the British position worsened the claim exaggerations got more unreal. The total RAF claim of 'Confirmed kills' over Dunkirk was 377 (later reduced to 262). The stark truth was that the Luftwaffe lost only 132 aircraft of all types to all causes, including many to ships' gunfire.

The Stukas made three mass attacks on beaches on 1 June and caused enormous losses on the evacuation fleet. On 2 June there was one last major Stuka attack at 1100. Flying with St.G.77, Plewig recalled to me:

We also supported the advance to Dunkirk. During this period one of our crews was forced to crash-land in enemy-held territory. They destroyed their machine and were then rescued by another Stuka who risked a landing to save them. Over Dunkirk two of our aircraft were shot down by anti-aircraft guns. These were mounted on a troop ship which was going to be used to take back the wounded. As a result this troop ship was sunk shortly afterward by the rest of the Wing. This made difficulties for me later on when a prisoner of war. As commander at the time, they held me responsible for sinking what they claimed was an unarmed hospital ship. Fortunately I was able, with the aid of the International Red Cross, to obtain photographs from OKL which had been taken the day of the sinking by two reconnaissance Dornier Do17s, which clearly showed the ship's guns firing at us first. These photo-reconnaissance Do17s always flew with all the operations at this time, thank goodness.

The team of Palisek and Sellhorn flying with the Stab unit had similar reports to make. At 0743 on Saturday 1 June they sortied from Rocroi for a 480 kilometre round trip attack. They peeled off over the crowded shipping at 10,000 feet and released from about 3,000 feet. Their attacks were devastating. An eyewitness described the result of attacks on one British warship, the destroyer *Keith*:

A British destroyer outside of us began to fire at the enemy planes and bombs began to fall near her as she steamed about. At full speed with her helm hard to port nine bombs fell in a line in the water, along her starboard side, and they exploded under water, heeling the destroyer over on her beam ends, but she was righted again and a sloop joined in the gunfire, also shore batteries, and as the raiders made off over towards the land they machine-gunned us and we returned the fire with our Lewis gun.

At this time I could see that another destroyer had been disabled to the west of the harbour, and plane had just dropped a bomb on a small oil tanker astern of the *Vincia* which went up in flames. A direct hit on the stern of the sinking destroyer [HMS *Basilisk*] blew up her depth charges and we made to the sailing barge *Tollesbury* which was signalling us.

An RAF fighter pilot viewed the Stuka attack from above:

I had just turned again at Dunkirk, and was heading back once more, when something moving on my left caught my eye. I looked round in time to see an aircraft diving down towards the shipping off the harbour. Coming hard round I dive after it, the rest of the squadron chasing after me. The aircraft flattened out over a destroyer for a moment and then turned, climbing towards the coast. As I followed there was a terrific flash below and a huge fountain of water was flung high into the air, to fall slowly back into the sea. As the disturbance subsided I saw that the destroyer had completely disappeared.

In fact the British destroyers *Basilisk, Havant, Keith* and the French *Foudroyant* were all sunk in this attack, as was the minesweeper *Skipjack*, gunboat *Mosquito* and several lesser ships. The British destroyers *Ivanhoe* and *Whitehall*, along with the minesweeper *Salamander*, were all badly damaged.

The Stukas that inflicted this devastation took few casualties. The return fire from the ships meant that Sellhorn's Stuka was hit again, the third time in two days, a flak splinter puncturing one tyre and another hitting part of the leg. Despite this, they landed back safely. Towards midday they made a second attack, this time diving against Allied transport steamers near Gravelines. Their target was the *Scotia* with about 2,000 French troops aboard. Her master, Captain Hughes, described the Stuka assault on his ship thus:

After passing No.6 buoy we saw enemy bombers coming from astern. They came in formations of fours, there were at least twelve of them. In each case they swooped low – the two outside planes machine-gunned, the two inner each dropping bombs, none of which scored a hit. The second formation of four passed over us, flying very low. The shots from their machine-guns dropped like hail all round the bridge and funnels and in the water ahead. One bomb struck the ship abaft the engine-room on the starboard side and another on the poop deck starboard side. Immediately the third four swooped over us and one of their bombs dropped down the after funnel while the others dropped on the stern. All these bombs had caused extensive damage and the ship was gradually sinking by the stern and heeling over to starboard. I therefore gave orders to abandon ship. The engines had been put out of action.

Again return fire was intense and Sellhorn's machine took a flak splinter high in the tail-fin. Undeterred, they were back in action against similar shipping targets near to Gravelines and Dunkirk that same evening. Gravelines was already in German hands by this time and the guns mounted there proved a hazard to the evacuation ships which had to keep to the swept and deep-water channels in order to reach the Dunkirk beaches themselves. Captain J.E. Fishe, of the tug *Empire Henchmen*, described his experience of being caught in the narrow channel on the sharp end of one of St.G.77's attacks, while towing an ammunition barge:

Fortunately neither the tug nor the barge was hit, but the terrific explosions of the bombs

The airfield at Maast was the base of I./St.G.77 during the final stages of the war in France. Only the rump of the French armies south of the Seine and the fortifications of the Maginot Line remained to be finished off. Here the Gruppen-kommandeur of I. Gruppe, Hauptmann von Dalwigk, discusses tactics and targets with the Staffelkapitän of 1. Staffel, Oberleutnant Bruck, and others. Note the staff car with unit pennants. (Sellhorn Archiv)

which were falling very closely all round the tug, which was in shallow water, resulted in violent concussions, which caused fractures to the connections of our fuel oil tanks, and serious leakages of oil into the bilges with risk of fire; also serious damage was done to the tug's electrical installation, pumps and compasses.

From the fading hell of the Dunkirk beaches, the Stukas were switched once more to take part in the final land battles to finish off what remained of the French and British armies still left south of the Somme. It took until 4 June to re-organise for this, then St.G.77 gave non-stop support for the German crossing of the rivers Marne, Seine and Loire and the battles that followed until hostilities ceased on 24 June.

Sellhorn was now flying with Oberst Hans-Joachim Lehmann, on loan from a sister unit and piloting the much patched S2+MH. They were flying from Crupilby airfield now at 1008 on 5 June they made dive attacks against French troop concentrations at Licourt eight kilometres to the north of Nestle. The next day saw three missions as the Stukas hit motorised columns at Roye, at Cressy

The high sortie rate meant that Stuka aircrew were constantly on call and had to take their rest when and where they could. Here the Staffeloffizier of the 1./St.G.77, Leutnant Hitz (left), and two of his men rest between missions at the height of the French campaign. (Sammler Kroll via Sellhorn Archiv)

The devastation wrought by St.G.77 at Esternay rail-way station west of Paris during the final campaign across the Seine in June 1940. (Karl Schubert via Sellhorn Archiv)

The still smouldering ruins of the railway station and marshalling yards of Esternay, on the river Seine east of Paris, demolished by I./St.G.77 in the final campaign in France, June 1940. (Karl Schubert via Sellhorn Archiv)

ten kilometres south of Nestle and at Marke-Allonarve five kilometres west of Nestle.

Hans-Joachim was a very experienced Stuka pilot, as he told me:

I had followed all the developments of the Ju87 as a technical officer from the very beginnings, through the various modifications to the end when I was General of the Attack pilots. Through all these different activities, and within the viewpoint of one who flew and tested all the flying equipment of the 'Stukawaffe', I have, in the course of my career, flown 32 different types of plane, and therefore I think I am allowed to have an opinion as to the best types of airplane for the Luftwaffe at that time. I have therefore come to the firm conclusion that the Ju87 was probably the best type of plane for the Luftwaffe. Only the Ju52 can be named as equally good. From a flying point of view it is established that all Junkers planes were strong, sturdy and reliable machines both in flying aspects and technical aspects. They were of slow speed, that is undeniable, but under certain circumstances, that could be an advantage. In action the Ju87 was able to fly and land despite the gravest damage. Many of my comrades count themselves lucky they were flying Stukas in such conditions.

On 7 June Lehmann and Sellhorn were involved in attacks on French troops sortieing from Noyon, at first light. A second mission that day was flown against Morcuil some 20 kilometres south of Amiens. By late afternoon they were airborne again, this time hitting the enemy positions in the village of Noyers St Martin, which is 18 kilometres north of Beauvais. Nor was that the end: a fourth strike was flown off at 1923 to hit enemy troops at Lassigny, 11 kilometres west of Noyon.

On 9 June they moved to yet another new foward base, flying to Contescourt that afternoon and from there, on 11 May, they flew to Maast. On 13 June they conducted offensive sorties against a village 20 kilometres west of Troyes, and their escorting Me109's destroyed nine French Morane fighters which tried to intercept them. A second mission that day was flown against Nestle St Oulgah, east of Romilly, and a third was delivered at dusk against French defences at St Parres, four kilometres south of Troyes.

The French were maintaining stubborn resistance for the last time and the fighting was as hard as any before they finally cracked completely. The Stukas

Left *This light tank came to grief in Versailles, which was used by I./St.G.77 as a base during the final stages of the campaign in France.* (Sellhorn Archiv)

Below *Radiomen relax in the sun with a bottle of Burgundy, aware that victory over the French is now in sight. Left to right: Bordfunker Uffzs. Sellhorn; Shuh; Bastian (the latter two to die in Russia on 9 October 1941); Muller; Steckel; Barsch (to die over Thorney Island on 18 August 1940); Gramlich; Mobius; and Palisek.* (Sellhorn Archiv)

were therefore fully utilised in these last days. On the afternoon of 14 June I./St.G.77 hit a French column at Raum-sur-Areis and next day cleared a stubborn block by bombing fortified houses and conducting low-level strafing runs at Auxerre. They then leapfrogged forward to Courgivause, a flight of 75 kilometres and began operations from there with an attack on French troop columns caught on the move south of the Loire. Another mission that day was against Dijon far to the south-east on the way to the Swiss borders, where the Ju87s strafed and bombed the enemy well dug in in deep bunkers and well protected by anti-aircraft guns.

On 18 June another move of base, a 30-minute flight to Auxerre and that same afternoon they were in action against a French column at la Chayselle d'Angillon, 35 kilometres north of Bourges, and an important road and rail junction between Orléans and Montluçon. This proved the last combat mission against the French for now the Panzers were once more rolling south through virtually undefended open territory. The *Blitzkrieg* was over .... but the war was not!

V
Flying against England

At the end of their stunning victories over the French, the German war machine, still hardly touched in terms of losses of men or equipment, turned to face their last, and most puzzling opponent. By this time Italy had joined the war on the side of the Axis, although that was to prove more an embarrassment than a help in the long-term. Penned into her island, her sea-links increasingly ravaged by U-boats and long-range bombers, her army shattered, its heavy equipment left behind in France, Britain's cause seemed hopeless. Hitler expected her to make peace, as did most other world leaders, but to his amazement the offer was scornfully rejected.

While Hitler toured the battlefields and distributed promotions and medals to his commanders, while army divisions were ordered to be disbanded and tanks and long-range bombers were rested and overhauled, for the Stukas there was to be no respite. Having led the way across western Europe, they were now to spearhead the assault on Great Britain. Firstly, they were to dominate the English Channel, drive away the British destroyer flotillas stationed at Portsmouth, Dover and Portland and thus leave the sea passages open to the invasion fleets that Admiral Raeder was laboriously (and unenthusiastically) assembling along the Dutch, Belgian and French coastline. Secondly, they were to obliterate with their usual precision attacks, the forward airfields of RAF fighter command in readiness for the landings. Finally, once the rest of the RAF had been brought to its knees by attrition, they were to resume this classic role of close support of the Army ashore.

In carrying out these three missions the Stukas were brilliantly successful in the first, did well initially in the second and no doubt would have been totally efficient in the third. But in the second phase they were thrown in against British eight-gun fighters whose bases, although heavily hit, were not abandoned or overrun by advancing ground forces. Subsequently they could be repaired and re-used quickly, unlike those in France. In truth, in using the supreme *tactical* air weapon in a *strategical* role, the Germans blundered badly. This was probably because they had no clear outline of where one phase started and the other began. 'Eagle Day' was grandly announced, but the vagaries of the English weather, the vital factor of British radar, and the fact that the British were fighting over their own home island, gave them a great advantage which they duly exploited to the full. The Battle of Britain was to be the hardest and cruellest test that St.G.77 was ever to undergo, for duelling with single-seater fighters 200 mph faster than they were, was *not* the role they were built or had trained for.

The Battle for France is won, the Battle of Britain has not yet begun in earnest. Here Unteroffiziers Sellhorn (right) and Maurer relax on the beach of the French resort of Bella-Riva, north of Caen, in July 1940. (Sellhorn Archiv)

Flying Officer Immerreich of the 2. Staffel, St.G.77, wearing his gas mask while working on the engine of his aircraft at a Caen airfield. (Immerreich via Sellhorn Archiv)

Low-level flying over the French beaches north of Caen in the summer of 1940 gave the Stukas experience in strafing coastal areas in similar conditions to those in which they expected to operate on the other side of the Channel once Operation Sea Lion was finally launched. (Sellhorn Archiv)

Throughout the end of June and early July 1940 the Stukagruppen, busy finishing off the last French resistance south of Orléans and the Loire, or, like St.G.77 themselves, attacking the actual Maginot Line fortifications by-passed at Sedan during the initial breakthrough, were steadily assembled at various arifields in the Cherbourg Peninsula in preparation for the first 'Channel Dominance' phase of the planned attack on Britain.

Under their new Kommodore, Graf Clemens von Schönborn-Wiesentheid, St.G.77 was regrouped and reorganized throughout this period to form a Geschwader of full strength. As part of this standardisation of units, the hitherto independent I./St.G.76 became, on 9 July, the III./St.G.77. The Gruppenkommandeure were: I.Gruppe, Hauptmann Friedrich-Karl Freiherr von Dalwigk zu Lichtenfels. (He was to be replaced on his death on 14 July by Hauptmann Meisel, who, in turn, was replaced on 28 August by Hauptmann Helmut Bruck;) II.Gruppe, Hauptmann Waldemar Plewig who had replaced von Schönborn-Wiesentheid on 15 May (until Plewig was himself shot down on 8 August); III.Gruppe, from 9 July 1940 Hauptmann Helmut Bode.

St.G.77 came directly under Fliegerkorps VIII, which had its headquarters at Deauville, and the whole group was based at various airfields in the Caen area, mainly at Flers, La Ferté and Maltot. This involved much shifting of equipment, stocking up and preparation in readiness for the assault.

With Feldwebel Knauer as his pilot, and Junkers Ju87 S2+EH as his steed, young Heinz Sellhorn, his first campaign behind him and now a veteran, flew overland from La Ferté some 145 kilometres to Théville early on 6 July and returned that same evening, a 45 minute flight. Next day a similar trip took them to Flers and back, another 40 minute hop.

Once firmly settled into their new bases both veterans and newcomers with St.G.77 had just days to prepare themselves for a wholly new type of warfare. Static bases, strong opposition, and overwater flying with the grim prospect of either ditching in the water or crash-landing in a hostile land with no hope of their comrades, either airborne or on land, being able to support or rescue them quickly.

Nonetheless, buoyed up with their already great achievements, the men of St.G.77 stood confident at the beginning of July 1940. Firstly the leaders:

Major Graf Clemens von Schönborn-Wiesentheid was to be awarded the Knight's Cross on 21 July for his work in Poland and France. He was to more than earn it over the Channel and in the Battle of Britain.

The 'old firm' of Helmut Bruck, who was to lead I./St.G.77 from 20 August, and his radio operator Franz Hettinger, were to clock up no less than ten missions over the Channel. Georg Jakob was to fly three missions during the Battle of Britain after completing 30 against Poland and 38 against France with the I./St.G.77. On 22 August he became Kapitän of the 2. Staffel.

There was Alex Gläser, with the 2. Staffel, preparing for the same battles as the unit's Kettenführer. Friedrich-Karl Freiherr von Dalwigk zu Lichtenfels, 'Chicken', was to prove himself hardly that as he made ready to lead his men out for the first attacks against British convoys while Helmut Bode was to fly his first missions as the Gruppenkommandeur of III./St.G.77 over the Channel. Gerhard Bauhaus was with the Stabstaffel of the St.G.77 but on 27 August moved to the staff of VIII. Fliegerkorps itself. Karl Henze was still the Gruppenadjutant of the

I./St.G.77 but flew regular combat missions as did Walter Stimpel, the Grup-penadjutant of the II./St.G.77. 'Ali' Orthofer had, throughout the French cam-paign, been with the Stab of the 7. Flg. Div, VII Fliegerkorps but, on 15 August, was to become the new Kommandeur of II./St.G.77.

Among the veterans were Herbert Dawedeit with 8./St.G.77. In May 1940, he had fought hard in the French campaign and was to carry out two major missions during the Battle of Britain. Oberleutnant Heinz-Günter Amelung, the Staf-felkapitän of 5./St.G.77, was to be similarly placed. Günter Hitz was to join the III./St.G.77 on 28 July before transferring to the I./St.G.77 on 22 August after several missions across the English Channel.

Ready to fight over the English Channel under those hot skies stood Gerhardt Bauer, 'Jonny' Jauernik with II./St. G.77, Paul Langkopf, Helmut Leicht, 'Piepel' Weihrauch with the 2./St.G.77, Hans-Karl Sattler with III./St.G.77, Alois Wosnitza flying with 2./St.G.77, Johann Waldhauser with III./St.G.77, who was promoted to Oberleutnant.

All now had wide experience of attacking land targets, but the new phase, that of driving the Royal Navy from their anti-invasion ports, was to call for a very dif-ferent skill from the dive bomber men. Some had already acquired that skill and were ready and eager to apply it to help their Army comrades in a new and novel way. Among such 'ship-busters' in St.G.77 were Rudolf Weigel, who had already personally sunk a destroyer and a transport off Dunkirk in June. Then there was Hans Meier, who with the 7. Staffel of the new III.Gruppe, had sunk a 12,000 BRT oil tanker and damaged a British flak vessel, also near Dunkirk, at the same time. Otto Schmidt, flying initially with I./St.G.76 and later with III./St.G.77, had destroyed several supply ships here and was to add to his score in the Channel battles.

Others came new to this task, but quickly established themselves with the best in shipping missions. Men like Staffelkapitän Kurt Huhn, who was to prove an outstanding pilot in attacking shipping in the Channel. There was Wilhelm Joswig, South African born from Johannesburg and one of the Stuka immortals. Like so many others he had joined the Luftwaffe from the police in 1935 and had spent the early part of the war as a flying instructor at the Stukaschule at Otrokowitz. In the summer of 1940 he thankfully joined on the 8./St.G.77 on the Channel coast and hit and sank an 8,000 ton freighter on one of his very first missions.

As always there were new faces taking the places of the fallen (although only 14 Stukas had been destroyed in the whole of the first week of the Blitz in the west, a negligible attrition rate). Among the newcomers later to make their mark with St.G.77 were Josef Grewe, a 31-year-old from Schuren-bei-Meschede in Westphalia. He had been a keen glider pilot nine years earlier, then had had pre-war power flight training with Luftwaffe. He was to fly his very first combat missions during the Battle of Britain, a harsh introduction to air warfare indeed! Adolf Weiss, from Munich, joined 4./St.G.77 that summer and also flew his very first combat sorties during the Battle of Britain.

There was young Theodor 'Bubi' Haker, a 20-year-old who was to join 7./St.G.77 in France as an officer cadet later that summer; also Josef 'Sepp' Huber from Kempten/Allgau, five years his senior, who had received Stuka pilot train-ing at his own request from March 1938. He was one of the many transferred into

The blockade of the English Channel, July 1940. Here an attack by St.G.77 leaves a British tanker sinking by the stern, her shattered hull leaking her precious cargo into the waters around her. (Scheffel via Sellhorn Archiv)

2./St.G.77 on the Channel coast in the autumn to fill the ghastly gaps left after the battle.

Horst Kaubisch, born on 3 December 1915 at Freital-Zaucherode/Sachsen, had joined Luftwaffe in 1936. After extensive dive bomber training he had been kept as an instructor at the Stuka School so did not reach active service until August 1940 when he joined 11./St.G.1. He was quickly transferred 3./St.G.77 but still saw no action. Fritz Neumüller, 24, from Herford/Westfalen entered the Luftwaffe in November 1937, for pilot training at Detmold. On 10 June he joined 4./St.G.77 but later became a flying instructor back in the Reich. Similarly Heinz Niehuus, from Hamburg, had pre-military pilot training in 1935–36 before entering the Luftwaffe. Promoted to Leutnant in January 1938, he served at the Luftnachrichtenschule but was also transferred to the Stukas in June 1940 as Oberleutnant and Staffeloffizier with the I./St.G.77.

Rudi Reussner, Norwegian-born from Bergen, had his initial pilot training at the Flieger-Ausbildungs-Regiment 42 in Salzwedel before transferring to the Stukaschule 1 at Kitzingen-Main on the outbreak of war. He served with the Erganzungs-Stuka-Staffel and then, on 9 June, joined III./St.G.76 (which formed the III./St.G.77).

The men were thus again ready. If Operation 'Sealion', the invasion of Britain, was to be a reality instead of a big threat and a bluff, these were the men who would lead the invasion troops ashore and then spearhead the drive on London. Meanwhile they had to deal with the Royal Navy and the coastal convoys of small coal-laden freighters that were still defiantly plodding up down between the Thames and the Atlantic. The hitherto remarkable immunity of these ships was about to come to a sudden end.

During July dive bombing attacks were mainly directed against the British destroyer flotillas that represented the Royal Navy's front-line defences against invasion. These attacks resulted in the sinking of the destroyers *Brazen, Codrington, Delight* and *Wren*, damage to many others and the abandoning of Dover as a front-line base for such ships. Working in conjunction with the newly-established radar sets set up on the Channel coast any surface movement by British ships, whether by day or night, was quickly spotted and both dive bombers (by day) and E-boats (by night) decimated these slow-moving targets. The British ships were mainly small coasters, their principal cargoes being coal for London and general products in return. They were given destroyer escorts but the RAF was reluctant to become involved initially, stating their job was the defence of Britain not the defence of the convoys. After one important convoy was decimated off Portland by St.G.1 early in July the Admiralty protested to Churchill and limited air cover was provided. The Germans used these attacks as a lure to draw out the RAF eight-gun fighters, but, unfortunately for the Stukas, they were the bait. The dive bombers also conducted attacks against harbour installations.

On 9 July, St.G.77 made its initial contribution to this campaign, twenty-seven Stukas being sent out against a convoy off Portland and being allocated targets at the naval base itself. With Feldwebel Knauer again piloting S2+EH, Sellhorn's first Channel combat mission took off from Théville at 1700 that afternoon. They had an escort of six Me110's and their targets were a convoy of ocean-going ships south of Portland itself. They were intercepted by Spitfires from Warmwell but the defending fighters gave them good protection in the main and only one Ju87 failed to return. In reply, the dive bombers hit and damaged the *Empire Daffodil* (7,085 tons) south of the port. It was the aircraft of Hauptmann Freiherr von Dalwigk zu Lichtenfels, the Gruppenkommandeur of I/St.G.77, that was reported missing in action when his Ju87 had vanished into cloud cover. It was much later confirmed that he had been shot down by a Spitfire of No.609 Squadron, piloted by Flying Officer D.M. Crook. The leader's Stuka was seen to have crashed into the sea with no parachutes opening. He was a popular officer and a great loss. Once his death was confirmed he was posthumously promoted to Major (on 19 July) and awarded the Ritterkreuz posthumously on 21 July.

The survivors returned to Théville at 1805 after a 65 minute round-trip of 270 kilometres. It had been a salutory lesson for St.G.77 that the easy missions were now definitely over, but far worse was to follow. Sellhorn's own aircraft survived and flew the 165 kilometre trip overland at 1915 to La Vente that same evening. Here the Staffel re-organised and did not return to Théville and the battle until the early morning hours of 21 July.

St.G.77 as a whole, however, was still to be fully committed. On 11 July they were, joining with St.G.2 in another attack on Portland, again escorted by the Me110's of ZG.76. The skies were again overcast and unsatisfactory and RAF Hurricane fighters were once more waiting for them. Two aircraft were shot down, both crashing into the sea in or just off the harbour itself. The Stukas hit and badly damaged two merchant ships: *Peru* (6,961 tons) and *Eleanor Brooke* (1,037 tons).

On 19 July the Stukas hit Dover, sinking the tanker *War Sepy* and *Crestflower*, and damaging the destroyer *Griffin*, while next day the Stukas were heavily committed against convoy CW.7 in the Dover area and one of the escorting destroyers, HMS *Brazen*, was sunk by them, a near-miss breaking her back, and the coaster *Pulborough* was sunk with the *Westown* damaged.

On 21 July, St.G.77, with Knauer and Sellhorn in S2+EH, returned to the fray and participated in a more successful anti-convoy strike initiated at 1545 from Théville against a convoy of 20 ships located off the Isle of Wight. They scored hits and a tanker, estimated at 12,000 tons, was sunk. The size of their target was

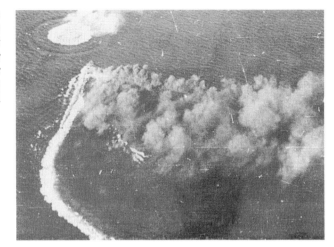

Closing the Channel. A British destroyer weaves and turns in vain, and is hit and set on fire by the dive bombers of I.St.G.77 to the south of the Isle of Wight in July 1940. (Sammler Kroll via Sellhorn Archiv)

Here Unteroffizier Sellhorn utilises an SC250 bomb as a library seat between sorties, at Théville near Cherbourg during attacks on the Channel convoys. (Sellhorn Archiv)

a gross over-estimation. In fact St.G.77's victims were the SS *Terlings*, a 2,318 ton steamer, which was sunk ten miles south-west of St Catherine's Point, Isle of Wight by Stuka bombs that day, along with the Norwegian vessel *Kollskeg*.

Again the hazy weather over the combat zone limited activity far more than anticipated. The Sellhorn logbook reveals nothing more than routine flights between the various Stukas bases, La Vente, Théville, Maltot by Caen and so on, at this period.

On 24 July attacks took place on convoys in the narrows off Dover again, the victims being the *Fleming*, and the trawlers *Kingston Galena* and *Rodino*. Also damaged was the Trinity House tender *Alert*. It was much the same story the next day when the coasters *Corhaven*, *Polgrange*, *Leo*, *Henry Moon* and *Portslade* were all sunk by Stukas and the *Tamworth*, *Newminster*, *Hodder*, *Summity* and *Gronland* were badly damaged. This day too, two of the last three fully active destroyers based on Dover, *Boreas* and *Brilliant*, were both hit and damaged by Stuka attack. Although eventually towed back to port they were effectively out of action. On 26 July convoys off Portland and the Isle of Wight were hit by

St.G.77 in repeated raids without serious loss.

There was a marked escalation on 27 July when three different Stuka Geschwader took place in several fierce attacks designed to drive the Royal Navy from Dover. The destroyers *Codrington* and *Wren* (the latter having just arrived as replacement for some of the lost ships) were both sunk and others damaged this day and the Admiralty was forced to withdraw what remained of the 1st flotilla from that port. Dive bomber attacks on Dover nonetheless continued on 28 and 29 July when the coaster *Gronland* was sunk.

Next day the destroyer *Delight*, lacking any air escort at all, sailed from Portland and was picked up by the German 'Freya' radar set at Audeville, near Cherbourg, at a range of sixty miles. Aircraft were promptly despatched and, at 1835 that evening, sank her off Portland Bill without any loss to themselves. They also despatched the patrol vessel *Gulzar* at the same time.

The weather once more took a hand and cloud and drizzle predominated until 5 August, with the result that few sorties took place. The Stuka crewmen enjoyed the period of inactivity by relaxing on French beaches and visiting the towns of the area in true 'Tourist' style. It was a welcome re-charging of batteries from the earlier batteries. For many it was their last ever time of relaxation for the bitterest battles were just ahead of them.

On 8 August the second phase of the Battle of Britain commenced with the major *Adler Angriff* offensive. However, the weather over the Channel intervened before decisive results could be obtained. Nonetheless heavy Stuka assaults were launched on coastal convoys.

The following extract from a German wartime interview with a Stuka crewman

The closing of the English Channel, July/August 1940. A series of near misses scored on a British tanker south of the Isle of Wight by the aircraft of St.G.77. She was hit and sunk by the next aircraft in line. (Scheffel via Sellhorn Archiv)

gives us a graphic description of Plewig's last mission leading II./St.G.77's across the Channel on this day:

At the briefing we were told that our target is a British convoy trying to force the Channel route. We were given a codename for our attack, 'Puma'. We had no proper location and so we had to fly our mission most accurately by compass. Our wing leader had to give each squadron commander short and accurate instructions from what he knew, then everyone got dressed. The most important piece of clothing is the life-jacket. Then, shortly before 1600 hours, the whole Gruppe is ready, the formation to take off being our Commander's formation. A small signal lamp flashes and, like a flock of large birds, the squadrons rose up one after another into the sky. We all circle our base and collect in formation, then head off toward the Channel battleground. After only a few minutes we are at the coast. Below us, as far as the eye can see, is the Channel. Once it was the busiest shipping lane in the world, now it is the largest ships' graveyard.

Water – nothing but water below us, we cannot see the coast or the enemy ships. Our thoughts are with our engines, those reliable, humming helpers in our operation. Our eyes go from instrument to instrument checking, water cooling, tachometer, pressure gauge, all are regularly checked. If our engine gives up there is only one thing for us and that is 'Ditch'. The Channel is large and wide and on the other side is the 'Island'.

There, carefully, one would like to say shyly, from the blue-green water a light strip, at first you can hardly make it out. The English south coast, the white cliffs of the steep shore. A few hundred metres above us fly some squadrons of fighters Me109s, and the long-range 'Destroyer' Me110s as protection for us. Half-right in front of us at about 3,000 to 4,000 metres higher, the first air battle has already begun. You can hardly tell friend from enemy. We can only see small silver specks circling. Now we must be especially alert. The coast is getting nearer, to the left, below us, the Isle of Wight and we also see already ten or twelve ships. They, as they in turn spot us, try somehow to avoid our attacks by zig-zagging turns. We fly steadily eastward toward them. Suddenly we hear through the WT: 'Number Four aircraft has crash-landed'. A corporal from our 4. Staffel has had to go down into the water; his engine must have failed. We hope everything goes well for them as we press on.

'Puma One – to all Pumas – Attack!' We are above the convoy, it seems to be all small ships, coasters. Our 1. Staffel has already started to attack. Now the formations pull apart. Each one of them chooses a ship that has not yet been hit by one of the other squadrons. Our Staffelkapitän's formation starts its attack dives, near to the coast. But what is this? Four aircraft? I cannot believe my eyes, there is also a third formation, which attacks from the left, the same picture. At the same instant I hear, 'Puma – Alert. Enemy fighter diving from above.' When we are diving and banking vertically the English fighters have virtually no chance to shoot our Stukas. So they always tried to intercept us earlier or catch us later and, on account of them being so much faster than us, we form up for mutual protection.

That's for later. Right now I select for my formation's target the most southerly ship of the convoy. Before I commence my dive I make sure by asking my radio operator if everything is clear behind us. I receive the reply, 'All clear'. Then we dive down without braking as in our perilous position we need speed to get back into our unit formation again. My bombs land close alongside the ship, my left-hand *Kettenhund* aircraft also scores a near-miss by a very small margin, but the third aircraft of my formation hits the ship square amidships with his bombs. Within seconds a huge flame shoots up from the ship and a large cloud of smoke bellows out of her insides. As we fly away, we can see her listing badly and on fire.

Now the English defenders are right on top of us. Spitfires, Hurricanes. From a distance you cannot distinguish these from our own Me109's. Above the Isle of Wight it makes for a terrible air battle. About sixty aircraft of all makes, German and English, fighting for their lives. Some of the English draw back toward the coast of England, on the left of me a 109 drops into the sea. The pilot is able to get out and slowly he guides his parachute towards the water. Another aircraft, the make I cannot see clearly, circles in flames like a bonfire above us, explodes and falls in many small pieces. You can only recognise the engine compartment.

When we all collect towards the south the English take us on. Only weaving helps if you want to escape the eight machine-guns of the English fighters. Our radio operators shoot whenever their guns will bear. Again and again the English attack from astern. Again and again I feel bullets striking my aircraft but I don't think the engine has been hit, the motor is quiet and smooth. The closer we get to the centre of the Channel the fewer English attack us. Our squadrons find each other bit by bit and we form up. To the left of us flies our 4. Squadron. One of the planes has a smoke trail behind it. The pilot gives the message, 'Aircraft damaged, going into the water.' At that moment a Spitfire comes from ahead, shoots, hits and down into the water the damaged Stuka goes. But the Englishman does not long enjoy his cheap victory and glory, as he veers away after his attack he gets hit by a Me109 and dives vertically into the sea.

After 30 minutes' flying we at last see the coast of Normandy. We all sigh with relief. My formation comrades approach to the side of my aircraft, nod and smile. Everything in our squadron seems to be all right. We land at our base. Unbelievably all the aircraft from our squadron have returned. Some had up to forty bullet holes in their fuselages and wings, but all landed safely despite this. We praise the sturdiness of the Stuka. After about an hour the Commander came back from the debriefing, very serious. 'The Commander, Major Plewig, is missing, a Hauptmann and an Unteroffizier also. We can't believe it. No one saw the CO ditch. After the attack we saw him with the Stab formation. From there no one knows anything. A few weeks later we found out that he was a prisoner of war in England, he had to ditch the plane which most likely hit and was taken prisoner.

The defending British fighters were mainly from Nos.43 and 145 Squadrons, RAF and they destroyed three Stukas. The British ships sunk in this attack were the *Coquetdale* (1,597 tons), and *Empire Crusader* (1,042 tons), both dive bombed and sunk some 15 miles south-west of St Catherine's Point, Isle of Wight. Two others were hit and badly damaged at the same spot, the *Scheldt* (497 tons) and the *Balmara* (1,428 tons) while the *John M* (500 tons) was also dive-bombed ten miles south of the Needles and also later hit by E-boat attack.

Plewig was later to tell me the aftermath:

My aircrews in St.G.77 did no more or less than any other Stuka crews. I carried out 220 short-range missions in the Junkers Ju87 before I was shot down on 8 August 1940 by a Hawker Hurricane. If anything the Ju87 B was 100–150 knots too slow, and the reason is that the development of the more powerful engine was not permitted to go ahead at full speed. I knew about the new engine being developed from Adlershof, and it would have made the new Stuka fighting fit by about 1941.

There is one final event which I will never forget. It proved that, between nations whatever the circumstances, and even in time of war, companionship and respect towards the human being will remain. For the achievements of my wing in Poland, France and the Channel fighting, I was one of the first Stuka officers of the Luftwaffe to receive the Knight's Cross for front line combat operations. This distinction we compared with the *Pour le Mérite*.

After I had been shot down I spent long periods in different military hospitals and interrogation camps in Great Britain. One day in January 1941, I was asked to attend, along with the German camp leader, Captain Lott of the German Navy, to see the British camp commander. All I had to wear was an old London tram-driver's trousers, a T-shirt, and a sixpenny cap while Captain Lott was in what remained of his naval uniform. I was

Calibrating the wing guns of a Ju87B of 1./St.G.77 at Maltot/Caen airfield, France, in the summer of 1940. (Sellhorn Archiv)

apprehensive, what had I done to be summoned so?

In the camp commandant's office all the English officers had assembled; the commander himself was from the Coldstream Guards and had been wounded many times in combat. He explained the purpose of my summons. Even though they were all British officers I somehow felt amongst fellow officers and comrades. 'In the absence of your Commanding Officer he cannot himself make the correct presentation. So I herewith solemnly hand you your just award. All the best, stay healthy and hopefully return in peace to your own home.' With all military honour I received the award from my enemies. I wore it in the camps right through to 1946 and it is still one of my proudest possessions.

Plewig remained at this camp, Shap Wells Hotel between Carlisle and Kendall, and was promoted to Major, still as a POW, on 1 April 1942. His target on the day he was shot down was what was to prove the final large-scale battle involving a coastal convoy before the Stukas were switched to land targets, involved convoy CW.9. It had sailed from Dartford on 2 August and had been badly mauled by E-boats on the night of 7 August. Given the codename 'Peewit', the survivors then faced an all-out Stuka assault during the daylight hours that followed.

On the morning of 8 August St.G.s 2, 3 and 77 took part in a running battle with this convoy off the Isle of Wight, during which three Ju87s were shot down by RAF fighters. Five more dive bombers were lost in afternoon attacks but the convoy was decimated. The *Coquetdale, Empire Crusader,* and the Norwegian *Tres* were sunk, while many other vessels were damaged.

Meanwhile increasingly detailed exercising was being undertaken by St.G.77 for the critical days ahead. The intensity of the exercises can best be gauged by

Top *2. Kette from the 1. Staffel St.G.77 is pictured returning to its forward operating base at Caen during the Battle of Britain. (Sellhorn Archiv)*

Above *A Kette of Junkers Ju87Bs from I./St.G.77 landing back at its base near Caen on 18 August 1940, led by the new Staffelkapitän Oberleutnant Trogemann-Gefuhrt. (Sellhorn Archiv)*

Left *After the attack on Thorney Island on 18 August 1940, many of the Stukas which returned to their base at Maltot bore the marks of the intercepting Spitfire and Hurricane squadrons. This machine from the 1. Staffel has lost the front part of one wheel covering, while the rest of it is liberally splattered with bullet holes. (Sellhorn Archiv)* the Sellhorn logbooks, showing both combat sorties and the many exercises in between, for the early of August.

115. Fw Knauer: Ju87 S2+EH, Overland, Maltot, 2-8-40, 1030–Mesnie Argentan, 2-8-40, 1050: 20 mins, 85 km.
116. Fw Knauer: Ju87 S2+EH, Mesnie Argentan 1545–Maltot, 2-8-40, 1615: 30 mins, 125 km.
117. Fw Knauer: Ju87 S2+EH, Maltot, 3-8-40, 0930–Mesnie Argentan, 3-8-40: 20 mins, 85 km.
118. Fw Knauer: Ju87 S2+EH, Mesnie Argentan, 3-8-40, 1910–Maltot, 3-8-40, 1935: 25 mins, 105 km.
119. Fw Knauer: Ju87 5108, Staffel exercise, Maltot, 9-8-40, 1013–1128: 75 mins, 310 km.
120. Fw Knauer: Ju87, 5108, Staffel exercise, Maltot. 12-8-40, 0915–1045: 90 mins, 380 km.
121. Fw Knauer: Ju87, 5108, Gruppen flying, Maltot, 12-8-40, 1330–1500: 90 mins, 370 km.
122. Fw Knauer: Ju87 5108, Overland, Maltot 12-8-40, 1935–Beaumont, 12-8-40, 2010: 35 mins, 145 km.
123. (39) Fw Knauer: Ju87 5108, Operation, 13-8-40, Beaumont, 0650–0830: 100 mins, 420 km.
124. Fw Knauer: Ju87 5108, Overland, Beaumont, 13-8-40, 0945–Maltot, 13-8-40, 1020: 35 mins, 145 km.
125. Fw Knauer: Ju87 5108, Overland, Maltot, 16-8-40, 1710–Tonneville, 16-8-40, 1740: 30 mins, 125 km.
126. Fw Knauer: Ju87 5108, Overland, Tonneville, 16-8-40, 1855–Maltot, 16-8-40, 1945: 50 mins, 210 km.
127. Fw Knauer: Ju87 5108, Overland, Maltot, 18-8-40, 1145–Tonneville, 18-8-40, 1220: 35 mins, 145 km.

To revert to the battle itself. On 9 August there was heavy cloud and rain and the preliminary orders for the launching of 'Eagle Day' on 10 August were cancelled. There was consequently little or no aerial activity until 12 August when the unofficial start finally got under way with fine and clear weather. An early success was the dive-bombing and disabling of Ventnor radar station but the Luftwaffe failed to profit by this or follow it up in any detail, an omission that helped lose them the subsequent battle.

It was not until the afternoon of 12 August that heavy attacks finally got going with Fliegerkorps VIII's dive bomber forces again leading the charge. RAF airfields along the south coast were heavily hit, including those at Eastchurch and Detling, which were wrecked, Thorney Island, Middle Wallop and Benson.

On 13 August the target for the 52 Ju87's of the Geschwader led by Graf von Schönborn-Wiesentheid, himself, was Warmwell airfield. They reached the assigned area at midday without mishap, but they were unable to carry out their dives owing to the target being 'weathered out' by heavy cloud cover at 3,000 feet. They returned back across the Channel with their bombs. Meanwhile III./St.G.77 had lost two Stukas on training exercises at Argentan and Tonneville airfields respectively, but these were merely normal hazards of training and no doubt similar accidents were being repeated on British training airfields as well.

On 15 August heavy dive bombing of both Hawkinge and Lympne airfields was carried out by 40 Stukas and badly damaged both places with the latter being out of action completely for 48 hours. No.54 Squadron's Spitfires intercepted the raiders.

It was clear that the early model Junkers Ju87 Bs lacked the necessary armour protection for their crews when directly pitted against the best British fighter aircraft. The upgraded B-2 model of the Ju87 B was being phased in at this time. It featured the Jumo 211 Da engine of 1,200 hp and featured broad wooden-bladed propellers. The protection problem was partly solved by the U-3 factory conversion kit (*Umrust-Bausatze*). This was the fitting of additional cockpit armour, mainly over the pilot's overturn structure and the gunner's canopy. Hauptmann Meisel, the new Kommandeur of I.Gruppe, had his own solution to this problem. He had earlier searched around Caen airfields among the wrecks of French aircraft strewn there. He had stripped armour plate from a pair of Morane fighters and had them fitted to his own steed. He felt confident they would do the trick even if they did slow his Stuka down still further. He was soon to get the chance to put his theory to the test. Next day attacks resumed in fine and warm weather with dive bombing of Tangmere, Gosport and Lee-on-Solent airfields as well as Ventnor radar site again.

There was another lull on 17 August but then came the climax of the fighting for St.G.77 the following day. That Sunday heavy raids were once more directed against airfields along the south coast with Biggin Hill, Ford, Polling radar station and Thorney Island all being targeted and accurately hit. A new bombing sight was introduced to take out Poling and it proved to be successful. But it was this day also that St.G.77 took what British historians have luridly called 'a staggering defeat' when they lost a total of 16 Stukas from the three Gruppen involved, I. and II./St.G.77.

The Stukas flew in over Selsey Bill but while forming up for their final approach to the Poling target were caught by the fighters of No.43 Squadron. More RAF fighters, Spitfires, Hurricanes even the odd Defiant, from, among others, Nos.152, 601 and 602 Squadrons, intercepted the other Stukas as they headed back out across the Channel. Their fighter cover failed to protect them and losses were heavy. Sellhorn himself flew with Knauer as his pilot in Ju87 No.5108, a reserve machine from the Stab unit, in this operation. They lifted off from Tonneville at 1430 to attack on Thorney Island near Portsmouth. They finally returned to Maltot airfield with the aircraft in a bad way but both men survived to fight again.

Among the many casualties was Herbert Meisel himself, his additional armour failing to save him. As well as those machines shot down at this time, two others were so badly damaged that they crash-landed and were written off while others got back but with wounded pilots and dead gunners aboard. Among such was Karl Henze, wounded during his attack on Fort airfield, near Portsmouth. Despite this he was to go on to become a Gruppenkommandeur and survived the war. Nor was it all one-sided; Helmut Bruck's gunner, the faithful Hettinger, nailed at least one British fighter on the way back over the Channel.

Naturally enough, after such a carnage, St.G.77 was immediately withdrawn from the combat. New crews and new aircraft were needed to re-build the force in readiness for their vital role of close support once the army had got ashore. An intense period of training took place during the rest of the August, both men and aircraft being pushed to the limit to be ready in time. But it was not to be.

VI
Through the Balkans to Crete

As the autumn of 1940 gave way to winter, time hung heavily for the Stuka crews of St.G.77. It was a time of re-building and intense exercising. Newcomers had to be absorbed into the Gruppe on a larger scale than had hitherto been the case. Mourning for lost friends and the transfer away of others made the transition harder to bear and the anti-climax, after the heady victories over Poland, Belgium, Holland and France, made the contrast even more obvious. The workload was intense during September when the invasion was expected almost daily. This training, and the influx of newcomers, lent itself to a higher than normal accident rate on the French airfields at this time. Two particularly bad air accidents occurred during diving trials at the ranges at Curfeulles in September which cost the lives of four crews. On the 11th of the same month another aircraft was written off in a taxiing mishap. On 18 October there was another bad crash involving two Stukas.

Gradually the realisation grew that the German aerial campaign by the long-range bombers, too, had failed. Although they could reach further inland and hit more distant RAF fighter bases, there were never enough of them to put the bases out of action for long enough periods, and, with no troops following up to take possession, these airfields were quickly made ready again and fresh aircraft and pilots flown in from the untouched bases in the Midlands and North. The only way the Luftwaffe could have won the battle was to kill enough young fighter pilots so that the RAF could not man their fighter defences; to knock out all the early warning radar stations and thus swamp the defences by mass attacks, and finally to knock out all the aircraft factories producing Spitfires and Hurricanes. It failed to do any of these things totally, although on occasion they came close. Moreover, the German Navy was never able to guarantee to transport and land, let alone constantly supply, a German invasion force of suffi-

Oberleutnant Trogemann leads the 1. Staffel on a training exercise with new aircrews following severe losses during the August fighting. (Sellhorn Archiv)

A Staffel exercise by three Ju87 Bs of 1./St.G.77 working from Caen airfields in September 1940. Training occupied the units for two months at high intensity before Operation Sea Lion was finally abandoned. (Sellhorn Archiv)

The Stuka of the Kommandeur of the Stabstaffel of I./St.G.77, Hauptmann Helmut Bruck, on a northern French airfield in December 1940. Both undercarriage mountings carry the sirens. The unit badge is carried just below the pilot's cockpit and the leader's stripe on the propeller boss. The engine now carries ejector exhausts on either side above the cowling. (Sellhorn Archiv)

cient size to establish a beachhead. Had that have been possible, then St.G.77 would have quickly transferred over the Channel and established themselves there. Once that was done the lethal Stuka/Panzer combination would have found very little to oppose them other than brave people indifferently armed with one-shot rifles and pikes!

The Sellhorn logbooks again best illustrate this period of relative quiet for the Stukas and of the intensity of the training which belies the much repeated statement that they had been withdrawn from combat as failures. On the contrary the tempo *increased* as their services were considered absolutely vital to a successful invasion. The only difference was that they were once more to be used in the correct role:

129. Fw Knauer: Ju87 5108, Ketten exercise, Maltot, 27-8-40, 1106–Caen-Maltot, 27-8-40, 1204: 58 mins, 204 km.
130. Fw Knauer: Ju87 5108, Ketten exercise, Maltot, 28-8-40, 0912–Maltot, 28-8-40, 1016: 64 mins, 275 km.

131. Fw Knauer: Ju87 5108, Ketten exercise, Maltot, 28-8-40, 1428–1530: 62 mins, 260 km.
132. Fw Knauer: Ju87 5108, Bombing range work, Maltot, 1-9-40, 0950–1032: 42 mins, 175 km.
133. Fw Knauer: Ju87 5108, Bombing range work, Maltot, 1-9-40, 1220–1303: 43 mins, 180 km.
134. Fw Knauer: Ju87 5108, Bombing range work, Maltot, 1-9-40, 1450–1518: 28 mins, 115 km.
135. Fw Knauer: Ju87 5108, Bombing range work, Maltot, 2-9-40, 1052–1130: 38 mins, 160 km.
136. Fw Knauer: Ju87 5108, Bombing range work, Maltot, 2-9-40, 1431–1548: 77 mins, 320 km.
137. Fw Knauer: Ju87 5108, Bombing range work, Maltot, 3-9-40, 1045–Maltot, 3-9-40, 1200: 75 mins, 310 km.
138. Fw Knauer: Ju87 5108, Bombing range work, Maltot, 3-9-40, 1440–Maltot, 3-9-40, 1540: 60 mins, 250 km.
139. Fw Knauer: Ju87 5108, Dive bombing exercises, Maltot, 5-9-40, 1005–Maltot, 5-9-40, 1035: 30 mins, 135 km.
140. Fw Knauer: Ju87 5108, Bombing range work, Maltot, 5-9-40, 1135–1225: 50 mins, 210 km.
141. Fw Knauer: Ju87 5108, Dive bombing exercises, Maltot, 6-9-40, 1510–1542: 32 mins, 130 km.
142. Fw Knauer: Ju87 5108, Bombing range work, Maltot, 8-9-40, 1025–1120: 55 mins, 230 km.

The pace of training continued through autumn and winter and by the end of the spring it was clear that, *if* any invasion was to come, then it would not be against England. Hitler's heart had never been in such an operation anyway. He had long stated that he had no real quarrel with the British Empire, which he regarded as a protective force for the Aryan race. His great obsession had always been 'living space' for his master race in the East, and that meant the wide open spaces of Soviet Russia, which he meant to colonise and clear as far as the Urals for his grand design. His pact with Stalin had been a brilliant coup, but an opportunist one to protect his back. With the West underheel or cowed, with British undefeated but totally unable to do more than nibble at his vast conquests, Hitler now turned his mind more and more to the final settlement with the hated Communist Empire in the east. As early as 22 June 1940 he was musing and dropping hints to that effect and, by the winter, preliminary plans were being drawn up for the great gamble, Operation 'Barbarossa', the conquest of the East.

Awaiting the call which never came. A Stuka of the Stabstaffel St.G.77 in its revetment at Maltot airfield in the winter of 1940-1. (Sellhorn Archiv)

For this vast and bold new battlefield, the Stukas were to lead the way to Moscow as they had done to Warsaw and Paris, and preliminary plans were made to secretly shift their bases eastward to advance fields belonging to Germany's eastern allies, Rumania, Hungary and Bulgaria. Rumanian oil as well as airfields was essential for Hitler's plans. Until he had conquered the Russian oilfields in the Caucasus he was dependent upon the Ploesti output. Most of the Balkan states were friendly towards his cause; all hated Russia of course and few dared oppose the new master of western Europe.

The only fly in the ointment for German preparations was the impossible situation that the Italians under Mussolini had got themselves into. In North Africa their vast army was chased back from the Egyptian frontier by a tiny British force, the only victory achieved by that nation's land forces. In the Mediterranean Sea defeat followed defeat and humiliation followed humiliation as the Royal Navy chased and hounded the Italian Navy back to its bases and then reached out and hit them there also, culminating in the stunning naval victories of Taranto and Matapan. Worse, from Hitler's viewpoint, Mussolini's grandiose invasion of Greece from Albania had turned into another defeat and the Greeks were winning hands-down. This enabled the British to send troops to Greece and once more establish themselves on the European mainland. This mattered little but for the fact that the RAF were now within striking range of Ploesti.

This the Germans could not tolerate. In talks with the Yugoslavian Prime Minister Hitler blamed the British for the impending doom coming to the Greeks, accurately predicting that: 'Only when our dive-bombers and armoured corps appear will they get out of Greece as hastily as they have on every other occasion we employed these means.'

One final factor tipped the scales. In Yugoslavia, a government favourable to the Axis cause, had been toppled in a sudden *coup d'état* after British agents had stirred things up and the new leaders of that nation threatened a hostile policy. Hitler decided to secure his fuel supplies and jumping-off positions against Russia, evict the British once more from Europe proper and rescue his bumbling ally, all in one swoop.

The invasion of Greece was already decided upon, Operation 'Marita'. On 27 March Hitler announced to his generals; 'I have decided to destroy Yugoslavia. How much military force do you need? How much time?' Within nine days the whole plan had been re-drafted to include this order. The date was set for 6 April.

As far as St.G.77 was concerned the fast moves of bases, aircraft and equipment for which they had long trained were smoothly put into effect. Immediately following the revolution at Belgrade on 26 March orders were given for the rapid transfer of flying units totalling nearly 600 aircraft including the two-dive bomber Gruppen from France. Nearly all these short-range units were to occupy bases at Arad, Deta and Turnu Severin in the extreme west of Rumania, within easy distance of Belgrade. The attack on Greece and Yugoslavia commenced on 6 April and most of the Stuka formations had arrived at their destinations with at least 75 per cent of their aircraft and were ready to operate at two-thirds strength on the opening day.

Such a feat was totally beyond the RAF and, indeed, most air forces at that time, as a British official pamphlet duly noted:

It will be seen that the Luftwaffe was on this occasion able to move a fleet of aircraft, comparable in size to a large Fliegerkorps, distances averaging 1,000 miles from bases far apart, so that about 40 to 50 per cent of the establishment number were able to be serviceable for operations in ten days from the date of the order for transfer. This accomplishment was only possible, first, because of the airfields at the destination were ready with assistance in M/T and ground personnel and were capable of being stocked up with fuel, ammunition etc from depots within reasonable distance, and secondly, because a large number of transport aircraft could be made available at short notice.

What that meant in practice to the men of St.G.77 is shown by the entries in the Sellhorn logbooks for this period:

182. Oblt Scheffel: Ju87 S2+DB, Overland, Théville, 31-3-41, 1100–Romilly, 31-3-41, 1235: 95 mins, 400 km. Complete Gruppe transfer.
183. Oblt Scheffel: Ju87 S2+DB, Overland, Romilly, 31-3-41, Strasburg-Cutzheim, 31-3-41, 75 mins, 310 km.
184. Oblt Scheffel: Ju87 S2+DB, Overland Strasburg-Cutzheim, 1-4-41, 1400–Erding, 1-4-41, 1525: 85 mins, 350 km.
185. Oblt Scheffel: Ju87 S2+DB, Overland Erding, 2-4-41, 1010–Gotzendorf, 2-4-41, 1145: 95 mins, 440 km.
186. Oblt Scheffel: Ju87 S2+DB, Overland, Gotzendorf, 2-4-41, 1255–Schwecherm, 2-4-41, 1300: 5 mins, 20 km.
187. Oblt Scheffel: Ju87 S2+DB, Schwecherm, 2-4-41–Gotzendorf, 2-4-41, 1415: 5 mins, 20 km.
188. Oblt Scheffel: Ju87 S2+DB, Overland, Gotzendorf, 2-4-41, 1650–Arad (north-west Rumania), 2-4-41, 1835: 105 mins, 440 km.

The actual command HQ was set up at Wiener-Neustadt south of Vienna. Here St.G.77 came under general command of General der Flieger Loehr, AOC of Luftflotte 4 with HQ at Vienna. Actual air operations were once again entrusted to von Richthofen, commanding Fliegerkorps VIII. By 27 March there were 120 Ju87s ready on the Bulgarian airfields.

Despite the losses over the English Channel nine months before, the bulk of the St.G.77 Stuka crews involved in this new venture were old hands.

There were newcomers to be sure, among them 21-year-old Dresdener Manfred Goetze. He first joined the 4./St.G.77 as a Leutnant in April 1941 and quickly made his mark. During a notable exploit on his first combat sortie he earned himself the nickname, 'The Lion of Banya Luka'. From Berlin came Günther Ludigkeit, the same age. He was to become a very well-known Stuka pilot, noted for his courage later in the war, but his very first missions were in the Balkans and at Crete with II./St.G.77.

There was Werner Roell, a 26-year-old French-born pilot from Ailly-sur-Noye, who became an Oberleutnant in the St.G.77 in 1939. In April 1940 he transferred to the Transportgruppe under Hauptmann Alewyn flying Junkers Ju52s but April found him back as the Staffelkapitän of 4./St.G.77. In May he was to become the Staffelkapitän of 4./St.G.77 at Crete.

Gerhard Stüdemann, born in 1920 at Rom-bei-Parchim, Mecklenburg, was nicknamed 'Stutz'. In October 1939 he had been a volunteer for the Luftwaffe, joining the Flieger Ausbildungs Regiment 10 in Neukuhren/East Prussia as an officer cadet. After his dive bomber training at the Stukaschule in Graz, Austria, a year later he joined the Erganzungs-Stukastaffel of the Fliegerkorps VIII before being transferred on 1 February as a Leutnant to 2./St.G.77 on the Channel

Coast. He saw no combat there and was one of the 'green' Stuka men still awaiting their chance.

Karl-Georg 'Schorschil' Geschwendtner was born in 1918 at Wollomos-bei-Aichach/Obb. He had volunteered for Luftwaffe in 1936 at the age of eighteen before going on to receive his pilot training. In July he was assigned to the 3./St.77 on the Channel coast as an Unteroffizier. His first of many hundreds of combat missions was flown in Yugoslavia. Herbert Rabben, from Oldenburg, had a similar background and flew his initial missions with I./St.G.77 in April 1941.

Hauptmann 'Bubi' Haker had joined 7./St.G.77 in France as an officer cadet in the autumn of 1940. He was also to fly his first mission on 6 April in Yugoslavia and was to go on to a total of six combat missions during the Balkan campaign. Josef 'Sepp' Huber was yet another to go into battle for the first time in Yugoslavia.

Among others we have met, but still lacking combat experience, were: Horst Kaubisch who had joined 11./St.G.1 in April and then transferred to the 3./St.G.77 on 18 August to make up their heavy losses; Franz Kieslic, who had transferred to 7./St.G.77 in France that summer but had seen no action; Hans Meier was there and so was Gustav Pressler, promoted to Hauptmann in September. Between October and December he had formed the Stuka-Erganzungsgruppe (dive Bomber Auxiliary Group) at Lippstadt. He became Geschwader I/a with the St.G.77 in Balkans in April. The Scandinavian-born Rudi Reussner was with III./St.G.77.

But most were veterans. As always leading from ahead, Clemens Graf von Schönborn-Wiesentheid. Helmut Bruck, since early 1941 the Kommandeur of I./St.G.77, and promoted to Hauptmann on 1 April. Gerhard Bauhaus was back. After a period from August 1940 to February 1941 when he had served a stint on the staff of VIII. Fliegerkorps he had joined 7./St.G.2 but came to the 8./St.G.77 as Staffelkapitän on 9 May. Here too was Heinz-Gunter Amelung, since August 1940 the Staffelkapitän of 5./St.G.77, 'Ali' Orthofer, who had served as the Kommandeur of II./St.G.77 since 15 August. Karl Henze, was still serving as the Gruppenadjutant of the I./St.G.77, Helmut Leicht who, between 6 February and 27 June, was the Staffelkapitän of the reserve Staffel, Heinz Niehuus, Oberleutnant and Staffeloffizier with the I./St.G.77 since June 1940.

Kurt Huhn, the Geschwader Ia of the St.G.77, Josef Grewe with the 9. Staffel of III./St.G.77, Günter Hitz was to again fight with I./St.G.77 at Crete, Herbert Dawedeit with 8./St.G.77, 'Jonny' Jauernik of II./St.G.77, Gerhardt Bauer serving with III. Gruppe, Adolf Weiss of the 4./St.G.77, Helmuth Bode, Werner Haugk, Karl Fitzner who had been promoted to Leutnant on 1 January, Alex Gläser, Paul Langkopf, Franz Hettinger the ace gunner, Georg Jakob, made Kapitän of the 2. Staffel on 28 August. He was to clock up seven missions in Yugoslavia and seven more at Crete.

There was Alois Wosnitza flying with the 2./St.G.77 in Yugoslavia, Greece and at Crete, Hermann Ruppert with the II./St.G.77, Johann Waldhauser, who was destined to make his mark as an outstanding anti-shipping pilot with a string of hits scored against such targets both in the Balkans and off Crete. And another outstanding ship-buster, 'Piepel' Weihrauch. The previous June he had been made Unteroffizier to the 2./St.G.77, but, following the casualties of the Battle of Britain, had been promoted to Staffelführer and Leutnant on 1 September. He

Arad airfield in Rumania on 5 April 1941, the forward base for I./St.G.77 for the opening of the Balkan campaign. Busy with the spray-can, run from a mobile compressor, painting yellow frontal parts of the engine cowling for easy ground recognition pur-poses, are radioman Ofw Hettinger and 1st Class Mechanic Fw Pauser. (Sellhorn Archiv)

Arad, Rumania, in April 1941. Preparations for a sortie against Yugoslavian targets during the brief Balkan campaign. Luftwaffe armourers are loading the bomb into the bomb swing rack from the cradle of the standard three-wheeled loading trolley. (Niermann via Sellhorn Archiv)

The Stuka of Oberleutnant Scheffel and Unteroffizier Sellhorn at Arad airfield, Rumania, on 6 April 1941, at the beginning of the Balkan campaign. Note the bold yellow markings adopted by the Luftwaffe for this campaign in contempt for Allied air opposition. The distinctive nose of the aircraft shows it is still, at this late stage, a Bertha–1. (Sellhorn Archiv)

St.G.77 ready for action at Arad airfield in Rumania, where they had hastily flown from northern France in April 1941 to take part in the Balkan campaign. From the left: Staffelkapitän Oberleutnant Georg Jakob; officers Schöngarth; Otto Schmidt; Horst Kaubisch; and Alexander Glaser. (Sellhorn Archiv)

was to claim to have sunk a British submarine and a minelayer during the fighting off Crete. Rudolf Weigel with 7./St.G.77, Hans-Karl Sattler was there again as was Otto Schmidt and Walter Stimpel, the Gruppenadjutant of the II./St.G.77.

The Stab/St.G.77 movements are of interest as representing the rapid transit the Stukas made across Europe to their new war zone. They also illustrate the advantage that Germany's central position gave her in thus being able to allow her short-range units to hop from one airfield to another as her war priorities changed. With Oberleutnant Kurt Scheffel as his pilot, and flying Ju87 S2+DB, Sellhorn and his unit flew from Romily in France on the last day of March 1941 and a 310 kilometre journey of 75 minutes' duration brought them to Strasbourg's Cutzheim airfield where they landed at 1550 that afternoon. After an overnight stop, they took off from Cutzheim at 1400 to fly another 350 kilometres to Erding, landing at 1525. Next day they were off again with a 440 kilometre hop to Gotendorf which took them 95 minutes. From there there was a five minute trip over to Schwecherm before they resumed their journey eastward. They finally touched down at Arad, in north-western Rumania, at 1835 on the evening of 2 April. Next day they prepared themselves for combat.

As we have already noted, half the additional Luftwaffe ground attack forces were placed under the Kommandeur of Stab/St.G.3, who also temporarily controlled II./St.G.77 for this operation, and worked from Austrian bases. Clemens Graf von Schönborn-Wiesentheid, as the Kommandeur of St.G.77, had the Stab, I. and III./St.G.77 also had a number of fighter and destroyer Gruppen under his command in Rumania.

The Yugoslavs did not think the Germans could possibly attack before 20 April. Commencing on 6 April, however, heavy Luftwaffe air attacks were made which wiped out most aerial opposition. With German air mastery quickly established, St.G.77 was assigned fortress and defensive positions in the vicinity of the capital, Belgrade as their initial targets.

First mission of the day for Scheffel and Sellhorn's S2+DB commenced at 0708 from Arad. Their actual target was the royal castle at Belgrade-Dedinge and they flew with a strong Me109 fighter escort as they expected strong resistance.

That same afternoon, a second combat sortie was launched and the Stukas made precision attack dives upon both fortifications and against the strategic bridge near Smederevo, which is south-east of Belgrade, at the confluence of the rivers Nera and Morava.

Yet a third combat mission that day had to be aborted on account of engine problems while they were on the way to the target zone and they were forced to return to Arad for repairs.

The next day, with the faithful S2+DB again fully combat-worthy once more, they took off from Deta airstrip, to the south of Arad, just after 0930 to attack a column of Yugoslavian troops located at Konigulilofs-bie-Topola, a place due south of Belgrade. This target was duly hit hard and dispersed with some panic. They refuelled then switched back to Arad airfield, before mounting the next attack. This was launched by the Stukas at 1140 and again was strongly escorted by Me109 fighters. Dive attacks were made enemy forces at the town of Jadija, which was an important rail junction, 25 kilometres north-west of Belgrade. Disruption of the Yugoslavs' means of moving their forces around in reaction to the German thrusts coming in from the north and east threw the slow-moving enemy more and more onto the defensive and caused chaos, which the Germans were quick to exploit.

With the bulk of their forces in the north, the Simovitch Government was caught flat-footed. It had immediately despatched reinforcements to the south on foot. These straggling and primitive horse-drawn armies became strung out through the narrow passes. Once they had become broken up into a 150-mile long plodding column, they presented easy targets from the air and from that point onward the Stukas efficiently harassed the retreating Yugoslavs and then their allies, both British and Greek, all the way back across to Corinth canal. What resistance there was left was progressively isolated and cut off. It became a matter of mopping up isolated groups still fighting among the mountains, and for this work St.G.77 was constantly on call.

In Greece it was much the same story. The dive bombers blasted Forts Rupel and Ussita and helped the crossing of the Struma river. With a rapid drive down the Vardar valley and also through the Monastir Gap, by 23 April the Greeks

The main road bridge into Belgrade demolished in a precision attack by the I./St.G.77. A pontoon bridge is being constructed by German army engineers alongside it. Note the short muzzled MG 17 wing machine gun fitted without a flash-muzzle on this machine. April 1941. (Sellhorn Archiv)

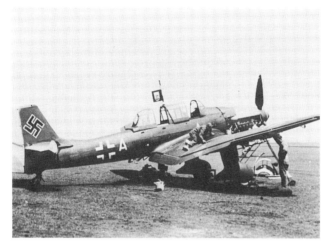

The Stuka of Oberleutnant Rudolf Neumann, flying with the 3. Staffel St.G.77, at Semlin airfield, Belgrade, during the Yugoslavian campaign in April 1941. Note the unit commander's metal pennant mounted on the cockpit of the aircraft which is undergoing engine maintenance. (Sellhorn Archiv)

Aircrew from the 2. Staffel St.G.77 enjoy a meal in their tented accommodation at Bijeljina, Yugoslavia, April 1941. From the left: Oberstleutnant Bader; Staffeloffiziers Leutnant Sudemann and Glaser; Staffelkapitän of the 2. Staffel, Oberleutnant Jakob; and Sonderführer Kriegsberichter. (Sellhorn Archiv)

The surrender of the 2nd Serbian Army by parley at the base airfield of the I./St.G.77 Bijeljina, northern Yugoslavia, to the west of Belgrade. Third from the right is the Oberwerkmeister of the 2. Staffel, Ofw Hackbath. (Oelshlager via Sellhorn Archiv)

were lamenting that: 'Numbers of Axis aircraft were able to attack our retreating troops at will without interference, and the state in their rear created difficult conditions for the continuation of the unequal struggle...' More bluntly *The Times* correspondent was to report: 'For two days I have been bombed, machine-gunned, and shot at by all and sundry. German Stukas have blown two cars from under me and have strafed a third...'

The British had landed 58,000 men (one armoured brigade, one Australian and one New Zealand division and British Corps artillery) to help the Greeks, 23,000 of which were supply and back-area troops of no combat value. A British wartime pamphlet explained this away thus:

The task of the British army was to establish itself in Greece in order to hold Greece, and therefore it had to compress into the peninsula which the Germans could spread over a larger space and longer land distances. The Germans were advancing, and, as in France, their spearhead of tanks was far ahead of its rations and lived on the country.

Translated in lay language, it meant that the British had learnt nothing from the 1940 débâcle about mobility of forces. The results were predictable enough. As for air power the RAF still relied on the Blenheim medium bomber which was a totally inaccurate weapons system, and had four squadrons of Hurricane fighter aircraft. They were soon overwhelmed and withdrawn.

Soon the British were clambering aboard their ships and sailing away. The Stukas hastened them on their way, sinking the troopship *Slamat* and the destroyers *Diamond* and *Wryneck* in the process. They had already sent the two Greek battleships, the *Kilkis* and the *Lemnos*, to the bottom of Salamis harbour on 23 April, along with several destroyers.

While the other German dive bomber units moved on down the peninsula and into Greece itself, Sellhorn's unit remained for a time based at Arad. On 14 April they mounted attacks against enemy forces dug-in around Pancevo, to the north-east of Belgrade. The following day they were in action again, bombing and strafing Yugoslav stragglers at Bijeljina, which is due west of the capital. They had to abort this mission, through problems with a badly running engine shaft. Bijeljina airstrip itself was used later the same day and, on 19 April, they flew overland from Pancevo to Belgrade's own Gemhin airfield.

They then flew to Vienna-Zwolfaeim field and then to Vienna-Aspern for repairs. Here they received orders for the Gruppe's transfer to take part in the planned airborne invasion of Crete, so Sellhorn hitched a ride with one of the many transports heading south. With Feldwebel Goral as pilot, Sellhorn took passage in a Ju52 transport from Vienna-Aspern to Belgrade-Lemlin on 24 May and thence, next day, to Thessaloniki (Salonica). Finally their lumbering old Ju52 landed at Athens at 1400. The final step, from Athens to the Stukas' operational airstrip at Gygea, was made on 25 May.

The decision to undertake an invasion of the island of Crete, to where the remnants of the British forces had fled by sea, was mainly an opportunist one. The German advance through Greece had been unexpectedly swift. The German General Staff had not even considered the occupation of Crete; even though they were fully aware that the British forces had long been established there and had set up a naval base at Suda Bay. They did not know just what the British strength on the island was, but they knew it was fairly formidable.

Doctor to the I./St.G.77, Dr Armbrust, in the summer of 1941. (Dr Armbrust via Sellhorn Archiv)

Operation 'Merkur' (Mercury) was really then the brainchild of Generaloberst Student, the AOC of the newly-created Fliegerkorps XI (Parachute and Airborne Troops). He it was who convinced his superiors that it was practical. With the Royal Navy forming a ring of steel around the island a sea-launched invasion was as out of the question as 'Sealowe' (Sealion) had been before it. But it was the Germans who were masters of the air in the Mediterranean. Ignoring the then current thinking, von Richthofen knew his Stukas could take on Admiral Cunningham's fleet – aircraft carriers, battleships and all. Thus an airborne invasion of the island was hastily presented to Hermann Göring. It was emphasised that German occupation of Crete would be another useful stepping stone for future expansion. The occupation of Cyprus and a link up with Rommel's drive across the North African desert to the Suez Canal was envisaged. There was also the pressure this would put on a wavering and nervous Turkey. With the Russian campaign imminent anything that would keep Turkish government friendly, or inert, was to be welcomed. Göring quickly saw glory for his Luftwaffe here and, at a meeting held on 21 April, he obtained the go-ahead from Hitler, with the strict proviso that the operation should be finished quickly so that the Stukas could be relased for Russia. It was to be strictly a Luftwaffe adventure and the parachute and airborne troops were to commence dropping on Crete by 16 May.

Again fast preparation was the keynote and, during the first three weeks of May, the German ground organisation in Greece worked round-the-clock to convert dry dusty strips into working combat airfields. Again the 150 Ju87's of von Richthofen's tried and tested Fliegerkorps VIII were to be given with the tasks of preparing the way for the parachute and glider troops and also for the task of tackling the Royal Navy off Crete itself.

The Stuka dive bombers and Me109 fighters were to be duly concentrated on these forward airfields, all of which were quickly constructed at Mulaoi, Melos and Scarpanto. These, however, proved insufficient and others were based at Corinth, Gygea and Argos airfields.

In addition to new airfields, the Stuka crews took the opportunity of the brief preparation period before the new assault to improve their weapons. A potent new development in the use of fragmentation bombs against troop and horse concentrations reached fruition in the Balkan campaign: this was the *Dinortstabe* percussion extenders. They were much used by St.G.77 and other units from this time onward. Oberst Friedrich Lang told me how these weapons came into being at this time:

The *Dinortstabe* were invented in the middle of May 1941 at the Molai airfield (South-East Peloponnese) where the I./St.G.2 were under the command of Oberst Dinort. They were supposed to detonate the bombs before they reached the ground thus scattering their fragments more effectively. The first trials were with 60 cm long willow sticks which we screwed into the screwhole on the point of the 50 kg bombs. The trial area was marked with a white sheet and was a wheatfield with some olive trees scattered in it. You could easily see the depth of the shallow crater, and the scatter effect around it by the damage to the wheat. The willow stick did not work out as it broke off and did not detonate the bomb before impact. The next trial was done with even lengths of round metal rod. That also did not come up to our expectations. The rod became embedded in the ground and the bomb detonated too late. We were successful with the third attempt. On the end of the metal rod we welded an 8 cm diameter metal disc. The bomb now detonated at about 30 cm above the ground. The scatter effect was high, as expected. The rods were at the beginning made in our workshop waggons, and first used when we attacked Crete. Later, they were made by industry under the name of *Zunderabstanstabe* or *Dinortstabe*.

Prior to the actual first landings on 20 May, a steadily increasing tempo of bombing missions took place against British positions and anti-aircraft guns located along the northern coast of Crete. These reached a climax on the morning of 20 May, and General Freyberg found his forces effectively pinned down and unable to move to reinforce his garrisons at Rethymnon and Heraklion and Maleme airfields, where a desperate struggle took place as the Germans landed transport after transport in an attempt to gain a vital toehold. Eventually they did so, but at a heavy cost. Even then the Imperial troops vastly outnumbered the German airborne men, who only had light weapons. But it was the Stukas that compensated, and more than compensated, for that lack. Any British soldier that exposed his position, any gun that revealed itself by firing, and kind of movement, was instantly pounced upon by the Junkers Ju87 and blasted out of existence. Once again superior numbers were rendered impotent by the close support air weapon.

May 1941. The main airfield for the 1. Staffel of the I.St.G.77 for the Crete battle was specially built at Mulaoi (Molai, on the north-western arm of Cape Malea). With their Stukas lined up in the sunshine in the distance, aircrew relax on ammunition crates during a lull between sorties. From left to right: Ofw Meier; Fw Gramlich; Ofw Schuh; Offz Maurer; Uffz Langdorf; and two unknown. (Schobert via Sellhorn Archiv)

Top *Stukas from I./St.G.77 pass over the rugged coastline of southern Greece on their way to attack British evacuation warships off Crete, May 1941.* (Sellhorn Archiv)

Above *The Stab of I./St.G.77 was a latecomer to the battle of Crete, but participated in the final battles against the Royal Navy in May 1941. This machine, with Gruppenkommandeur Hauptmann Bruck and his radioman, Feldwebel Muller, is* en route *to the island.* (Sellhorn Archiv)

Just how much the Junkers Ju87 dive bombers were feared and detested by their opponents is reflected by a group of tough Australian infantrymen evacuated from Crete by the Royal Navy's anti-aircraft cruiser *Coventry* in conversations with their rescuers.

On the mess decks they met the Australians, who were in wonderful form, and unable to find enough words in praise of the Royal Navy. With beatific smiles they guzzled tea, and one soldier said, 'You don't realise how wonderful that stuff tastes – we haven't had any for weeks. We found out that as soon as we started to fire, the Stukas were on us.' Said another, proffering a blue woollen jersey to a sailor, 'You take this mate. It might be some good to you, but whenever I wore it, the bloody Stuka pilots sorted me out for special attention.' The hate for Stuka pilots was exemplified by three grinning men who proudly displayed some very greasy currency notes. 'See that fat?' said one of them, 'It boiled out of one of the bastards that we managed to shoot down.' The Australians could not sufficiently curse the fates, that had put them against an enemy who pinned them to the ground with Stukas, while they never saw a single aircraft fighting for them.

The St.G.77 with Scheffel and Sellhorn flying with S2+DB from Gygea, was heavily involved in the closing stages of the land battle on the island when the scales were finally tipped in favour of the invaders. At 0723 on 26 May they took off and conducted an attack on positions at Alikami and this was followed by a second combat sortie against strongpoints located in a small village some four kilometres distant from Canea. A third mission followed late that afternoon with a free-ranging patrol.

Next day they were over the island's approaches at midday in a 400 kilometre round patrol without sighting any suitable target. A similar patrol followed between 1617 and 1755 that same afternoon. When, after the week of fierce fighting, Freyberg threw in the towel and retreated over the mountains to the southern coast to be picked up by the waiting Royal Navy, the dive bombers turned their attentions full time to taking on for the first time, a whole naval fleet. The contest was a bitter one, but in the end the dive bomber won hands-down. Three British cruisers and six destroyers were sunk outright, two battleships, an aircraft-carrier and numerous other cruisers and destroyers were hit and badly damaged as the fighting at sea continued without respite.

Scheffel and Sellhorn's unit conducted one sortie against the evacuation fleet on 29 May. They left Cygea at 1400 and conducted a diving attack against Admiral Rawlings' battered cruiser force south of the island half an hour or so later.

Some impression of just what it was like to be aboard the British warships that were under the lash of the Stukas off Crete in those days can be gleaned from the cold stark words of the official report of the cruiser HMS *Orion* on 29/30 May:

At 0736 during an attack by a large formation of Ju87s there were several very near misses, mainly forward. It is with the deepest regret that I report that during this attack Captain G.R.B. Back received wounds from which he subsequently died, and that Midshipman J.C.R. Poundsford who had been gallantly serving at No. 2 Pom-pom was killed by a machine gun bullet.

Between 0830 and 0905 attacks were intense, coming continuously at very short intervals. At 0905 one aircraft, coming down unusually low, scored a direct hit on 'A' turret, and crashed into the sea about 50 yards away. At the same time there were very near misses on both port and starboard sides, approximately abreast of the bridge.

Summarised in general terms, the immediate effect of this bomb was as follows:

'A' 6 inch turret demolished as far as and including the lobby. 'B' turret out of action, guns distorted, breech-blocks blown out. Elevation circuits to 'X' and 'Y' turrets out of action. The 4 inch gun control table out of action for about a quarter of an hour. Port 0.5 inch AA guns put out of action by a splinter. Fire between decks in vicinity of turret trunk. Forward 6-inch magazine and 'A' shellroom had to be flooded. Forward air compressor room flooded. Apart from the turret crew themselves, there were considerable casualties to naval, and particularly military personnel amongst those who were in the vicinity by the turret trunking.

Fortunately, after 'A' turret was hit, there was a temporary lull of about 45 minutes which enabled much good work to be achieved in all departments comparatively undisturbed, particularly in regard to the fire.

At 0955 further attacks developed, followed by others at 1010, and then the final Ju87 attack of the day at 1043. This was particularly fierce and closely pressed home, and it was during this attack that a bomb hit on the port side of the bridge, passed through the next deck in the vicinity of the plot, through the deck of the sea cabin flat into the canteen compartment near the recreation space, then through the deck of the sick bay bathroom and stokers' messdeck, finally exploding with great violence in the lower conning tower lobby.

The immediate effects of this bomb were far-reaching. Summarised generally they were as follows:

(i) *Casualties*. Very large casualties were inflicted on naval and military personnel, the latter largely as a result of the very congested state of the stokers' and boys' messdecks which were crowded with soldiers and which were much effected by the explosion. Lights in this area were temporarily extinguished, the boys' and stokers' messdecks were on fire and the whole area full of smoke and fumes. The forward sick bay was wrecked and both medical officers who were there at the time had very narrow escapes, one requiring attention himself. The first Lieutenant, 3 engineering officers and the captain's secretary (plotting in the lower conning tower) were all killed. It was under these conditions that commenced a struggle between decks, extricating and tending wounded, extinguishing fires, restoring lighting, and maintaining the steaming capacity of the ship, and repairing communications. Personnel directly affected, personnel freed from their quarters no longer capable of firing, naval passengers, military personnel, all joined in with a spirit of courage, initiative and determination which reflects the highest credit on all concerned.

(ii) *Damage to Armament*. 6-inch and 4-inch tables flooded, 4-inch magazine flooded, though this had been reported empty ten minutes earlier.

(iii) *Damage effecting Control of the Ship*. Lower Conning Tower demolished. All normal communications to Engine Room destroyed.

(iv) *Internal communication*. Telephone exchange destroyed. Some direct telephones left intact.

(v) *External communications*. Visual Signals – All S.P.'s were put out of action, two being got into action later. Only two halyards remained serviceable.

W/T. (a) Auxiliary W/T and Fire Control Office demolished.

(b) Three receivers in main W/T supplied from generators forward temporarily out of action until changed over to battery supply. This meant that reception for Routines, Admirals and Fighter frequencies was temporarily lost.

(c) All transmission in second W/T office out of action. This was being used for Fighter frequency. Receivers were also out of action due to aerials being down.

(d) All aerials were brought down in the course of the day, but were replaced as opportunity arose.

The Gruppe doctor, Dr Armbrust, poses with Oberleutnant Karl Henze in front of a Bertha of the 2. Staffel in the summer of 1941. (Dr Armbrust via Sellhorn Archiv)

Aircrew await the start of the Russian campaign — 3. Staffel at Biala, Poland, summer 1941. Note the camouflage netting on the machine's wings. (Immerreich via Sellhorn Archiv)

(e) D/F out of action as supply came from Auxiliary Office which was wrecked.

(f) All receiving lines from R.C.O. destroyed.

HMS *Orion* suffered 262 men killed and 300 wounded in these attacks. She was out of action for over a year, repairing the damage in South Africa, the USA and Britain.

The next day was a busy one for all St.G.77's aircraft, and one mission was carried out, again against one of the evacuating Royal Naval flotillas, commanded by Admiral King's squadron. The Australian cruiser *Perth* was hit and damaged in her boiler room but survived.

Sellhorn flew two final missions against the Royal Navy, one on the morning of 31 May and another early the following morning but the seas were empty. By the time the last stragglers were being rounded up ashore Crete was in German hands, and was to stay that way for the rest of the war.

It had been a stunning and remarkable victory. And as in Poland and France it had been a cheap victory, the occupation of the Balkans and the clearing of Crete had only cost the lives of 42 Stuka crewmen. Once more the Stuka had changed the face of warfare, this time maritime warfare, just as it had revolutionised land warfare the previous spring. But the victors were not allowed long to enjoy their fresh laurels. Already more complex movements were in train to shift the dive bombers rapidly northward toward their new field of endeavour. 'Marita' and 'Merkur' were completed, but 'Barbarossa' awaited them.

VII
'Barbarossa' – Strike to the East

The movements of St.G.77 toward the new battle zone called for their rapid re-deployment from the sunny Mediterranean back to the northern reaches of oc-cupied Poland. As usual it was carried out with speed and efficiency. The route taken by Scheffel and Sellhorn in Junkers Ju87 B, S2+DB, reflected this. On 2 June they left Cygea at 0532 and flew to Athens airport. Here was a brief refuel-ling stop and then they took off again and flew the second leg which took them to Salonica, where they landed at 0812 after a flight of 295 kilometres. No rest here for they again took off almost immediately and continued their flight across the Bulgarian border, arriving at Sofia airport at 1034.

Next day the pattern was repeated. Take-off from Sofia was at 0720 and their first stop was Lemlin, which was reached at 0840. Within a quarter of an hour they were off again; this time a hop of 210 kilometres took them to Kecskemet in Hungary. Less than an hour here to freshen up and then away again, touching down at Olmitz just after midday, with another 370 kilometres on the clock. In under half-an-hour they were off again, flying overland and arriving at Sprottau at 1400.

The dive bombers themselves were followed by the ubiquitous Junkers Ju52/3m transports which hauled both the ground crew and vital equipment, but all the heavy gear was, perforce, following by rail. The time taken to get this all in place at the forward Polish airfields to which they went direct, gave the Germans time to refurbish and re-equip at their central German bases in readiness for the new conflict. Thus almost a fortnight could be spent in this manner before they moved out to their Polish airstrips and the opportunity was also taken to give a much-earned leave to the Stuka crews themselves.

Forward bases had been under preparation long before this transfer. Under the clandestine *Ostbauprogramm* (Eastern Construction Programme) initiated as early as October 1940, construction work had been pressed ahead in occupied Poland. From March onward this work was accelerated and flak units moved in. By the end of April the new airfields were ready for their squadrons, but these, as we have seen, were busy to the south. It was planned that the actual movement of the aircraft themselves should be delayed until the last minute to avoid giving away the German plans. Training fields had been set up in Poland and these air-craft were exchanged for combat machines and moved west to hide the build-up. Fake signals were sent by cadres left in France to convince listening operators that the squadrons were still there. Even so British intelligence got wind of it and repeatedly warned Stalin. The Soviet dictator, however, closed his ears to what he dreaded to hear and no special precautions were taken on the Communist side of the border. The Russians had been equally assiduous in building up their defences and these were formidable, especially facing the Germans across the new border and centred on the powerful fortress of Brest-Litvosk.

In the afternoon of 19 June Scheffel and Sellhorn, still flying the faithful S2+DB, flew with the whole Gruppe, 122 machines, from Sprottau to Deblin in Poland. This was an airfield close to the Vistula river, south-east of Warsaw and north of Radom and Lublin, between the two cities. Next day they moved on their forward base to Biala-Podlaska in Poland, which lay just over Polish border from their first and principal target, the enormous fortress complex of Brest Litovsk in Russian-occupied territory. Tension was now high, with the actual attack imminent.

At 0300 on 22 June 1941 the invasion commenced. By the end of the day 1,811 Soviet aircraft had been destroyed, the bulk of them caught on their airfields, for the loss of only 35 German. It was the greatest air victory of all time. The bulk of these kills were achieved by the aircraft of Luftflotte 2 which had accounted for 1,200 of the enemy by midday.

St.G.77 had been placed under Luftflotte 2, commanded by Kesselring. He had the most powerful concentrations of striking power, Fliegerkorps II and Fliegerkorps VIII, with which to support Army Group Centre under Feldmarschall Fedor von Bock, which had the toughest job: the drive through the strongest Soviet defences along a 250-mile sector between the Romintener Heide and the Pripet Marshes towards Vilna and Smolensk. Their part of the overall 1,000 mile front bristled with forts, trenches and concrete bunkers and many million Soviet troops stood ready to meet them.

Losses in the Balkans and at Crete had been minimal but there were still a few new faces, as the Gruppe began its most prolonged and severe test. Among them was Horst 'Macki' Görtler, born in 1921, at Dresden, who had started his flying

St.G.77 fought almost exclusively at the southern end of the 1,000-mile Russian front from July 1941 onward. Here a Soviet vehicle is picked off on a road crossing the featureless steppe, September 1941. (Orthofer via Sellhorn Archiv)

On the main arterial road to Moscow in June 1941. A huge Soviet tank, the 52 ton KV–2 armed with the 15.2 cm cannon which came as one of many nasty shocks to invading German armies, has been knocked out by St.G.77 with a near miss bomb which shredded its tracks. (Luibel via Sellhorn Archiv)

training in October 1939 and a year later had moved to Bad Aibling to convert to Stuka flying. Between May and October 1941 he was serving with the Erg. Staffel of the St.G.77, before moving over to 7./St.G.77. The 22-year-old Karl Zellner hailed from Hangalzesberg/Bayerisch Wald and was another replacement who joined 1./St.G.77 that autumn. He was destined to remain with this unit until his death. Otto Heinrich, born in 1920 at Alt-Valm-bei-Neustettin, had volunteered for the Luftwaffe in August 1940. On completion of his basic pilot training he went on to undertake his specialised dive bomber training at Stukaschule 1 in the winter of 1940/41 before joining 8./St.G.77 in the summer.

Among many youngsters joining at this period was Osmar Griebel, a 21-year-old from Nuremberg, who had volunteered for the Luftwaffe and received his basic pilot training. He was to fly his first missions with 1./St.G.77 in June 1941 and to become one of the most outstanding pilots in the Gruppe. Kurt Rick from Ebersteinburg near Baden-Baden, celebrated his twenty-second birthday on 22 June by joining I./St.G.77. Hanns Luhr, 26, from Nieder Kasbach-am-Rhein, joined III./St.G.77.

An Austrian pilot, Leutnant Theodor Langhart from Graz, had been the Kompanie-Offizier as well as an instructor with the Flieger-Ausbildungs-Regiment 32 but in the autumn joined III./St.G.77 in the East. Kurt Stifter, another Austrian, from Vienna, came to III./St.G.77 in July in Russia. He was to fly as a pilot in the 7. and 9. Staffeln. Later he became the Gruppenadjutant in the Stab of the III./St.G.77. He was to repeatedly distinguish himself in close support missions with that outfit. Christian Schutt, 25, from Terkelsbull, also joined 1./St.G.77 in June at the very beginning of the Russian campaign

Finally there was Herbert Schmidt, an 'old' man at 33. From the East Prussian town of Nautzken, he had been a professional forester, but during the Munich crisis he had joined the Luftwaffe and received his pilot training at the A/B Flugzeugführerschule at Kamenz. In November 1940 he went to Stukaschule 1 and, on qualifying, was transferred to 1. Staffel of the reserve Stuka-Gruppe in April 1941 where he remained until 26 June. On that date Herbert joined 1./St. G.77 in the east. Despite his extra decade he quickly established himself as one of their most outstanding pilots.

The first strictly military targets for Major Graf von Schönborn-Wiesentheid's Stukas were enemy fortified lines along the river Bug and these were hard hit. A counter-attack by wave-upon-wave of Russian aircraft that had somehow survived was witnessed by Herbert Pabst just after 6./St.G.77 had landed back after their first sortie. 'They went on coming the whole afternoon,' Pabst was to recollect later. 'From our airfield alone we saw twenty-one crash, and not one get away.' All these enemy aircraft were immediately shot down without doing any damage to the parked Stukas.

Sellhorn was now flying with Feldwebel Werner Weihrauch and they flew two combat missions on 23 June the first against Kobrin, just north-east of the Brest Litovsk fortifications. Over the next few days they were operating between Biala-Podlaska and Prushany supporting strikes on that citadel. The fortress had proven a very tough nut to crack and repeated artillery bombardments and mortar fire had failed to breach its walls. Assault after assault failed and was beaten back. Finally, on 29 June, the whole of St.G.77 was sent against the eastern fort on the river's Northern Island which still held out against the Germans. The 93 Stukas made accurate dives with 1,000 lb bombs and scored numerous direct hits, but the thick old walls still withstood this blasting. Special 4,000 lb bombs had to be employed and this time they did the trick, the defences crumbled, breaches were opened, the defenders came out with their hands up, all save the officers who fought to the last man. This was hard going, but once the front-line had been breached and the Panzers surged triumphantly forward again they soon got caught up in the rapid moves and re-deployments that were now a part of the Stukas' routine.

As usual, the Luftwaffe was to concentrate its forces and support the Army in a series of enveloping operations which would nullify the vast Soviet superiority in men and machines by more sophisticated application and more combat experienced men. As with all operations to date, the initial target of all the German aircraft on the first days of the battle was the elimination of the Soviet air force. But St.G.77 was also totally committed to smashing the enemy defensive works and lines of communications. Sortie ratios achieved in France were to be doubled and combat sorties of six missions per day were soon to become commonplace for the Stukas.

The strain was intense. There was no 'tour of duty' for the Stuka men as there was in western air forces. The crews kept flying day-after-day, six times or more each day, week-after-week. It was hoped that Russia would go under in a lightning campaign lasting weeks. The pace could have been maintained, had it worked out thus. In fact, gross under-estimation by the Germans of both numbers and types of equipment held by the Soviets led to a far tougher campaign than hitherto fought. The weeks turned to months and then to years and the élite German forces were to be ground down on the Eastern Front. But this of course was unknown as, in the last weeks of June 1941 and on through July and August, the men of St.G.77 once more led their soldiers into battle. 'Where the infantry goes, so goes the Stukas' was the proud cry, and it was to be made good time and time again in the grim years ahead.

Among the many fresh innovations introduced with the start of the eastern campaign was the Panzer Verbindungs Offizier (Tank Liaison Officer), later to become a commonplace feature of close air support, but at that time quite a striking concept. In order to keep in touch with advancing tank columns Stuka pilots rotated on a duty in which they accompanied the armoured spearheads in their own tanks with direct radio-contact with the dive bombers who could thus be more readily directed against targets of opportunity.

An official Air Ministry pamphlet noted how smoothly this combined operations work now worked for the Germans.

The rapid advance of the German ground forces through Poland into White Russia called for the highest degree of mobility of the part of the close-support forces, and ground organisation of the German air force in the field proved itself fully capable of maintaining the serviceability and operational efficiency of units under these conditions. The German air force was in fact being employed on the now classic lines evolved by pre-war theory and confirmed with such striking success in practice in previous campaigns... Reconnaissance extended deep into the Russian back areas as well as covering the fighting zones and the German headquarters were constantly able to form a clear picture, not only of Russian movements and of troop and tank concentrations, but also of the general situation on an extensive front, where the fighting was often extremely confused.

New aces appeared in these circumstances. Adolf Weiss was quick off the mark in June destroying the first of what was to be a personal scoreline of three important bridges and 32 Soviet tanks.

We have already commented on the strength and durability of the Junkers Ju87. These features are often ignored but proved vital assets in all the varying conditions that the Luftwaffe fought in World War II. Such qualities are equally as good as high speed, defensive armament and the like so emphasised in the west. In fact in conditions in Russia, with primitive airstrips and atrocious conditions, such attributes as these were more important and enabled the Stukas to fly and fight when aircraft far superior on paper would have been grounded for days and weeks at a time.

As well as its ruggedness, giving it the ability to use any stretch of level field or roadway as a temporary airstrip, the serviceability of the Stuka was excellent. The whole engine compartment for example could be quickly unbolted, the engine lifted out whole by means of a simple mobile hoist and a new engine fitted within hours. Such features ensured maximum effort by the dive bombers despite the enormous number of flying hours they were engaged in.

Nor was the opposition to be despised. Even if they had lost hordes of aircraft on the opening days of the attack the Soviets seemed capable of inexhaustible reinforcements, as was the case in both men and tanks. In the field of anti-aircraft gunnery they were lavishly equipped and indeed every rifleman seemed to draw a bead on the Stukas. Intense flak was, and remained, a feature of war on the Eastern Front and Stuka losses from ground fire far exceeded losses to enemy fighter aircraft, which remained largely impotent throughout the war. Casualties therefore began to mount.

Helmut Leicht, Staffelkapitän of the Auxiliary Staffel of St.G.77 was one of the first when he was hit and seriously wounded on his first combat sortie in Russia on 28 June during the great twin enveloping battles of Bialystok-Minsk.

There were also many daring and sometimes lucky escapes. Indeed these became commonplace. Gustav Pressler, for instance, was forced to bail out when his aircraft was hit near Kishinev in July. After five days' hiding and moving he managed to reach German lines and re-joined his unit. After recovering none the worse for this adventure he was transferred to take over as the new Kommandeur of III./St.G.2, following death of Hauptmann Steen at Krondstadt in September.

It had always been the unwritten code of the Stuka crews not to abandon their comrades if they could help it. The ability of the Junkers Ju87 to land in the poorest of conditions plucked many shot-down crews from the jaws of death. The bitterness of the ideological struggle between Germany and the Communist state made the fate of any such airman a grim one with little or no mercy being shown by the Soviets to any Stuka men they caught alive.

On 25 August Otto Schmidt landed his Stuka in a daring rescue of a downed radio operator from his Staffel from behind enemy lines. Such bravery was common. Schmidt went on to become Staffelkapitän of the 7./St.G.77 in December.

While their comrades continued to support the centre front, at the end of June I.St.G.77 had been pulled out of the central sector battles now underway and rapidly moved back down through the Balkans to support the southern end of the vast battle front. Flying S2+CB, Scheffel and Sellhorn accompanied the rest of their unit in short legs from Biala-Podlaska on 29 June down via Kecskemet in Hungary, then across Rumania by way of the Iron Gate through the Carpathian Mountains via Craiova and on to Bucharest's Digera airport, where they arrived on the evening of 3 July. From there it was a 400 kilometre journey on 4 July to their forward Rumanian airbase at Tudora. Here they were to support Army Group South, under Field Marshal Karl von Rundstedt, in its drive to take Kiev capital of the Ukraine.

The plan was to wipe out all the defending Soviet forces west of the River Dnieper. The initial German thrust, however, owing to Rumanian sensibilities, had to be delivered on 22 June by the northern wing with General Paul von Kleist's 1st Panzer Group being the hammer and the infantry of the German 6 and 17 Armees the anvil. Von Kleist began moving south-east below the Pripet marshes and 11 Armee, under General von Schobert, crossed the Prut and headed east.

However, bad weather conditions and lack of sufficient armour meant that, by 30 June, the German advance had become bogged down opposite Russian forces holding the 'Stalin Line' defences. I./St.G.77 had been rushed down to this front to provide the necessary close air support punch. On 4 July they flew their first combat sorties before moving up to Jassy on 6 July where they dive bombed vital railway marshalling yards at Barschtschy that afternoon. In heavy fighting on 7 July some progress was made but at Starokonstantivov the German tanks again needed Stuka support.

Flying with the Stukas at this time were many outstanding pilots we have met already: Josef Grewe, with the 9. Staffel of III./St.G.77; Josef Huber was also serving with 9./St.G.77; Kurt Huhn was to quickly make his mark in the huge battles of envelopment at Bryansk-Wyasmathat that were to take place on the central sector; Gerhard Stüdemann served with him all that time; Johann Waldhauser, the Staffelkapitän of the 9./St.G.77 at the start of the campaign; 'Bubi' Haker was there right from the start and was to soon see hard action; Herbert Rabben flew from day one right to end of war in the East in both the 1. and 3. Staffeln of St.G.77; and Hauptmann Gerhard Bauhaus, Staffelkapitän of the 8./St.G.77, who was to shine at the battles of Feodosia and Eupatoria.

On 7 and 8 July the Stukas were heavily engaged working from Jassy against hordes of Russian armour. By 9 July the Stalin line was penetrated at Lyuban and the drive to Dnieper was pushed forward Stuka strikes being put in this day at Pemter. By 16 July the Panzers had reached Belaya Tserkov and on 1 August Novo Arkhangelsk. They thus trapped three Soviet armies in the Uman pocket and annihilated them. This victory led to the opening up of the whole Black Sea coastline from the Rumanian border to Odessa, Nikolayev and beyond.

Following the advance as usual, I./St.G.77 moved base across the frontier to Beltsy on 17 July and from here they conducted numerous strikes. Three missions were flown that day, against Mogilev Podol'skiy on the Dnieper, and against enemy artillery positions at Floreshty. Next day they flew further attack missions before returning to Jessy from where they flew a long-range strike at the enemy at Orgijev.

But this was but the prelude to an even greater encirclement battle around Kiev itself, where the Germans surrounded one million of the enemy whom Stalin had forbidden to withdraw. On 1 September the Stukas were instrumental in opening up the way for 4 Panzer Division which repelled the fierce counter-attacks by the Soviet 40 Army.

By 14 September only a 30-mile gap lay between the two German thrusts. The Soviets tried to keep this gap open but at 1300 I./St.G.77 led the final advance of elements of 6 Panzer Division to meet those of 16 Panzer some 130 miles east of Kiev. Thus the German armoured pinchers closed at Romny and Sencha and, on 19 September, after more hard fighting, the city itself fell. Five Soviet armies had been smashed completely. The way to the Donets basin, the river Don and the Crimea lay open.

Hitler had laid down the objectives of the southern front armies in 1941 as the over-running of both the Ukraine and the Caucasus, because he wanted the grain and oil conquest that these regions would bring. With the annihilation of vast enemy forces at Kiev, it seemed that the way to achieve those grandiose objectives had been amply prepared. 11 Armee, along with its Rumanian allies, was given the task of liberating Bessarabia (which the Russians had seized from Rumania in 1940) and then to advance along the littoral of the Black Sea coast by forcing the Dnieper river basin and driving on past Odessa which was surrounded and put under siege.

The overall aim was to capture the whole Crimea peninsula, including the most powerful fortress in the world, Sevastopol. While this was being accomplished, the main German armies would thrust eastward along the Nogay Steppe on the shores of the Sea of Azov. The forces of General von Kleist von Stülpnagel and General Kael would meanwhile push down from Kremenchug, Dnepropetroysk and through Stalino to outflank the enemy at Melitopol, Berdyansk and Taganrog thus opening the way to Rostov-on-Don. Kharkov and Belgorad to the north of the Donet basin, would be directly assaulted by 6 and 17 Armees. It was a bold concept and the Germans tackled it to the letter.

Maritime strikes began to feature more and more as the drive along the northern Black Sea coast gathered momentum. Here St.G.77's experience off Crete began to come in handy against a new enemy fleet. On 18 August 1941 the Soviet submarine *D6* was damaged by Stuka bombs off Sevastopol. She had to be docked but this was only a short reprieve for she was to be finished off by the dive bombers while still in dock there on 12 November. On 7 September, during attacks on the Soviet fleet, the destroyer *Sposobny* was damaged by a near-miss bomb in her after engine room at Odessa.

The Luftwaffe was now being widely stretched to cover such a vast war zone effectively. That it did so says much for its organisation but the strain was beginning to tell. The RAF recorded in a pamphlet:

The intensive scale of these air operations gave further proof of the German determination to employ their Air Force to the utmost in order to achieve their objective; the ability of close-support units to follow up the advance provided a further striking instance of their success in maintaining mobility and operating at short notice from field landing grounds. At the same time operations also showed that the resources of the German Air Force on

Below *An attack by the II./St.G.77, September 1941. Russian columns on the move were hit again and again during the initial advance eastward.* (Orthofer via Sellhorn Archiv)

Bottom *A Kette of Ju87 Bs from St.G.77 banks over its forward southern Russian airfield on completion of a fresh sortie, on 19 September 1941.* (Sellhorn Archiv)

the Russian front still remained insufficient to allow strong forces to be maintained at all points; a difficulty increasing contended with by concentrating the main air effort in support of local operations at the expense of other sectors, thus establishing air superiority where considered most necessary.

But there was nothing new in the Luftwaffe's philosophy in the application of such concentration; it had always formed the basis of their policy. It was only that the area left uncovered was now much greater.

New weapons and ideas continued to be developed and deployed on the Eastern Front. The new SD2 4 lb fragmentation bombs for example. They contained between 50 and 250 shrapnel particles and could be detonated on impact or just above the ground. The spread range of each bomb was confined to a 40-foot maximum circle, but large numbers could be dropped at once with devastating effect. They were mainly carried on the Stukas' underwing racks and proved formidable when employed against the massed ranks of the Soviet infantry on the open steppe. The Stuka crews christened them 'the Devil's Eggs'. More useful against Soviet armour and thin-skinned vehicles were the 20 lb SD 10 fragmentation bombs. Although machine gun was still the most effective way of disabling tanks, a great deal of thought was being put into producing a suitable cannon capable of firing a shell capable of penetrating even the armour of the Soviet T-34s.

Two things worked against the steady German progression. By the end of September the ominous signs of the dreaded Russian winter were becoming manifest, mud and rain made the poor roads almost impassable, and the Russians still showed limitless reserves of men and machines with which to block their progress. Despite these factors, and with superhuman efforts, the advance continued with I./St.G.77 keeping up its pressure, but struggling to maintain its full operational efficiency at the end of long and problematical supply routes.

On 30 August the Dnieper was crossed at Berislav and this remarkable feat was covered by the dive bombers, now operating under Luftflotte 4, which attacked Russian defence works at first light. Quickly pontoon bridges were thrown across and the advance rolled on.

On 11/12 September the Soviet cruiser *Krasny Kavkaz*, while shelling Rumanian positions off Odessa, was taken under attack several times but escaped without any damage. By way of some compensation the Stukas operating on 19 September caught the Soviet monitor *Udarny* in an attack near Tendra Island and sank her.

Despite this, the Russian Black Sea fleet made attempts to intervene in the land battle. On 21 September the Soviets made a seaborne landing with No. 3 Naval Regiment behind Rumanian lines near Grigorevka. The cruisers *Krasny Kavkaz* and *Krasny Krym*, with 3 Marine Rifle Regiment embarked, had left Sevastopol escorted by four destroyers. Off the Tendra Peninsula one of the destroyers, *Frunze*, and the Soviet gunboat *Krasnaya Armeniya* were caught and attacked by the dive bombers of St.G.77. Both were quickly hit and sunk, along with the tug *OP-8*.

This little victory failed to stop the enemy attack and, on the night of 21/22 September, the Russian landing took place and the Rumanian positions at Fontanka and Dofinovka were stormed and taken. Again St.G.77 was called in

A Kette of Stukas from the II./St.G.77 attacks the lighthouse and fortress at Ochakov, eastward along the northern coast of the Black Sea from Odessa, September 1941. (Helmut Grosse via Sellhorn Archiv)

The wreck of the Soviet destroyer Frunze *sunk by II./St.G.77 led by Alois Orthofer in the Black Sea near Grigorevka, west of Odessa, 21 September 1941. (Frau Orthofer via Sellhorn Archiv)*

Stukas of the II./St.G.77 attack and sink a Soviet transport ship in the Black Sea in September 1941. (Helmut Grosse via Sellhorn Archiv)

Gruppenkommandeur of the II./St.G.77, Hauptmann Alois 'Ali' Orthofer, on his 100th combat mission on 22 September 1941. 'Ali' went on to become Geschwader-kommandeur of St.G.77 until his tragic death in a random bombing attack on his airfield in the Caucasus on 26 July 1942. (Frau Orthofer via Sellhorn Archiv)

to rectify a serious position. Early next morning the dive bombers located the remaining three Soviet destroyers which were bombarding along the coast in support of their troops ashore. In quick succession the Stukas scored hits on the bows of the *Besposhchadny* and near-misses on the *Bezuprechny*, damaging both so that they had to be towed back to port.

The neck of the Crimea at Perekop Isthmus was reached on 12 September and was found to be strongly protected by the 'Tartar Ditch' earthworks. Two Soviet armies counter-attacked here but were in turn taken in their rear by Kleist's advance and between 5 and 10 October the battle of Chernigovka resulted in their decimation. But for a time it had been touch and go and it was clear that the Axis advance had shot its bolt. Once more the Stukas of St.G.77 were flung in to help stem the tide. In the thick of the fighting in the Donetz region was Heinz-Günter Amelung. His unit was called on again and again to give close support to both German and Roumanian troops here. By the end of this period Amelung had to his personal credit alone the destruction of 27 tanks, 16 field guns and 12 AA gun batteries as well as 6 vital bridges knocked out. During attacks on the river crossings and the Black Sea ports he was also credited with bomb hits on several river monitors and armoured patrol boats, as well as military transports and Soviet supply ships. In December 1941 he was awarded the German Cross in Gold for his outstanding work, and two months later was promoted to Hauptmann.

Another of the Gruppe's stalwarts, Adolf Weiss, earned a similar reputation at this period; he destroyed a total of 32 enemy tanks as well as three strategic important bridges. During attacks on the Soviet fleet at harbour that autumn he was credited with sinking an enemy warship.

Further north Kharkov fell on 24 October, but, back on the coast, von Kleist had swung up towards Rostov which his troops finally took on 20 November. Meanwhile the German 11 Armee was left to tackle the Crimea itself. Far to the rear Odessa was abandoned by sea by its defenders on 16 October. This enabled German reserves to be moved up for the new assault but it took over a week of hard fighting to achieve the breakthrough to the peninsula itself.

On 14 October, during the evacuation of Odessa, the troopship *Gruziya* was hit by bombs and badly damaged and in follow-up raids against the evacuation convoys on 16 October the troopship *Bolshevik* was in turn bombed and sunk.

Further attacks ranged wider afield and on 31 October the Soviet cruiser *Voroshilov* was hit by two bombs at Novorossisk and badly damaged. She was towed to Poti in the Caucasus for repairs. On the same day St.G.77 attacked the destroyer *Bodry*, which was bombarding German positions near Nikolaevka. Near-misses caused 50 casualties among her crew, including her captain.

The Soviets withdrew into Sevastapol and its hinterland and prepared for a long siege. Von Rundstedt was unable to take this powerful defence work 'at a rush' and from mid-November he commenced elaborate preparations for a grim, step-by-step reduction of the fortress. And all the time the weather was worsening.

Recognition of the outstanding work being done by the St.G.77 flyers was made during this time. Hauptmann Helmut Bruck was awarded the Knight's Cross on 4 September, and had then achieved 200 missions. On 1 September Franz Kieslich, who had covered most of the eastern front battles up to that date, was promoted to Oberleutnant. On 10 October Hauptmann Helmuth Bode was awarded the Ritterkreuz having achieved 145 battle flights. Alex Gläser and Karl Henze both received the Honorary Cup on the 24th of that month, and Hans Meier on the 26th.

A further naval operation by the Black Sea fleet took place between 10 and 12 November. The Soviet cruisers *Chervona Ukraina* and *Krasny Krym*, with the destroyers *Nezamozhnik* and *Shaumyan*, undertook shore bombardments during the German assault on Sevastopol. To silence their guns at midday, 'Ali' Orthofer led I./St.G.77 in a series of accurate dive attacks against these ships and they scored three direct hits on the *Chervona Krasny*, sinking her. For 'Ali' this marked another milestone in an outstanding career. It brought the total number of warships destroyed by his unit to ten, in addition to 27 auxiliary vessels with total tonnage of 50,000 BRT sunk so far in the Black Sea. On land they had been responsible for the destruction of at least 140 Soviet tanks, 45 anti-aircraft gun and 43 field gun positions completely destroyed. The well-deserved award of the Knight's Cross was made to 'Ali' on 23 November in recognition of this work, after he had completed his 150th combat sortie of the war.

The raids on the harbour continued and, on 12 November, the damaged destroyer *Sovershenny* was hit by bombs in the south drydock at Sevastopol and capsized, while the *Besposhchadny* was badly damaged again.

The winter campaign was wearing on both machines and men. Not surprisingly fresh crews were drafted in to replace the losses in both at this time while the veterans were given leave after an intensive six month combat period. Among the newcomers were some who were to make their mark with St.G.77

in no uncertain manner in the years ahead.

Ignaz Schweizer was a 22-year-old from Rosswangen/Wurtt. He was given the nickname 'Natz' and first joined II./St.G.77 at this time. Almost at once he was in action in the grim conditions at the Crimea. Of the same age was Anton Andorfer, an Austrian from Linz. He had first joined the Luftwaffe on 1 October 1939 and had gone on to train as a Stuka pilot. He was transferred to I./St.G.77 that winter.

Werner 'Blackberry' Honsberg, was an older man. Born in 1914, he was a Brandenburger from Eberswalde. He flew his very first combat mission with 1./St.G.77 on 27 December and was destined to fight with this same Staffel for a further three years on the Eastern Front. Rear-seat man Leonhard Burr, soon universally known as 'Leo' of course, was a year older, from Zindorf-bei-Nürnberg. He was a very experienced crewman and had flown as early as 1938 as a member of the Legion Kondor during the Spanish Civil War. On 13 September he became the replacement radio operator/gunner to Otto Schmidt, the Staffelkapitän of the 7./St.G.77 and this team was destined to fly a total of 328 missions in the East. In fact 'Leo' finally established the record for the highest number of radio operator combat sorties of all the St.G.77 Oberfeldwebel, no mean feat.

By December the temperature was down to 20 degrees below freezing. Assault followed assault but the defences proved just too powerful and too strong. Finally the attempts had to be broken off. General 'Winter' had won for the time being. More, Soviet assaults had re-taken Rostov and overrun the German armies before Moscow. For the first time in the war the German armies were on the retreat. They finally stabilised the line, but the Stukas had been taken out of the battle for rest and refurbishment in the interim.

In continued combined operations on 4 January 1942, the Soviet cruiser *Krasny Kavkaz*, which was part of a Soviet naval squadron which had earlier landed supplies for the Sevastapol garrison and carried out shore bombardments, was attacked off the port of Feodosiya, on the neck of the Kerch peninsula in southern Crimea, by six Ju87s of St.G.77 and was badly damaged by four near miss-bombs off her stern.

By now the veteran flyers were all clocking up impressive combat totals despite the dangers. On Boxing Day for example Helmut Bruck made another landing behind enemy lines, to pick up downed men from his unit. Leutnant 'Cherry' Brand with 8./St.G.77 flew his 200th mission attacking shipping at Feodosia harbour in January 1942. Otto Schmidt continued to fly bravely and was made Staffelkapitän of the 7./St.G.77 on 20 December. Rudolf Weigel was to reach a total of 271 missions, 169 of them flown in Russia by the spring. Franz Kieslich became Gruppenadjutant of the III./St.G.77 on 14 February.

Among those of St.G.77 who received the German Cross in Gold at this period for their outstanding work was Walter Stimpel. Early in the new year he became Staffelkapitän. Oberleutnant Hermann Ruppert was Staffelkapitän of the 6. Staffel and they had been credited with the destruction of five Soviet warships as well as four freighters totalling 11,000 BRT in attacks around the Black Sea coast. During one such mission Ruppert's Stuka was hit by flak and he was forced to ditch. They survived and took to their dinghy but had to endure several hours afloat in enemy waters before they were rescued. Nothing daunted Ruppert was

Above *A view below the surface of the Ju87 B. Clearly visible are the national markings, from the underwing surfaces over the dive brakes themselves; the faired-off siren mounting on the undercarriage; and the two SC 50 (110 lb) bombs with whistle attachments to their tail fins. The snowy landscape indicates that this is the winter of 1941–2.* (Schobert via Sellhorn Archiv)

Right *My best friend! An abandoned Russian puppy adopts Feldwebel Becher of 3. Staffel in Russia 1941.* (Immerreich via Sellhorn Archiv)

Above *The 3. Staffel of the St.G.77 flying from Kharkov-Rogan airfield in May 1942.* (Sellhorn Archiv)

Top Left *Flying personnel of the I./St.G.77 line up for food at the snowbound Kharkov-North in the bleak winter of 1941–2. Note the use of scarves as earmuffs, the blue-zipped top jackets over standard brown flying overalls, and the burnt-out hangars offering little relief from the Russian winter.* (Gohmann via Sellhorn Archiv)

Middle Left *The Gruppe front line base of the I./St.G.77 at Kharkov, during the winter of 1941–2.* (Dr Armbrust via Sellhorn Archiv)

Bottom Left *A Ju87 Bertha from the 1. Staffel prepares to take off from the snow-covered Kharkov-North with 50 kg bombs fitted with Dinortstab extended fuses in the bitter spring of 1942. 'Happy Easter 1942' reads the message for the enemy on the bomb in the foreground.* (Dr Armbrust via Sellhorn Archiv)

back flying combat sorties the day after. His courage was rewarded with the award of the Knight's Cross on 23 November. Oberleutnant Hans-Karl Sattler also repeatedly distinguished himself and became Staffelkapitän of the 8./St.G.77 early in 1942. He too earned the Knight's Cross which was presented on 16 March after he had flown more than 400 Stuka missions. Oberleutnant Karl Henze received the German Cross in Gold in January.

They also lost some valuable men, not to enemy action but promotion. Georg Jakob had been presented with the Honorary Cup in September, followed on 22 November by the award of the German Cross in Gold. He was promoted to Hauptmann on 1 March but left St.G.77 next day to take up his new position on the staff of Luftflotte 4 as Generaloberst Freiherr von Richthofen's aide-de-camp.

In compensation some faces re-appeared at the front, one of these being Fritz Neumüller who had left his job as a flying instructor in Germany in June and was once more back in action with 4./St.G.77 in the central and southern sectors of the front, including the Crimea. Helmut Leicht had made a full recovery from his wounds and, on 3 January became Staffelkapitän of 2./St.G.77 and deputy Kommandeur of the I./St.G.77

Despite the re-taking of the Kerch peninsula by the enemy, the Germans held the Crimea when the front ground to a halt. Fresh German assaults were planned for the coming spring. In this grim struggle St.G.77 was once more to be in the forefront.

VIII
The reduction of Sevastopol

As the grim winter of 1941/42 passed and the Germans faced the unappetising prospect of a long war in the East and not their usual 'lightning war', St.G.77 again prepared itself for a third spring offensive as the powerhouse of the planned German assaults for 1942, Case 'Blue'. This time Hitler was forced by losses, events and a certain unpalatable realism, that the vast goals he had set for 'Barbarossa', the attainment of the 'A-A' line from Archangel on the Baltic Sea in the far north to Astrakhan on the Caspian Sea in the south, were not possible. Although fresh armies could be raised by using more and more of his unreliable allies at the front, and new tanks and guns could be produced, the impetus had been lost. The more modest goals set for the new year's offensives were therefore those of an advance to the Don and the destruction of the Soviet armies there, then drives to the Caucasus and the Caspian oil fields at Baku. The initial goal was the securing of the Crimea; then the drive to the Volga.

Hitler summarised this by stating that, once the spring mud had dried up sufficiently, the German Army and Luftwaffe were to attain these new objectives by first cleaning up and consolidating the entire Eastern Front and the rearward military areas. 'The next tasks will be the clearing of the enemy from the Kerch Peninsula in the Crimea and the capture of Sevastopol.'

This was all well and good provided the enemy had no plans of his own. But the Soviet military machine, undeterred by the staggering losses of the previous year, was busy mounting offensives of its own which had to be dealt with first. All these plans were made at a time when just to hold the existing front was still in the balance. The situation was especially critical around Kharkov, where a January offensive had threatened to overwhelm the Axis positions based on that city, with fierce fighting at Belgorod to the north and across the river Izyum to the south, at Balakleya and Slavansk. And the focal point of that battle became the small village of Cherkasskaya.

St.G.77 moreover, still had to fight the new battles planned for 1942, with the same basic aircraft in which it had fought the battles of 1939, for no replacement for the ageing Junkers Ju87 Stuka had yet appeared. As long ago as 7 November 1938, Jeschonnek had lain down that future eight planned Sturzkampf-geschwader to be ready for the year 1942, would be equipped with the Messerschmitt Me210 dive bomber and later this number of units was increased to twelve. In reality the twin-engined Me210, designed to replace both the Ju87 and the long-range 'Destroyer' Me110, was a disaster. There were numerous development faults with this aircraft, perhaps not surprisingly as it had to double as a long-range fighter *and* dive bomber with dive brakes, two hardly compatible roles. The original specification dated back to 1938 and, on the second and fourth prototypes (V2 and V4), slatted dive brakes had been fitted for trials. Dive bombing tests were held throughout 1940 with the Me210 in this configuration before the dive brakes were removed from these two machines.

Even so, the replacement of the Stuka idea remained firmly in place and further dive bombing trials were conducted with the V12 machine, while early production models, the Me210-AO, were constructed with this role in mind. They could carry two 1,100 lb bombs on underwing racks. But finally the Germans did not actually use the Me210 for this purpose. When test pilots put the machine into the tight turns necessary in combat conditions many went into flat spins and crashed. Ernst Udet, way in over his head and charged with getting the machine into action, wrote to Messerschmitt himself in July 1941 that the Me210 had caused, 'unnecessary vexations and intolerable wastes of time'. Four months later Udet committed suicide.

In the end the Luftwaffe pushed the Me210 into series production and fifteen were completed by December 1942. The first unit to employ them (III./ZG.1 in North Africa) did not even begin to equip with it until October 1942. Nor did it shine in action the following month and it had to be withdrawn. Major Bruecket, one of the Luftwaffe's most experienced close-support fighters, described this aircraft in no uncertain terms as, 'the most unsatisfactory aircraft Germany ever built!'

Strangely enough it was left to one of Germany's allies on the Eastern Front actually to employ the Me210C as a combat dive bomber. This was Hungary, who licensed-built the aircraft with dive brakes and actively employed them with their 102 Group in the east in 1944. Back in Germany a much modified version, the Me410, was developed, but only entered service in small numbers, and then not until 1943.

The other German replacement close-support aircraft hope was based on their own bitter experience at the hands of the awesome Soviet Ilyushin I1-2m3 *Shturmovik*. They copied its heavy armour protection for the crew and equipped it with a tank-busting Mk 101 cannon in addition to bombs or machine-gun packs. This was the Henschel 129 B, another twin-engined machine, equipped with captured French Gnome-Rhône 14M radial engines. This aircraft *did* enter service (with 4. Schlachtgeschwader 1 on the Eastern Front in the summer of 1942) but in too small a number to make much difference. Again, the engines proved themselves unreliable and the twin-engined Hs129 was only 22 mph faster than the much-derided Junkers Ju87! In addition the first Hs129 pilots themselves were not fully trained on the use of the new weapon. It was replaced by the much more efficient 30mm Mk 103 cannon later. This had a higher muzzle velocity and penetrating power, which proved a much better tank killer, but it was all far too little, much too late.

And so the faithful Stuka had to soldier on, not only through 1942 but into 1943 and beyond. If no replacement could be provided for the Junkers Ju87, then at least attempts were made to improve its performance all-round and the many changes asked for by the front line units between 1939 and 1942 resulted in the 'Dora' model which was to be widely used by St.G.77 in the East over the following two years of war.

As early as 1939, when the results of the Polish campaign had been analysed, the Technical Department of the German Air Ministry was calling for an improved design to give the crew much better armour protection from ground fire, a better defensive armament than the 7.92 mm MG15 machine gun and a cleaned-up, and more aerodynamic, profile to match a larger and much improved power-plant. The need to lift heavier bomb-loads to deal with targets like concrete gun emplacements and other tough defences had been made obvious time and time again, the last occasion at Brest-Litovsk. All these factors were co-ordinated by the Junkers Flugzeug und Motorenwerke company at their Bremen-Lemwerder factory. By the summer of 1941 over 1,000 of the new D-1s were on order, but little progress had been made on production, due to troubles with the new engine.

The engine designed for the *Dora* was the 12-cylinder, liquid-cooled, 1,400 hp Jumo 211 J-1. This had several refinements over its predecessor (see Appendix One). In practice, some of these, including the new Heine variable-pitch three-bladed propeller, didn't stand up to combat conditions in the middle of a Russian winter and had to be replaced, in this case by a Junkers VS 11 three-bladed wooden propeller.

In weaponry the *Dora* featured two fixed forward-firing 7.92 mm Rheinmetall-Borsig MG17 machine guns and in the after cockpit the radio man now wielded the 7.92 Mauser MG81 Z (twin) on a GSL-K 81 flexible mounting. The *Dora* could now heave up to a maximum weight of almost 4,000 lb of bombs into combat in various combinations, with a single 3,968 lb PC 1800 bomb as its most awesome payload slung under the fuselage. The usual combinations of 550 lb and 110 lb bombs could be carried as before, along with 92 of the 4.4 lb fragmentation bombs in underwing wooden containers. Two new additions to the Stukas inventory were to be introduced in Russia, the 'watering can', an underwing weapons' pack which housed three MG81 Z machine-guns inclined downwards at fixed, but varying angles, to spray troop concentrations was one. Later came the 'Tank Cracking' 37 mm Flak-18 cannon, which spawned a whole new sub-type of Stuka, the *Gustav*, of which more later.

Extra cockpit armour was worked in all round the sides, the floor and the pilot's seat, with the gunner's sliding canopy incorporating the GSL-K armoured turret. Range was increased through the new internal tanks to more than 500 miles. The new engine gave the *Dora* a top speed of 255 mph. With the fitting of two 300 litre underwing tanks, this could be further increased to 953 miles. This extra reach was rarely used in combat however, save for strikes at the remnants of the Soviet Black Sea fleet sheltering at Tuapse.

There were a number of problems with the new landing gear, which proved far less tough than those fitted to the *Bertha*. This resulted in a number of crash-landings early on and the gear had to be strengthened, but it was never really satisfactory in service. The tailwheel also failed, and generally the *Dora* was less rugged than the *Bertha* had been. The streamlining of the cockpit had resulted in more cramped conditions for the crew and was not popular. Nor was the restriction of the previously excellent all-round vision, so vital to dive bombing. But the inclusion of 50 mm armoured glass for the windshield was a plus factor.

In the nightmarish conditions of the Russian winter each Gruppe was issued with 14 heated tent-like covers to fit over the engines. Even so, there were endless problems with temperatures that plunged to below minus 30 degrees F. The 'black men' of the ground crew had to start and run the Stukas' engines several times each night to ensure they would be ready for combat the next morning. Oil and fuel lines fractured and cracked and there was trouble with the starter motors themselves. The 'line abreast' take-offs, adapted the previous summer to cope with the choking dust, came to be applied with equal efficiency to the powdered snow that now clogged the airstrips. This 'flying from the tablecloth' as the Stuka crews termed it, called for a new skill from them, as did landings on icebound fields after battle damage. All these factors added to the normal hazards of combat and had a wearing effect on their operational efficiency. The return of the mud in spring meant that even the modified wheel spats of the *Dora* were often removed, partially or completely, and missions were flown without them to prevent their clogging up.

As 1942 progressed the D-1 gave way to the D-3 (D-2 was a glider-tug adaptation, see Appendix One). This featured several modifications to the D-1, mainly the fitting of yet further armour protection along the undersides of the ventral fuselage, the engine and radiators. The undercarriage leg fittings for the 'Trombone of Jericho' sirens was done away with, as this device had lost much of its original effect on the opposition. In all, some 1,559 of the D-2s were built up to the end of production in 1944, and it became the most widely-used model of the Stuka.

I./St.G.77 itself first began to re-equip with the *Dora-1* in the middle of March 1942, while it was in its rest and recuperation period back on its home base airfields at Boblingen near Stuttgart. The 6./St.G.77 was to be the first to take delivery and all other Staffeln of the Gruppe progressively re-equipped before being moved back to the Eastern Front in readiness for the May offensive.

As we have seen, I/St.G.77 was based near General Fritz von Manstein's 11 Armee's operational headquarters in the Crimea at Sarabusy village; their actual forward airstrip was Sarabusy-South field, near Sinferopol. Here they began their training programme to prepare both men and new machines for the softening-up of the Soviet defences of Sevastopol in readiness for the planned final assault.

On 2 May Sellhorn and Scheffel crewed S2 + AL, and the whole Gruppe held a 55 minute exercise flight from Sarabusy-South; on 4 May there were three more such practice missions. Another training exercise took place on the next day. The Gruppen were also assigned roles to assist the re-clearing of the Parpach isthmus and the Kerch peninsula. Here three Soviet armies had established formidable defence works across the 11-mile neck of land. Behind a 16-ft deep, 11-yard wide anti-tank ditch and deep minefields were trenches, machine-gun posts and gun positions, which could not be outflanked. It was considered impregnable by the Soviet commander, Lt-General Koslov.

The German attack was put in against the southern end of the isthmus with 22 Panzer Division and five infantry divisions, spearheaded, as usual, by the Stukas of St.G.77. The first dive bombing attacks went in on the afternoon of 7 May, the Ju87s flying for these attacks from the airstrip at Grammatikowo. The Stukas' targets were enemy anti-tank batteries located by Tulumtshak. A second strike was made at 1730 against Soviet defence works three kilometres from the strategic Hill 253.

All this was but a prelude to von Manstein's carefully thought-out feint to get across the formidable enemy defences under cover of darkness on the night of 7/8 May in readiness for the all-out assault that morning. Sappers in assault boats were launched in silence in the early hours and at 0315 the main bombardment commenced. St.G.77 was awake before the dawn and their attack took off from Sarabusy-South at 0315 and delivered their ordnance in screaming power-dives against the Soviet emplacements. Under cover of this the assault boats sailed into the anti-tank ditch and took the enemy positions by surprise.

Once established across that obstacle much fierce fighting was still required to break through the fortifications beyond. The Soviets held this land with a density of nine men to a yard and they were well prepared and dug in. I./St.G.77 was in constant demand and on call throughout that day and the next. Sellhorn, Scheffel and their comrades flew no less than five more combat sorties from Grammatikowo on 8 May alone.

The second mission of the day took off at 0607, a ground strafing attack one kilometre from Paysatih. With take-off at 0823, the next target was dug-in troops at the village of Gwork near Armaa-Eli where a Soviet armoured brigade was discovered. At 1130 the Stukas hit again at anti-tank batteries holding up the advance at Hill 638, Paysatsih and, at 1330, Soviet field positions at Hill 566 south-west of Arma-Eli was the target. The final mission flown that day was against enemy columns moving up from reserve at Hill 465. The German attack then swung north, as planned, to mop up the rest of the enemy defence line from the rear.

This became a pattern, with five more missions flown on 9 May, starting with a 0355 take-off from Sarabusy-South to hit field works three kilometres from Paysatik. This was followed with strikes delivered at 0720 against trenches and strongpoints a kilometre north of Arma-Eli and another against flak batteries three kilometres north of the same village at 0820. Their fourth sortie, launched from Grammatikowo at midday, was aborted due to the fluid position on the ground where the rain had set in turning the battlefield into a quagmire. At 1505, they were airborne once more, their target Russian field works seven kilometres south-west of Paysatsih. That evening they flew the 145 kilometres back to Sarabusy.

On 10 May they returned to Grammatikowo in mid-morning, but undertook no actual missions, despite the fact that it was this day that strong Soviet ground attacks were launched. I./St.G 77 resumed their fight the next day at 0729 with the dive bombing of enemy positions one kilometre south of Ak-Monay on the coast, in support of 22 Panzer; this was followed by two further midday strikes against artillery positions and infantry columns. Early that afternoon, around 1440, they made a precision attack which wiped out key Soviet Army staff in their headquarters at Tschaltemier. This caused widespread panic among the Soviet high command and Koslov's command disintegrated. The last Stuka attack of the day was made against fleeing enemy columns which they caught at Kerch itself. The town fell to the Germans on 16 May. The last contribution made by the Stukas to this stunning victory, achieved against all odds, was made on 12 May against those stubborn Russian batteries at Palaysan which were still holding out alone and were hit once more. But the battle was all but over, the way to the Caucasus was opened and another ten Soviet divisions were in the bag, with 170,000 prisoners, 1,138 guns and 258 tanks captured.

None of this was achieved without some cost to the Stuka flyers however. One of the saddest losses was that of Johann Waldhauser, Staffelkapitän of 9./St.G.77. During a dive against the last remnants of Soviet resistance on the Kerch peninsula at Vasilyevka Johann's aircraft took a direct hit from enemy anti-aircraft batteries and did not pull out. Both he and Martin Kleinert, his long-time radio operator, were killed outright. He had received the Knight's Cross just four months earlier for his outstanding work. He had flown 312 combat missions in the Stuka, and achievements in that time included the sinking of a destroyer and 31,000 tons of shipping.

St.G.77 had meanwhile been rapidly switched north to assist in the threatening situation around Kharkov. Here the powerful Russian offensive had commenced on 14 May. Spearheaded by no less than 14 Soviet armoured brigades, this attack soon threatened the German hold on that city. But the Germans were experts at this form of armoured warfare and reacted almost without breaking stride. Rapid counter-blows were mounted by von Kleist's 1 Panzer Armee and Hermann Hoth's 17 Armee on 17 May which rapidly saved the situation.

Once more it was St.G.77 that was to contribute to the German recovery by which the dangerous Russian salient was itself pinched off. On 13 May they left Grammatikov at 1015 and flew the 270 kilometres north to Lazovaya and then from there to the centre of the cauldron landing at Kharkov's Rogou airfield at 1315 the same day. Combat missions commenced the next day at 0416 with a strike at advancing Soviet troops located at Falusinge and Nepokrytaja. Every sortie was now vital; the Soviet advance had to be blunted to give the Germans time to readjust and take counter-action. At 0700 the second strike of the day was made against enemy tanks at Nepokytaja and the third at 0930 hit mobile batteries at Molowoje. A second strike against the same guns was made at midday and a third, at 1430. Sellhorn and Scheffel were now flying a new mount, S2+BL, but it was rapidly becoming a veteran. Sellhorn's 109th combat mission was flown between 1600 and 1648 and the Stukas hit T-34s massing at Walche, two kilometres to the north of Petrowskoje. Enemy infantry at Wesseloje were strafed at 1740 for the day's final attack.

Thus the tempo continued. On 15 May there were seven sorties made by I./St.G.77 as they tried to turn Timoshenko's armoured tide sweeping in towards Krasnograd and Poltava. The first was at 0835 and the last at 1756; the targets were always the fast-moving Russian armoured formations, tanks caught out in the open some four kilometres south of Petrowskoje; tanks and armoured vehicles in the same position at Walde four kilometres north Petroskoje; tanks at Krassnyj; tanks and tracked vehicles at Kolnnen near Wesseloje; tanks by Krassnyj; tanks and armoured cars at Kolnnen near Wesseloje; enemy thrusts at Molodowoje. It was a desperate, non-stop shuttle as the German aerial arm attempted to blunt the Soviet armoured masses alone. And they succeeded!

Now was the time for the right hook coming up fast from the south and delivered by von Kleist from positions to the south of Izyum, led by 1 Panzer and 17 Armee. A day of rest and then St.G.77 was again there to lead this counter-blow on 17 May.

Enemy field works and armoured vehicles at Raime, west of Peremoga, were their first objectives this day. At 0722 they flew against enemy troops near

Many post-war historians have claimed that Stukas were not very effective against tanks, especially Soviet ones. The following photographs show they are wrong.
Left A Soviet tank offensive stopped cold by a Stuka attack: an assortment of T.34 corpses. (Dr Armbrust via Sellhorn Archiv)

Right Wrecks of 'Stuked' Soviet T.34s south of Kharkov, May 1942. (Dr Armbrust via Sellhorn Archiv)

Left A Stuka bomb demolished the bridge with this T.34 on it. (Dr Armbrust via Sellhorn Archiv)

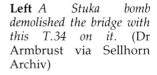

Left A nicely decapitated T.34 caught in the open by the I./St.G.77. (Dr Armbrust via Sellhorn Archiv)

Newkanoje. The third and fourth missions were once more against the Soviet tanks on the steppe, six kilometres south of Wesseloje, then at 1421 massed infantry two kilometres north-west of Nepokrytaja. At 1707 they were off again, bombing mobile artillery south of Isarokin; and finally, at 1830, they hit more tanks west of Perenoga.

On 18 May, take-off from Kharkov was at 0534 and the Stukas' targets this time were large numbers of enemy in the woods south of Temovaja. Yet more Russian armour was attacked at Hill 1990 near Nepokrytaja and in positions three kilometres north of Nejskvyta, tanks in woods by Feverowka; tanks and mobile artillery again at Feverowka; tanks by Feverowka and Krassnyji and, at 1800, tanks close to Termouaja: eight combat sorties for the day.

May 19 was yet another day devoted exclusively to T-34 smashing. Again the story is the same with four missions flown that morning against huge numbers of Soviet tanks caught in laager by Petschanoje. A fifth mission was flown off at 1430, but S2 + AL had to abort due to engine trouble.

This was fixed, and the following day saw a repetition of this endless and desperate air-to-ground fighting. Mission followed mission with brain-numbing routine. Tired as were both men and machines they knew tens of thousands of German soldiers were depending on their halting the Russian onrush. They did not let them down. And all the time salvation was coming up from the south behind the confident enemy columns. St.G.77 pinned them to the ground; von Kleist then hacked their necks off with his Panzer columns.

Enemy field works at Arajsowka-Ploskoje were the target of the first strike of the day, quickly followed at 0730 with hits on Soviet tanks still held up at Hill 1990; then the Stukas twice bombed tanks east of Wesseloje, others east of Minou; yet more four kilometres north-west of Temorvaja and, at 1805, tanks south of Arajsowka-Ploskoje.

On 22 May their targets were batteries of the much-feared 'Stalin organ' rockets located at Temowaja which they wiped out. On 23 May they destroyed the vital bridge at Lewkowka in an early morning attack and then turned their attentions to mobile armoured units to the east of Scheblinka. At 1722 they flew a mission against the village of Kaminka.

After a short lull, St.G.77 resumed operations from Kharkov at 0701, hitting

The dive bombing of the I./St.G.77 was also as effective as ever when Soviet artillery columns were caught on the move and summarily dealt with in fine style. Dr Armbrust via Sellhorn Archiv)

The 'Watering Can', a useful way for the Stukas to combat the hordes of Soviet infantry on the open steppe. The WB 81A or B weapons container held three twin MG 81Z machine-guns set to fire at different, set angles downward and were fixed one under each wing for low-level ground strafing. Each gun had a circular 250-round ammunition box, which necessitated a small exterior bulge on the otherwise neatly stream-lined canister. (Immer-reich via Sellhorn Archiv)

mobile guns and infantry columns near Losowenka, and, at 1215, destroying the Donetz bridge at Isawinzy. Retreating enemy tanks and supply waggons were caught and punished south of Schushunvka, by Hill 1562. Next day only one mission was flown to pick off another vital Donetz bridge south of Isawinzy while their final sortie of the Kharkow battle was put in against the strategic village of Schotomlja.

By now the battle was won. Again Stalin had refused to allow his troops to withdraw in good time. As a result a critical situation was turned into another victory and the Germans took another 214,000 prisoners, 1,246 tanks and 2,026 guns. The Germans could now carry on with their own methodical step-by-step advance and Sevastopol again became the priority. Another rapid switch for I./St.G.77, back to Sarabusy-South, followed with equal speed. On 31 May they flew the 620 kilometres from Kharkov to Sarabusy in one leg. There was to be no let-up, with two battles won in a month, but already an even tougher one looming up ahead of them.

Awards continued to flow into the St.G.77 for their work. Alexander Gläser, Werner Haugk and Hans Meier received the German Cross in Gold on 25 May, the latter pair on 4 May, the former being promoted to Staffelkapitän. Kurt Rick was also awarded the Honorary Cup, on 1 June. Georg Jakob received the Ritterkreuz on 27 April after 520 combat missions. Otto Heinrich received the Honorary Cup on 29 April after rescuing two shot-down aircrew from behind enemy lines, one of whom was his Staffelkapitän. This was Horst Kaubishch of 9./St.G.77. Kurt Stifter, Günther Ludigkeit and Christian Schutt received the Honorary Cup on 2 April.

General von Manstein was to finally launch his assault on Sevastopol on 7 June. Some 90 years before the British and French had laid siege fo Sevastopol for almost a year and the bloody battles of those distant times rang familiarly in the ears of the German attackers in 1942: the river barrier of Belbek to the north of the Star Fort, the ravines and gulleys that scored the bare Inkerman heights, at the foot of the River Tchernaya to the east of the fortress town itself, the fortress overlooking the valley of Balaclava on the south coast, and the many forts themselves around the perimeter. All these natural defences had been modernised and improved upon fourscore and more by Stalin's troops and Sevastopol was now the most powerful defence work in the world.

These works spread over 15 miles in three deep zones and incorporated some 3,600 fortified positions. There were huge casemates constructed with giant guns, like the four 305 mm guns of the 'Maxim Gorki' battery, firing from armoured cupolas commanding all approaches, anti-tank ditches and endless chains of deep, timber-backed, slit trenches, 220 miles of them, studded with machine gun posts, mortar positions and pill boxes, all covered with mountains of wire and minefields and reached by underground tunnels so that reserve troops could move up without being sighted by their opponents at all. There were rocket mortars emplaced in caverns hacked out of the solid rock and all but impregnable to normal air attack, myriads of anti-aircraft guns and light weapons emplaced; reinforced concrete bunkers sunk deep in the earth and proof from bombardment, deep storehouses and arsenals.

The Soviet commander, General Petrov, had eight divisions of army troops for his garrison plus three naval brigades of marines to hold these defences. But there were vulnerable points as well. Guns and machines depended on electricity supplies, men on water and other basics, all of which were wide open to air attack. The defenders relied on seaborne supplies from the Black Sea fleet to keep them going and provide extra fire support, but St.G.77 had already proved itself adept at dealing with warships.

General von Richthofen, with Fliegerkorps VIII faced no aerial opposition of any note; the 53 Soviet fighters were soon eradicated and then the Germans had the skies to themselves. The Stukas and the rest of his 600 available aircraft were thus free to mount continuous shuttle bombing sorties to smash down position after position. By the end of the 28–day battle the Luftwaffe would have flown more than 25,000 sorties and have dropped 125,000 bombs. This was in addition to the 46,700 heavy shells pumped in by artillery and mortars, including the awesome two 60 mm 'Karl' mortars and the super-heavy 'Gustav' 80 cm railway gun, which could fire 7 ton shells at the rate of three an hour into the inferno. Nonetheless, it was a slow and bitter struggle that the German 11 Armee now undertook to pound its way into the heart of this great defence work.

Well prior to the actual assault, I./St.G.77 had been conducting the usual 'softening up' orchestration. They termed these non-stop attacks conducted over a long period, 'conveyor belt' raids as they were termed. The well-oiled team was by now working perfectly and the intensity of the Stuka operations, up to eight sorties a day for a month, although arousing much comment by post-war western historians, had already become the norm for men like Scheffel and Sellhorn and excited no comment. They just got on with the job. With Ju87 S2+AL as their normal reliable mount, the team gradually saw the tempo increase in the week prior the main attack.

On 2 June they made a high-altitude approach at 6,000 metres sweeping out to sea and coming in from that unexpected direction to deliver their attack against the seaplane base and naval barracks at the harbour itself. A second sortie at the same height was conducted between 0906 and 1030, with their targets this time being the submarine base and also the great electricity works at Sevastopol. For the third attack of the day, carried out in the later afternoon, they flew at 6,300 metres and struck targets marked on their detailed maps as square F 9D in Sevastopol town itself to destroy a water works.

Meticulous photo-reconnaissance flights had been conducted time and again over the town and the Stuka crews were lavishly equipped with detailed aerial views of the various sectors with their targets clearly marked out and defined for them to hit. Von Manstein had established his command post in the north of the Belbek river, on the dominating hill christened by the Germans the 'Mount of Olives'. The main thrust of the German attack was to be delivered across the Belbek Valley from the north. In their way lay the first of a whole string of forts, 'Makim Gorki' on the coast being the most powerful and most advanced. Behind lay 'Molotov', 'Cheka', 'GPU', 'Stalin', 'Siberia', 'Volga', 'Ural' and 'Northern' with the old 'Star' fort (Severnaya Kosa) on the northern tip of the bay overlooking the town to the south.

The second prong would be delivered from the old British battlefields against the southern ramparts, against another line of forts stretching from south to north up from the southern to Gaytany on the Tchernaya river, 'Eagle Hill', 'Sugarloaf' mountain, 'Northern Nose', the Kamary caves, 'Rose Hill', Cinnabar and Fort Balaclava. The old British cemetery to the south of the town had unceremoniously been hacked through with further trenches and fortifications and the Russian defenders and German attacks fought and died in hand-to-hand conflict among the bones of these former besiegers.

On 3 June, I./St.G.77 struck three times at the enemy anti-tank batteries hidden in the rocky gorges to the west of Kamary to the south-east of the town. In between these strikes they also dive-bombed a Soviet warship of about 1,000 tons off Sevastopol harbour and sank her. She was part of a Russian naval relief force including a cruiser and two destroyers which brought in 1,759 fresh troops and took off 1,998 wounded and 275 civilians.

Next day the Stuka targets included strikes on defence works five kilometres south-west of Iservernaja, and two attacks on Sevastopol itself, one directed against the electricity works, the other another high altitude flight over the harbour area. A further three missions were conducted on 5 June, this time in the northern sector of the front, against fortified positions three kilometres south of the Kamyshly Ravine, just across the Belbek Valley to the south-east of Belbek itself, and at a railway and bunkers three kilometres north-west of the same

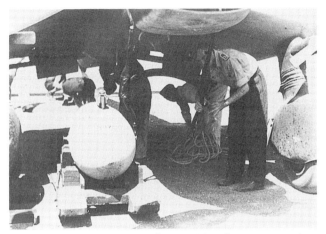

Crimea, June 1942. St.G.77 required special super-heavy 1,400 kg bombs to crack the powerful fortress at Morlele-Bashma which were held in Sarabus-North, so the unit had to exchange bases for these missions. Here the Stuka's spring-loaded cradle is prepared to take this large weapon resting on a primitive towing sledge. (Sellhorn Archiv)

village. Finally on 6 June three more sorties were flown. The first was against enemy positions a kilometre south of Hill 'Deukmekbucke', the second against 'Linkbacher' Hill south-west of Balaclava and the third against fortifications on the southern slopes near the Soviet airstrip at 'Balaklava II'.

At first light on 7 June the main assault began. The artillery, mortars and Stukas combined to rain down steel and explosives by the ton on the defenders. The German infantry assault on the northern defences commenced at 0350 across the Belbek and against the various forts. The battle was fought in sweltering heat with little relief. For a fortnight the murderous slogging match continued. Clouds of dust drifted inland as the whole peninsula on which the fortress stood seemed to vanish in smoke and flame and debris. Into this cauldron the Junkers Ju87s of St.G.77 climbed, wheeled and dove time and time again.

Their first target this day was the main electricity turbine house located 500 metres south of Krymskiye, then an attack to support an assault two kilometres north of the Mekensiervy-Gory. The third sortie took place between 0657 and hit field works at Haccius Korumm in Mekensiervy-Gary. The fourth attack was against Soviet positions on Hill 1045 one kilometre south of Belbek, and the fifth against Russian positions west of that town. As the advance was contested, a sixth and a seventh sortie followed, against enemy troop positions at Olberg, south of Belbek, and an eighth against yet more fortifications and the railway at Mekensiervy-Gory.

The same targets occupied them on 8 June, with strikes on fortifications south-east of Mekensiervy-Gory, and bunkers and the fortified village of Raume to its south. At 1130 they bombed and strafed bunkers at Sevastopol, at 1355 and again at 1630 positions at Panserberg and Pansergarben. On 9 June they flew five sorties, hitting positions on the 'Neuhaushohe' twice, at Mekensiervy-Gory, against one of the forts two kilometres south of Bartenjewka, and gun batteries at Nowfort by Bartenjewka. Next day they flew three sorties, all against battery positions at Morlela-Bashma.

June 11 saw I./St.G.77 temporarily shifting their base to the nearby Sarabusy-Kow field and from here they again bombed the stubborn battery positions at Morlela-Bashma with 1,400 kg bombs; they used the same weapons to smash a

The Crimea, summer 1942. This sequence shows the approach, attack and aftermath of St.G.77's assault on the main naval base, between 1101 and 1137 on 14 June 1942.
Top *Stuka over Jushnaja Bay.* (Sellhorn Archiv)
Above *Dive bombers go in to attack the Soviet 30.5 cm heavy gun battery Maxim Gorky II, as the first bombs explode on the ridge.* (Sellhorn Archiv)
Top right *Stuka bombs explode right on top of the gun batteries atop the ridge.* (Sellhorn Archiv)
Above right *More bombs explode on the gun positions.* (Sellhorn Archiv)

Coastal artillery battery located a kilometre south of Michajli. On completion of these special bombing sorties they returned to Sarabusy-South.

On 12 June a particularly satisfactory attack was made on the Russian army staff itself at Gaftari. These pin-point targets, designed to cause the maximum disruption, were something of a speciality for the Stukas, but unfortunately they failed to nab General Petrov himself this time.

They now shifted back to Sarabusy-Kow again for further high-level missions with the armour-piercing 1,400 kg bombs and they flew two missions against the

coastal artillery batteries at Noweigolel Strelezzkaja and against another located at Morlea-Bashama, west of Sevastopol which overlooked seaward approaches from Cape Khersonesskiy. A quick ten minute hop back to the normal airstrip and they were again in operation with conventional weapons on enemy positions east of Kamary.

Early on 13 June they attacked the main naval base at Sevastopol in a high-level flight and also struck a fortified postion two kilometres north of Kamary. Next day they bombed two bunkers located in the woods north of the arterial road and enemy armour close to 'Maxim-Gorky' on two occasions, as well as a Bastion just north of Sevastopol. Field artillery caught on the Balaclava to Sevastopol road one kilometre from Gabelhohe was the next day's target and they also struck at field artillery to east of Kavykowka. On 16 June they hit further artillery bunkers three kilometres north of the same village.

Despite all their effort and much hard fighting the outlying Soviet positions stood fairly intact. Although 'Maxim-Gorki' had now been smashed, it had not yet completely fallen. Its broken 11-inch gun barrels pointed aimlessly to the

Feldwebel Heinz Sellhorn of 3./St.G.77 with the wrecked 30.5 cm heavy gun barrels of the giant Russian fort Maxim Gorky (Sellhorn Archiv)

The Crimea, summer 1942. In a long-range strike against the enemy reinforcement convoy operating in the Black Sea, the I./St.G.77 attacked five Soviet warships about 100 km south of Balaclava on 18 June 1942. (Sellhorn Archiv)

skies, but fighting down in its bowels beneath the ground continued. German casualties had been heavy, and progress slow. There was a brief pause in the intensity of their activities as they re-grouped and re-gathered themselves then, on 17 June, the offensive recommenced with new violence along the northern front.

Fort Lenin was their main target on 17 June, as well as the village of Mekensievry-Gory once more. At 1050 they dive bombed the North fort overlooking the harbour itself. The German attack was now steadily progressing and the end was in sight. Anti-tank batteries south-east of Gretschichina were also hit. The following day two missions were flown against Fort Balaclava.

Soviet warships again occupied their attentions: five warships were attacked on the 18th some 100 kilometres to the south of Balaclava point and the flotilla leader *Kharkov* was near-missed and had to be towed away by the destroyer *Tashkent*. Theodor Langhart was credited with sinking a destroyer at this time. The second attack of the day was against another coastal gun battery. By this time, the German infantry had battled their way through to the head of

St.G.77's precision attacks on the Soviet main oil storage depot at the naval base of Severnaya Bay, 20 June 1942.
(i) The Stukas watch the fires from 2,000 metres height as their target blazes fiercely. (Sellhorn Archiv)
(ii) As the dive bombers depart, the fires spread. (Sellhorn Archiv)

Severnaya Bay at Gaytany and the second line of defences had been breached. In helping to achieve this, four missions were flown by I./St.G.77 on 20 June. The Northern Fort fell this day as did Konstaninovskiy battery at the seaward end of the bay.

   Their work did not go unnoticed. Osmar Griebel and Karl-Georg Geschwend-tner had been presented with the Honorary Cup on 1 June and they both continued to distinguish themselves in the Sevastopol attacks. Günter Hitz was flying with the Erganzungstaffel between 9 and 27 June, Kurt Huhn was promoted to Gruppenkommandeur and awarded the Ritterkreuz on 15 July, while Walter Stimpel was awarded his on 7 June after more than 250 sorties. Werner Weihrauch also distinguished himself flying against 'Maxim Gorki' and 'Stalin' forts, the Inkerman defence positions and the Sevastopol power station.

   'Bubi' Haker took over the leadership of 3. Staffel at this time and was also deputy leader to 2./St.G.77. He sank a 3,000 ton Russian freighter off the port that month, while Werner Roell was credited with the destruction of a light

The Staffelkapitän of the 3./St.G.77, Oberleutnant Scheffel, with Bordfunker Sellhorn, a team which saw much action together, pictured at the airfield of Sarabus-South in the Crimea during a short break between the relay attacks against Soviet batteries at Cape Fiolent on 21 June 1942. (Sellhorn Archiv)

cruiser of the 'Frunze' class off the Crimea. This was the *Molotov*, which was badly damaged and had her stern replaced by the incomplete hull of the *Frunze* herself after damage in August. (However the Italians claim this damage was caused by one of their ships.)

As well as all these short-range operations, St.G.77 occasionally flew long-range missions against Tuapse to try to stem the work of the Black Sea fleet in keeping Sevastopol supplied. This account of one such high-altitude attack is credited to Herbert Pabst, while serving with St.G.77 in the Crimea at this time.

Out of bed at 0400 hours. A wash, coffee, one fried egg, and then into the cars to drive us to our planes. At top speed we fly eastward over the Crimea. Then the Kerch Peninsula: everywhere destroyed villages, burned-out vehicles, the terrain ploughed over by bombs, innumerable pits, trenches and other positions. Shortly before reaching Kerch we land at a forward airfield to refuel. Then we take off again, flying southward across the Black Sea, climbing higher and higher, with nothing around us but clouds and the sea below.

Altitude 13,000 feet. Suddenly, punctually to the minute, the fighters are with us which are to escort us from here on. We are still climbing in a wide arc. We don oxygen masks in order to remain wakeful and fresh. Below us nothing but water. Then the coast comes into sight and we see the port which is our target. With quiet engines up in the blue skies, we approach the target. Yes, there are the ships at the jetty! We set our dive brakes and adjust our sights.

Our dive becomes steeper and steeper. Then they discover us and we see the muzzle flash on their anti-aircraft guns. Altitude 17,000, 13,000, 10,000 feet. Before us black puffs of anti-aircraft shells are bursting. I swerve my plane to the left to take shelter above a cloud and dive blindly through it. Then we are at 6,600 feet and I see again the jetty before me. Speed boats have started their engines and are dashing out to sea in wild curves. 1,100 feet. A large ship alongside the pier comes into my sights. I press my thumb. Now we level out and immediately our plane shoots upward at a sharp angle. The Russian anti-aircraft guns are firing wildly and blindly. I start to climb in a zig-zag course; then the flame of a bomb striking in the middle of the ships can be seen. Flying on towards the sea we can observe blood-red flames and black smoke rising at an angle with the wind.

Flames and smoke of other explosions from hits on other vessels follow, made by the squadrons which followed us.

Georg Jauernik was also credited with heavily damaging a 7,000 ton freighter at Tuapse in this attack.

On 21 June Scheffel and Sellhorn with I./St.G.77 flew three missions against anti-tank batteries and two days later they caught and destroyed a whole horse transport column accompanied by a few tanks in ravines at Inkerman identified

Above *Last-minute cockpit check for the Kommandeur of the Stab I./St.G.77, Hauptmann Bruck before the last mission in the Junkers Ju87 B. (Dr Armbrust via Sellhorn Archiv)*

Right *Radioman's domain. The twin MG 81Z of the Ju87 with a full belt of ammunition loaded. Also recognisable in this view is the VE–22 gunsight, the mirror and the tail-gunner's restricted view through the apertures in the integral rear-armour plating of the GSL–K 81Z turret itself. This turret rotated beneath the normal rear canopy.* (Sellhorn Archiv)

on their aerial maps as M3C and M6C. Unable to winkle out Russian defenders in these natural caves and caverns of this region, St.G.77 sealed them in, blocking the exit tunnels to one such system at map reference G9B with some precision bombing. Another horse transport column along with tanks and troops was decimated in ravine N2C.

The number of sorties flown by Sellhorn was not exceptional. Gerhard Stüdemann flew seven combat sorties on 22 June, the first at 0340. The last from Savalus ended at 0540 next morning.

They switched back to cracking tougher nuts on 26 June, hitting the coastal batteries at the east of Severnaya Bay and also bombing the enemy dug in at the western end of the village of Kadykowka, to the west of Balaclava, the same day. An enemy observation post was wiped out at map reference G9C that same morning while the fourth attack was against anti-tank guns south of Gretschi.

At 1800 they were sent out over the Black Sea and carried out attacks on an enemy destroyer and a submarine some fifty kilometres south of the Yalta. Here Herbert Dawedeit made his mark yet again. He had already flown 120 combat missions over Sevastopol and had participated in the attacks on Bastion 2, 'Maxim Gorki' and Bunker 4, as well as blowing up an ammunition dump in one of the Inkerman ravines. In his attacks on the harbour and offshore had personally despatched five supply ships totalling some 17,200 tons while damaging three others with near misses.

His eye was still true when it came to shipping, and he had sunk an enemy landing craft single-handed earlier. Now he homed in on his target unfailingly; it was the Soviet destroyer *Bezuprechny* which was bringing in further supplies to the defenders. Dawedeit's Stuka bored in closer and closer in his near vertical attack, despite the angry stream of light flak hosing up from the twisting destroyer. Lower and lower until the dive bomber almost seemed to scrape the mainmast of the ship before it pulled clear. At such a low altitude Herbert could not miss and his whole bomb load was either hits or very near misses; the destroyer broke up and sank in smoke and flames almost instantly. Such bravery was noted not only by his comrades but given prominent display in the German Army Daily Bulletin. Not surprisingly, Herbert was awarded the German Cross in Gold on 21 August, and he still had much fighting ahead of him.

His comrades turned their attentions to fresh prey, the submarine S.32, and,

A Junkers Ju87 D returning from yet another operation against Sevastopol on 6 July 1942. Operating from Sarabus-South airfield, near Simpferopol in central Crimea, the primitive conditions necessitated the removal of the whole of the wheel-fairing. (Sellhorn Archiv)

A unique event. In stacked-up echelon close formation, the 7. Staffel of St.G.77 flies from its forward base of Sarabus-South against the Soviet fortress of Sevastopol in July 1942. This mission was the last flown with the reliable Bertha, for the Staffel was subsequently re-equipped with the D model, Dora. (Borde via Sellhorn Archiv)

riddled with hits and near misses, she also quickly went down south of Feodosiya.

The final attacks were launched on 27 June, and once more were preceded by the Stukas which blasted a path for 22 and 24 Infantry Divisions which took the much battered power house then moved on.

In complete contrast they were picking out tunnels to the south-west of the town of Sevastopol on 28 June. The same day they also attacked field works on the main inlet of Sevastopol and in a gorge south of the eastern defence lines, as well as a serpentine two kilometres north-west of Norvi Schirh. Next day they hit field works four kilometres south-west of Inkerman, smashed tank traps three kilometres south-east of Inkerman by the English cemetery. Two further strikes were made at dug-outs and transports in the English cemetery in conjunction with its assault by 420 Infantry Regiment. Further attacks this same day included flak positions 1.5 kilometres south of Nikolajerwka, a bunker 500 metres south of Inkerman, heavy gun positions a kilometre south of the town of Sevastopol and then a final attack on the English cemetery tank traps which were still holding up the advance.

Fighting continued unabated but the writing was clearly on the wall. Even the enemy could see it and General Petrov had scuttled out on board a motor boat on 30 June. The remaining defenders fought grimly on however so the Ju87s experienced no slackening of effort. They flew six combat sorties this day, against bunkers and field positions south of Sevastopol town and flak batteries in the town itself as well as more horse transport columns on the shore six kilometres north of Cape Fiolent.

On 1 July at 0445 they took off and struck a fort a kilometre south-west of Sevastopol, landed then flew against fresh Soviet naval forces. They bombed and sank a small warship 100 kilometres south of Balaclava; Helmuth Bode was credited with the attack that did the damage and claiming a small destroyer sunk. By 1000 that same morning they were attacking emplacements in the western part of town of Sevastopol.

Some of the surviving Soviet units fought on until 3 July but at the end of the day Sevastopol was in German hands. It had cost them over 24,000 casualties but they had destroyed two Soviet armies and taken 95,000 prisoners, along with 467 guns and 758 mortars.

IX
Disaster at the Volga Bend

With the summer already well along, Hitler's timetable for 1942 would allow no delay to Case 'Blue' and, by early July, while St.G.77 was still finishing off the rearguard elements in the Crimea, von Richthofen and the staff of Fliegerkorps VIII were already moving northward once more to establish new headquarters at the city of Kursk. Here it came under the operational control of Luftflotte IV and rail and supply routes were utilised to the maximum to stockpile bombs and stores in readiness for the forthcoming attack towards Voronesh.

Under the overall direction of Field Marshal Fedor von Bock, commanding Army Group South, the left wing, General Baron Maximilian von Weichs's Second Army, planned to drive south-east from Livny towards Voronezh. This was an important road, rail and river junction and after its capture it would serve as the pivot on which the rest of the battle swung. For 4 Panzer Armee, under Hoth, was to thrust straight from Kursk in a wide scooping arc and rendezvous with von Weichs to the east of that city in one of the now standard German enveloping battles, the Voronezh Pocket. While these movements were taking place the southern flank of von Bock's force, 6 Armee, under General Friedrich Paulus, was to move forward in alignment with Hoth and then, once the initial battle had been concluded, was to execute the second phase of the grandiose scheme, driving northward to meet the other two arms of the German attack as they turned south-east along the Don and entrapped the enemy in the area of Staryy Oskol.

The campaign was in fact already compromised before it began when a light plane carrying an officer of 23 Panzer was shot down over enemy territory. He had the complete operational objectives with him in a briefcase. Nonetheless 'Blue' kicked off on 28 June with the drive on Voronezh as planned, with 214 Panzer Division at its head. The vital Tim and Kshen river crossings were taken 'at the run', and meanwhile, on 30 June, 6 Armee commenced its southern swing from Volchansk across the Oskol toward Rossosh and up toward Voronezh also. By 4 July a bridgehead over the Don had been established and by 7 July the Germans were fighting hard to cross the river Voronezh and take the town itself. Far to the south, 3 Panzer Division took Rossosh the same day.

This time, however, the Russians had finally learnt from past disasters and did not hold their ground. They retreated and the two arms closed on largely empty air instead of the two Soviet armies as planned. The Führer was completely fooled by this change of tactic. He now sensed victory. Convinced the Russians were at their last gasp, the German plan was hastily re-drafted at Hitler's behest in his Directive 45. Leaving 6 Armee to continue to thrust across the Don at Kalach and then to move on to take and destroy the city of Stalingrad (now called Volgagrad) on the Volga alone, 17 Armee, along with 1 and 4 Panzer Armees, were to thrust southward from Rostov-on-Don, Konstantinavskiy and Tsmiyanskaya into the Caucasus, aiming for Batum on the Black Sea coast and Baku on the Caspian.

The Germans also planned to thrust down the western bank of the Volga to reach the southern end of the 'A-A' line at Astrakhan, while 11 Armee would break out across the Kerch Strait to link up with the drive south toward Tuapse, but this was cancelled and 11 Armee put on trains north, their new mission, to take Leningrad! Unfortunately for the Germans, the splitting up of their southern armies' objectives in this manner meant that each arm was in turn, just too weak to carry out the task assigned to it. Although the initial stages of the Caucasus drive went well, none of the final objectives was finally reached.

St.G.77 was still in the Crimea on this day, far from the scene of these fresh battles. Sellhorn and Scheffel, for example, took a leisurely photo-record of the fallen city of Sevastopol this day, flying their Leica-equipped Stuka for 75 minutes over the fallen fortress and recording its death pangs and broken defensive positions for posterity. Next day, however, the news came that they were to move north-east urgently to join the attack and, on 9 July, they began flying northward by way of Sabarosch to their new base at Chazepetowka airfield.

On 10 July they were once more in action, attacking enemy troops concealed in rare woodland at Perpsiyanowka in the morning and dive bombing dug-in infantry positions in the northern part of the village of Kremenaja that afternoon. Next day the conducted similar sorties against southern part of the village of Gretschichkiu and against Soviet troops in Nova-Aidar.

On 12 July the German Army Group 'A', under Field Marshal Siegmund List, attacked the Soviet defences north of the Sea of Azov at Krasnyy-Luch, northwest of Rostov, and smashed through. I./St.G.77 attacked the railway station at Sutagino this day. The battles along the western bank of the Don continued as 1 Panzerarmee forced its way south-east. List's 52 divisions gradually closed on Voroshilovgrad, where some of the Soviet forces stood for a while and fought a brief rearguard action. Not until 17 July was Voroshilovgrad in German hands and, on the same day, German troops reached Tsimlyansk, far upriver from the confluence of the Donets and the Don outflanking the remaining Soviet units.

On 13 July I./St.G.77's targets were initially goods trains and rail wagons at the Dolsheuskaja marshalling yards, and then, late in the afternoon, dug-in gun positions at Scherowka village. The following day saw them in action again smashing enemy entrenched positions three kilometres south-west of Mount Ivanowka. Two further attacks were made that same day, against Krassnaja-Polyana and the fortified town of Rowenki. On 15 July a mid-morning attack was made which was to bomb and strafe a battery of 'Stalin organs' causing difficulties just west of Voroshilovgrad, north-east of Krasnyy-Luch. In the same area they hit a battalion of T-34s which had debouched from the town itself in a counter-attack. That afternoon they struck at Asarowka village, some three kilometres south-west of Voroshilovgrad. Missions against the towns of Norvo-Birharhowka, Wassigewka and Woroligrad occupied them next day.

Once again the men fighting in the ranks of St.G.77 in that blazing and fateful summer campaign included old and new faces. Among the former were Stuka

Even Stuka men got the odd day off between battles. Here officers enjoy wild-fowling in the south Russian marshlands. Centre is the unit's doctor, Dr Armbrust, and on his left the Staffelkapitän of the I./St.G.77, Hauptmann Henze. (Dr Armbrust via Sellhorn Archiv)

men who already stood out, men like Heinz-Günter Amelung, the Ia of St.G.77. By July 1942 his personal tally stood at six vital bridges, 27 tanks, 16 field guns and 12 anti-aircraft gun batteries destroyed. Rudi Reussner was still prominent with III./St.G.77, Kurt Rick was now Staffelkapitän of 2./St.G.77, Werner Roell led the St.G.77 Stabsstaffel, and he transformed this Me110 equipped unit from a pure reconnaissance outfit into a destroyer Staffel, flying fighter cover, providing il-luminations and flares for night bombing and engaging in locomotive-hunting operations, while sometimes stepping in as deputy leader of the I./St.G.77. Rudolf Weigel was to be promoted to Leutnant on 1 August. Kurt Huhn had been ap-pointed as Gruppenkommandeur on 1 July, Hans-Karl Sattler, the Staffelkapitän was to achieve his 500th mission while flying with 8./St.G.77 on the southern front.

The new faces at the mess table included Heinz Welzel, born 22 years earlier at Breslau. He had volunteered for the naval air wing (Seeflieger) on 2 January 1939, and, after the usual non-commissioned officers' course, had been sent to the naval fliers training school at Warnemunde on 1 April of that year. After dive bomber training in readiness for Ju87 carrier work, he had later transferred to the Luftwaffe's Stukas and joined 4./St.G.77 in Russia. There was also Ernst Orzegowski, a year his senior, from Hamburg. He was to fly his very first war mission with 4./St.G.77 that summer. Similarly was the story of Robert Bumen, born in 1918 at Freiburg. He too joined the 1./St.G.77 as a pilot, but, to give a scale of the intensity of operations at this period of the war, by the end of the year he had already clocked up 302 missions.

There were empty chairs also. One of those the Gruppe was mourning was Oberleutnant Hermann Ruppert, the Staffelkapitän of the 6. Staffel. He and his radio operator Unteroffizier Erwin Schallenmuller, were both killed when their Stuka was destroyed by Rata fighters and crashed in flames east of Golubovka, about 90 kilometres north-west of Stalino.

On 17 July List's forces finally took Voroshilovgrad while 1 Panzerarmee ex-ecuted a wheeling lurch that took it to the north of Kamesnk before turning back down south once more to concentrate on Rostov itself.

I/St.G.77 again gave its best close support in this drive to clear the whole of the northern coast and re-take the vital gateway city of Rostov-on-Don in order to

open the northern gateway to the Caucasus and the Kuban. During the afternoon of 20 July they dive-bombed the fortified village of Isultan-Isaly, some 12
kilometres to the north-west of Rostov and next day were striking at first half-
light, 0400, at enemy positions south-west of Isambuk. Later that same day they
shifted base to be within a better striking range of the new objectives, moving the
185 kilometres from Chazepetowka to Lakedemonowka air strip. From here, at
1030, they again dive-bombed the village of Isoltan-Isali and then strafed and
bombed large formations of Soviet tanks and troops caught out on the open
steppe north-west of that village. The next mission that day was a high-altitude
bombing of Rostov itself.

The Soviet commander, Timoshenko, was now pulling out of the area between the Donets and the Don as fast as he could and at Millerovo, north-east of
Voroshilovgrad, these eastward-scurrying brown masses clashed briefly with
weak German encirclement forces. As the centre of operations moved steadily
south down to the great Don bend so the clashes became more bitter. Heavy
fighting took place to the north-east of Rostov during the next few days as the
Germans came up against and then tried to smash through the three defensive
circles thrown up by the Soviets in a last-ditch attempt to hold that vital city and
deny the Germans the river crossings southward.

At 0330, on 22 July the Stukas took off for a high-level attack against these
defence works, but Sellhorn's aircraft had to abort after half an hour on account
of a failure in Oberleutnant Scheffel's oxygen mask. However, they took part in a
second strike, made at 0730, which bombed defence works located in the
western section of town. A counter-attack by Soviet T-34s made dangerous progress towards midday and I./St.G.77 conducted two sorties against the enemy
armour that afternoon. The T-34s were wedged into a corridor near the
Toihalteir-Thym suburb and here I./St.G.77 attacked them with splinter bombs
twice to good effect, thus halting their advance. The Germans were then able to
resume their pressure down the Stalino road and took Rostov airfield itself. It
would not be long before the Stukas were operating from this field instead of
attacking its perimeter.

None of this was achieved without a price being paid. St.G.77 paid with the life

*A machine of the
Gruppenstab I./St.G.77 in
the summer of 1942. Its
landing gear stripped down
for ease of operation in
quagmire conditions, it
heads home over the fea-
tureless Soviet steppe. (Dr
Armbrust via Sellhorn
Archiv)*

of Hauptmann Gerhard Bauhaus. He had shone in daring attacks at both Feodosia and Eupatoria and, on 25 May, had been awarded the Ritterkreuz because of these actions and more than 300 other combat sorties. But on 22 July his aircraft was hit by flak over Rostov town. Although he managed to survive Gerhard was very badly burnt. He was rushed to Taganrok hospital for emergency treatment to his terrible wounds and then quickly flown back to Germany to the Luftwaffenlazarett at Greifswald in Pomerania on 20 August. Despite all the specialist care lavished on him here this very brave pilot finally died of his wounds on 2 September and was buried at Jüterbog.

Fritz Neumüller and his radio operator, Unteroffizier Wolfinger, had also been attacked by Soviet Ratas near Cherkassy. They crash-landed 50 kilometres behind enemy lines but fortunately were soon rescued by another Stuka crewed by Oberleutnant Horst Schnuchel and radio operator Feldwebel Muller. Fritz himself therefore survived to later receive the Honorary Cup on 22 August.

The dive bombers flew four combat missions on 23 July. The first took off from Lakevemenowka at 0317 with enemy defence batteries guarding Batataysk on the other side of the Don being their target. A second strike at 0900 also carried out ground-strafing attacks south of Bataysk. The third sortie was flown off at 1130 and was a dive bombing attack was made on Russian defenders holding up the advance in the Rostov's eastern suburbs in support of 22 Panzer. The final attack was made in the early evening when a Soviet transport column was located and heavily strafed south of Aksawkaja.

By the following day Rostov had almost finally been cleared with vicious and bloody hand-to-hand fighting, but the essential bridges, and especially the great causeway across the Don to Bataysk, still lay in Russian hands. In order for the drive south into the Caucasus to succeed that bridge had to be taken. The Germans planned to make a final assault on the night of 24/25 July. I./St.G.77 was to play an essential part in blasting a way through for the Brandenburg Regiment's assault force. In preparation for this, at 1020 on the 24th, the Ju87s made a preemptive dive bombing strike against the defending Soviet anti-aircraft batteries guarding the causeway.

At great sacrifice and loss of life volunteer storming parties got across the river next morning but were well pinned down and threatened with massacre by strong Soviet machine-gun positions. To smash these, I./St.G.77 was sent in at 0630 to make one of their famed precision attacks. A second was made at 0930 on enemy reinforcements massing at the village of Olginskaja. And then a third strike followed, against smashing enemy flak positions three kilometres south of Bataysk. As one German historian has recorded, 'The Stukas arrived in the nick of time. Then the first reinforcements came up over the causeway and the bridge.'

Following up these attacks towards the Kuban, St.G.77 conducted dive bombing strikes on 27 July, the first attack being against Soviet troops dug in around the village of Olginskaja, while later the same day they hit enemy positions at the coastal hamlet of Kwostraud-on-Asov.

I./St.G.77 was sent in to deal with a flotilla of four gunboats on the river Don at Salsk, west of the Donez Delta on 28 July. In the first attack, launched at 0735, two of these boats were hit and were claimed to have been sunk. A second attack was sent off that afternoon against the two survivors in the same area, and

near-misses were scored on one of them. Both these missions were led by
Heinz-Günter Amelung who claimed direct hits on several monitors. As a direct
result of these attacks, the Soviet gunboats *BKA. 201*, *BKA.202 (ii)* and *BKA.205*
were so badly damaged that they had to be blown up by their crews to avoid falling into German hands. On 15 July Amelung was duly awarded the Ritterkreuz
for this excellent shooting, and for achieving over 300 combat missions. Franz
Kieslich received the German Cross in Gold on 2 August and at the end of the
same month was promoted to Staffelführer.

'Ali' Orthofer kept going. On 1 May he had been promoted to Major and in
August returned from his short stint at the Stuka school as the need for men of
his dive bombing experience was paramount at the front. He became the popular
Kommodore of St.G.77 which he was to lead with his usual panache for a
tragically brief period. 'Schorschl' Gschwendtner was also honoured by the
award of the German Cross in Gold on 27 July. His missions with 7./St.G.77 had
likewise been notable against ground and naval targets. He had already survived
being shot down twice and being wounded when baling-out of his damaged
machine.

Other veteran pilots were steadily adding to their tallies. 'Blackberry'
Honsberg had destroyed 30 tanks, an armoured train, and damaged a Soviet
cruiser. Otto Schmidt, Staffelkapitän of the 7./St.G.77, was to achieve his 500th
mission by August, as did Alois Wosnitza.

They were soon to lose Otto Heinrich, but not through enemy action. That
autumn he returned to Germany to be trained as a fighter pilot. But his loss was
softened by the return of Georg Jakob from von Richthofen's staff when the
General was replaced as commander of Fliegerkorps VIII and sent to the
Mediterranean area later that summer. Georg was to be made Gruppenkommandeur of the III./St.G.77 on 26 August. Another replacement who
arrived from the Stukachules at this time was Heinrich Zwipf, a 22-year-old from
Pirmasens. He had joined the Luftwaffe as an officer cadet in 1935 and later
converted to a Stuka pilot, seeing combat in Poland before going on to become an
instructor. In August he was transferred to I./St.G.77.

As the German advance re-gathered its momentum the Stukas once more
moved their base forward again on 29 July, flying from Lakemonowka to Rostov
airfield itself, a quarter-hour hop of 60 kilometres. Once there, they immediately
continued their close-support missions, with an attack on Soviet emplacements
located in the south part of the village of Proletarskaja. Sellhorn and Scheffel also
undertook an 85 minute aerial search in the vicinity of Rostov front between 1720
and 1845 that day in a desperate search for Oberleutnant Heine, whose aircraft
had crashed behind enemy lines, but they found no traces of him.

Hitler had directed on 25 July, that, in Operation 'Edelweiss', Army Group A
was to encircle and annihilate the 'weak' Soviet forces now in full flight to the
south and south-east of Rostov and that the Tikhoretsk to Stalingrad railway line
must be cut.

Several Stuka missions were flown by St.G.77 in pursuance of these orders:
the first, on the morning of 31 July, was a dive bombing strike on Pjestschanop-
skoje village; the second was a strategical mission, their targets being the
locomotives and other rolling stock at a marshalling yard ten kilometres north-
west of Tikhoretsck. The next day they conducted a similar mission, dive bomb-

ing Tikhoretsck railway station. Two further strikes were made against enemy troops dug in in the centre of this town during the day and the railway station was bombed yet again on 2 August. On 3 August they strafed and bombed enemy troops concentrations close by Dobrenkaj.

During the great offensive battles in front of Rostov Herbert Dawedeit has made a great impression. It had been he who scored several direct hits on a vital enemy fuel dump, which set it ablaze. His Stuka had also led the devastating dive bombing of Bataysk railway station against massive concentrations of Soviet anti-aircraft batteries and fighters. In the resulting aerial mêlée over the Sea of Asov the German and Russian pilots slogged it out all the way back to Taganrog. Nothing daunted, Herbert remained in the thick of the new fighting and, between 25 August and 23 September, he led his Staffel due to the enforce absence of the Staffelkapitän.

Among those who received awards at this period were Kurt Stifter, Gruppen-adjutant in the Stab of the III./St.G.77. He had made outstanding contributions to the close support operations and on 21 September received the German Cross in Gold. Leutnant Günther Ludigkeit and Hans Luhr also received well merited German Crosses in Gold on 7 and 5 September respectively. Oberfeldwebel Christian Schutt received the German Cross in Gold on 22 September.

There were also Hauptmann Helmut Leicht, who was awarded the Knight's Cross on 3 September after completing more than 400 missions; Osmar Griebel, who won the German Cross in Gold on 7 September; Anton Andorfer, who received the Honorary Cup on 22 September; and Hauptmann Otto Schmidt, Staffelkapitän of the 7./St.G.77, who received the Ritterkreuz on 3 September after more than 527 combat sorties. He left shortly afterwards to serve with the Stab of Luftwaffenkommando Ost.

Among others who left St.G.77 at this time was Helmuth Bode, who in November was to be appointed leader of the temporarily revitalised naval experimental Stuka flight for aircraft carrier *Graf Zeppelin* at the Travemunde trials centre.

Newcomers joining St.G.77 for the Stalingrad battle included Paul Haidle, born at Stuttgart in 1919. He was, ironically, himself a former Navy flyer who had transferred to the Luftwaffe that autumn. He joined III./St.G.77, serving with the 8. Staffel. Ernst Orzegowski was the same age, from Hamburg and had only flown his first mission with 4./St.G.77 that summer. On 12 September he had so distinguished himself in action that he received Iron Cross, second class, and a month later, on 22 October, was to win the Iron Cross first class. Two years his junior, Leutnant Herbert 'Quax' Piske was also from Hamburg-Osdorf but was a veteran flyer. He had flown as a fighter pilot with II./JG.3 on the Channel coast in the Battle of Britain and later and during 125 fighter missions had survived being shot down on three occasions. The third time meant that he could no longer operate with the fighter units, but he could still fly brilliantly and, after dive bomber training, he came east to join 5./St.G.77.

The German advance now resumed in two great prongs, south and north. In the south the occupation of the Caucasus proceeded with the capture of Krasnodar on 9 August and the wrecked oilfields of Maikop also fell and the mountain peak of Elborus had the swastika flag planted atop it on 21 August. I./St.G.77 was engaged in support this drive throughout the month but the number of sorties was comparatively low.

On 3 August they flew from Rostov in support of 3 Panzer Division who took Voroshilovsk in the central Kuban plain north-west of the Kuma Canal. The Stukas hit enemy troops dug in at the small town of Leningradskaja. Two days later the Gruppe moved its base from Rostov to Bielaja-Glina. From this dusty strip they flew three combat sorties over the Kuban steppe, the first on 6 August, and two days later, they attacked the villages of Dondukonskaja and Kelezmesskaja 20 kilometres north of Maikop itself. They shifted base firstly back to Malitopol and then to Kerch from where they conducted two more dive bomber missions against enemy artillery positions at Taman. Despite their efforts the last bastion of the Soviet Black Sea fleet at Tuapse still remained beyond the grasp of General Ruoff's 17 Armee, and very little further progress was made before the first snows in the foothills began to fall. The taking of Baku was put off until the following year. On 20 August I./St.G.77 was pulled out of this faltering advance and flew north-east from Kerch, via Tanganrog, to their new operational base of Obliwskaja, 150 kilometres west of Stalingrad itself, where they landed at 1445 that afternoon.

The German drive to the north had also faltered. Here the ultimate target became the vast and sprawling city of Stalingrad (now known as Volgagrad) and, at the beginning of August, it seemed it must fall quickly. Originally the occupation of the city was seen as no more than a happy by-product of the establishment of a strong flank to protect the drive to Baku and the Caspian. But steadily it became, for the Germans, firstly an obsession with Hitler, then, on 30 July it became the main target and finally it was a nightmare.

Fliegerkorps VIII, now commanded by Generalleutnant Martin Fiebig, was fully committed on a narrow front in the initial attack which was made against Voronesh and then on down the Don toward Stalingrad itself. The crossing of the Chir and the taking of Kalach on the Don marked the preliminary movement of the Stalingrad tragedy.

General Paulus's 6 Armee had romped some forty miles and gained the bank of the Volga north of the city on 23 August. This breakthrough was achieved with massive dive bomber support which struck repeatedly at Soviet defence positions on the city outskirts. I./St.G.77 made two attacks on 22 August, both were

A Luftwaffe mobile 2 cm anti-aircraft cannon at Chisinau (now Kishinev) August 1942. (Immerreich via Sellhorn Archiv)

directed against Tindutova, 20 kilometres north-west of Stalingrad itself, the first strike hitting the railway station and an afternoon attack being made against a concentration of T-34s south of the town. This opened the way for General-leutnant Hass Hube's tanks.

Next day the Stukas were again out in force for the attack launched at 0440 against the northern suburb of Spartakovka. However, General Hoth's 4 Panzer Armee, pushing across the dry and dusty steppe to the south, ran out of fuel some way short of its target. The Soviet defences thus had time to harden and a street-by-street defence of the city was organised. For Sellhorn and Scheffel and the faithful S2+CL, the battle was temporarily over. They accompanied their Gruppe west for a much-needed period of rest and refurbishment. They left Obliwskaya on the morning of 26 August and flew via Artemosky, Melitopol, Nikolayev, Uman in the Ukraine, Lemberg in Poland (now called Lvov) to Breslau. Here they remained for the best part of six weeks. Meanwhile their comrades in II. and III./St.G.77 carried on the fight for the disputed city.

Although General Paulus and 6 Armee was fighting in the suburbs by September there was to be no *coup-de-main*. Added to this was the obvious reluctance of the German generals to throw their men into the assault whole-heartedly. Instead relatively small forces were fed in driblets piecemeal, ground down and replaced. The whole front became static and only the Soviets could gain anything by such delay.

The dive bomber force was repeatedly thrown in wholeheartedly during September to try and force a decision, four or more sorties a day being the norm, as at Sevastopol. On 3 September an all-out assault was launched against the city, supported by the dive bombers of all three Stuka wings, 1, 2 and 77.

General der Flieger Martin Fiebig of Fliegerkorps VIII established his advanced HQ and target plot in the western sector of the city next to an Army observation post. Co-operation, always excellent between the ground troops and the dive bombers, was now further refined to an art. The city was marked out in grids, and radio requests from the front-line troops were instantly responded to by

Oberleutnant Hans-Joachim Lehmann on the award of his Knight's Cross on 23 November 1941. After earlier service with St.G.2 'Immelmann', in Poland, France, Greece, Crete, Russia and North Africa, this veteran Stuka pilot joined St.G.77 on 1 August 1942 as a special duties officer. On 14 October he left to become the acting Kommandeur of I./St.G.2. (Author's collection via Gisela Lehmann)

standing patrols of Stukas whose pilots flew with maps in their hands. They had strict orders not to release their bombs until absolutely certain of their targets, so closely intwined were the two armies in the rubble. The supply lines were greatly extended over the previous year's campaigns. There were problems of spare and fuel supply accentuated by the normal wastage and damage of such intense and prolonged activities.

The slowness of the house-by-house advance through the battered streets of Stalingrad prolonged such attrition into the winter months and thus aggravated the situation still further. That the city was not cleared more quickly was as much through the timidity and half-heartedness of Paulus as through the resistance of the communists, as Feldmarschall von Richthofen's (promoted to command of the whole of Luftflotte 4 which contained Fliegerkorps VIII), ever-more despairing diary entries make clear. As early as 10 September Richthofen was writing that, 'The throttling of Stalingrad gets slower and slower.' By the end of October he was claiming that: 'The main reasons lie in the weariness of the combat troops and commanders, and in the army's pedantic tolerance of a ration strength of twelve thousand men per division, of whom only a thousand are actually in the front line.'

Far to the south I./St.G.77 had returned to the fray on 8 October, operating this time from their new base of Beloretschenkaja, 30 kilometres north-west of Maikop in the Kuban. Despite the long period that had elapsed since they last flew here, little progress had been made and Army Group A was only just across the line of the river Terek and was still stuck in the Caucasian foothills guarding Tuapse, Poti and Batum on the Black Sea coast down to the Turkish border. Hitler was enraged that his master-stroke in the south had petered out in the same manner as his sleight-of-hand on the Volga. Fresh troops were ordered into the bridgeheads in another attempt to force the issue.

The Stukas began flying missions from here four days later. Sellhorn flew with Hauptmann Zwipf, the Staffelkapitän of 3./St.G.77 in S2+BL. Their targets this day were flak positions four kilometres south of Hill 1664. Two more missions followed the next day against flak positions at the Goitsch pass through the mountains. Here they were joined by elements of St.G.2 'Immelmann', including Hans-Ulrich Rudel himself.

Back on the Volga the re-estimated time for the fall of the city was now predicted as 10 November, but long after that date one of von Richthofen's diary entries recorded how the dynamic Luftwaffe leader continued to chafe at seeing his magnificent Stukas wasting away in mission-after-mission without resulting concrete advances by the ground troops. He noted that he had telephoned General Kurt Zeitzler, Chief of the Army's General Staff, urging the need:

... for really energetic leadership in the battle for Stalingrad, or for the attack to be called off otherwise. If the mopping-up is not done now, with the Volga icing over and the Russians in Stalingrad in dire distress, we will not pull it off. Besides, the days are getting shorter and the weather worse.

He continued:

I stressed to Zeitzler that the commanders and combat troops in Stalingrad are so apathetic that only the injection of a new spirit will get us anywhere. I suggested the com-

Stalingrad, autumn 1942. Unteroffizier Hirsch is congratulated by Uffzs Rabben, Schjlote and Polaskek in the 100th combat sortie. This was the first of St.G.77's attacks on the city. (Sellhorn Archiv)

Stalingrad, autumn 1942. Oberleutnant Scheffel of St.G.77 prepares for take-off with help from 1st Class Mechanic Uffz Schwarz. (Sellhorn Archiv)

manders – who are otherwise trustworthy enough – should be sent on leave for a while to let very different types take their place.

It was all in vain. The build-up of Soviet forces on the eastern bank of the Volga became more and more obvious. Fresh armies were gathering north and south of the city where the only opposition lay in the doubtful fighting qualities of Germany's Italian and Rumanian allies. On 19 November the Soviet artillery bombardment commenced to the north of Stalingrad. Huge swarms of T-34s swamped the Rumanian defences and those units that did not die to the last man fighting were soon in full flight. The Rumanian 3 Army soon ceased to exist. Two days later a similar storm of steel was unleashed to the south of the city and very soon 6 Armee was surrounded.

The relief operation which had been launched on 12 December by General von Manstein failed to lift the enemy noose. A fresh Soviet offensive broke the Italian 8 Army holding the line south of the city and the Don front burst asunder. Hastily transferred again to slow this new deluge, the dive bombers were badly stretched. Their own advance bases were at first threatened and then overrun, with ghastly consequences for the ground staff trapped there and massacred. As the dive bombers were forced to pull back their operational air strips, so these short-range aircraft could less and less hold back the brown tide that lapped and flowed over westward, threatening even greater disasters to the whole Don and Caucasus fronts.

Every effort was thrown in to stemming this tidal wave by knocking out its armour spearheads. The main Stuka base at Kalatsch was overrun and much vital equipment lost forever. A similar problem was faced at Karpovka when weather conditions precluded the Ju87s from having their usual devastating effect on the enemy columns. Soon even Obliwskaya was threatened with envelopment when the vital Tazinskaya airfield far to its rear fell to the enemy on Christmas Eve. The Stuka units based at Morosovskaya were hastily pulled back from the Novocherkassk strip and operated with great effect that day. The Soviet tanks were caught once more in the open steppe, clearly not expecting the Junkers Ju87s to be operating so close to their advance. By skilful and dedicated flying the Stukas smashed these armoured formations and forced them into temporary retreat so saving the day yet again.

In the southern sector I./St.G.77, although wearied by months of unceasing campaigning, now had to go on flying such missions at an even greater intensity

Radio operator and rear-gunner Heinz Sellhorn, who served with the Gruppenstab I.Sturzkampfgeschwade 77 throughout its whole career, and who took part in almost 1,000 Stuka sorties. This 1943 photograph shows him in full dress uniform with all regalia, as well as the Crete battle honour cuff title, well merited Iron Cross and campaign ribbons from Poland, France, the Channel battles, Balkans, Crete and Russian service. (Sellhorn Archiv)

from makeshift bases. To their ultimate credit they did not falter. Sellhorn was now flying as rear-seat man to Helmut Bruck in S2+AB. They flew from Limowiski and then, on 6 January 1943 back to Gigant near Ssalsk. By the end of the month they were flying missions from one of Rostov's airfields against the thrusting Soviet hordes which had now reached Manytschskaja itself. Other Stukas had to be quickly pulled out of Pitomnik airfield when the Soviets overran it on 16 January.

Amid the crumbling snow-covered ruins, in the cellars and bombed-out factories and houses of Stalingrad itself, there was no hope. Only by fighting on could they take some of the pressure off their comrades outside. And so the trapped German army fought on in its pathetic remnants until the end of January 1943, when the survivors surrendered. It was the end of Hitler's dream in the East.

For St.G.77 the New Year did not bring an end to the fighting; rather, it intensified and all-out efforts again had to be made to stem the tide. This time the Luftwaffe was better prepared for the Russian winter, but even so the serviceability of units rapidly fell off. The frequent shifts of base rearward, the interruption of their supply lines, the vastness of the enemy offensive, all took their toll.

The bitter fighting at Stalingrad and in the simultaneous drive deep into the Causacus gave St.G.77 survivors many stories to relate. For instance, Alex Gläser flew his 500th mission over that city in December. Early in January he was forced to crash-land his damaged aircraft far behind enemy lines. His fate seemed grim, but, despite all the odds, Alex managed to not only evade capture by the vengeful and unforgiving partisans for over a week, but, after eight days, had worked his way across the barren country to reach the safety of German lines. Franz Kieslich, Staffelkapitän of the 7./St.G.77 since 14 October, also flew his 500th mission near Stalingrad.

The Staffelführer of the 8./St.G.77, Theodor Langhart, had another amazing story to relate. During desperate fighting over the river Don on 19 December, Theodor's mount was shot down by Soviet fighters. Skilful as always Langart got his crippled aircraft down in one piece in the deep snow of 'no-mans-land' between the two front lines. Another Stuka from his Staffel gallantly landed close alongside him and Langhart himself flew off under the very noses of the enemy with the little dive bomber lifting not only both aircrew to safety but also a solitary German infantryman they discovered lost and cut off in the same area!

'Leo' Burr had flown a total of 328 rear gunner combat missions on the Eastern Front by the end of August 1942. At that time he became the rear-seat man for Oberfeldwebel Gschwendter who was to count himself lucky when, one December day, he found a Soviet MiG-3 on his tail over Stalingrad. All seemed lost but 'Leo' kept his nerve and by good shooting was able to destroy the much faster fighter.

Leutnant Karl Fitzner, Staffelführer of 1./St.G.77, firmly established himself as one of St.G.77's most prolific 'tank-busters' and an authority on the T-34's weak spots. After 565 combat sorties, he received the Ritterkreuz for his good work in this field on 27 November. Likewise Immo Fritzsche, Staffelkapitän of the 8./St.G.2, also stood out for his dedicated and selfless work during the ghastly defensive battles that followed the Russian breakthrough, giving close support to infantry units. Unteroffizier 'Macki' Gortler, who was serving with the 8. Staffel, carried out 233 missions before being transferred to the 8./St.G.2 at the end of February 1943.

Like the tens of thousands of doomed German soldiers on the ground who died amid the ruins of that cursed city during the autumn, or were lost in the snows and freezing conditions of the following winter hopelessly trapped and abandoned in their pocket, Stalingrad and the Caucasus cost St.G.77 much in the ways of lives and equipment. Some of their best pilots and crews failed to return after missions over the Volga and Don.

Perhaps the most grievous loss was that of Alfons Orthofer. Major 'Ali' was seemingly indestructible and was a most popular Kommodore. On the last day of September he had flown his 400th mission from Belorechenskaya airfield in the Caucasus. Soon his score stood at 432 and it seemed he would go on for ever; any man who had survived the Battle of Britain should have been immortal. Alas, he was not. Nor did 'Ali' plunge to his death in a blazing Stuka carrying out a last courageous attack. Instead he fell victim to shrapnel when Soviet bombers staged a sneak attack on Belorechenskaya on 12 October. He was rushed to the Luftwaffe field hospital at Maikop but died that same evening. The whole Gruppe was deeply shocked by his passing. 'Ali' was promoted to Oberstleutnant posthumously on 1 October.

Leutnant Ignaz 'Natz' Schweizer was wounded in action but survived and, on 21 December, was awarded the Honorary Cup. Not so fortunate was Kurt Stifter. On his 482nd mission he was making a low-level attack on the Soviet positions three kilometres east of Fissenkovo (17 kilometres south-east of Rossosh) in the face of heavy anti-aircraft fire. His aircraft received a direct hit and crashed. Both 'Natz' and his long-time radio operator, Unteroffizier Reinhold Schewe, died outright.

Another famous name doomed to pay the ultimate price that winter had been Oberleutnant Theodor Langhart. After his amazing courage and grit just three days earlier, he had returned to combat duty once more. It seemed totally unfair and unjust therefore when, the following day, 22 December, he was killed in action on his 342nd combat mission, in the Rossosh area. His Stuka was leading yet another assault on the same enemy positions on the Don front, attacking troop concentrations dug-in some five kilometres north-east of Fissenkovo. Soviet flak was again murderously heavy and his Ju87 took a direct hit. Theodor never pulled out of his attack dive but went straight in, his stricken machine exploding on impact and burning out.

Both Stifter and Langhart were awarded posthumous Knight's Crosses on 22 January.

It was not all tragedy. The awards continued to flow St.G.77's way as would be expected. Horst Kaubisch, Staffelkapitän of the 9./St.G.77, was another Stuka ace. By 6 November 1942, when he was awarded his Knight's Cross, Horst's tally from more than 500 missions was 137 tanks, 9 trains, 19 gun batteries, 6 important bridges destroyed, in addition to the earlier sinking of 10 enemy ships of 43,000 tons, and the destruction of one flak escort ship and 4 ferries.

Not all the medals were earned at Stalingrad for II./St.G.77 was giving close support further south in the faltering drive towards Tuapse and beyond. 'Jonny' Jauernik, for example, clocked up his 500th mission from the advance Caucasus airstrip at Beloretchenskaya on 10 November. He was to be awarded the Ritterkreuz on 27 November.

The South African born Wilhelm Joswig, who had flown with 8./St.G.1 on the Channel coast, in Sicily, North Africa and at Crete in 1940 and 1941, had been forced to ditch after a hit in the engine by flak off Crete on 25 May 1941. He was rescued after 26 hours in the sea by a Dornier 24 seaplane. By June he was back flying combat ops and had to crash-land his Stuka near Smolensk following a direct flak hit and became prisoner of the Russians. Fortunately he was freed by advancing German troops six days later. After a period as an instructor at Stukaschule established at Diest in Belgium, he went on to create a special night-fighting Staffel of Stukas at Coxyde. This little-known unit carried out several successful nocturnal actions against British coastal shipping using searchlights to mark their quarry. He was again seriously injured in flying accident on the night of 11/12 January 1942 but seemed to bear a charmed life. Nothing could keep him away from his beloved Stukas and on 17 June 1942 he was back in the thick of the action with 8./St.G.1 at Leningrad, Wolkhov and Lake Ilmen. Amazingly Wilhelm was shot down three more times on 3, 7 and 11 August by Soviet fighters and flak, managing to bail out safely on each occasion. In October 1942 Wilhelm joined St.G.77, an outstanding pilot for an outstanding unit. However, he only flew four war missions with them before again transferring, this time to the 9./St.G.2 on 6 November.

Konrad Fechner received the Honorary Cup on 7 December; Walter Stimpel was to fly more than 330 Stuka sorties on the Eastern Front alone, while, by 8 October, Herbert Schmidt had already flown 244 missions. He was promoted to Leutnant on 1 January.

Among the St.G.77 'regulars' who flew throughout the Stalingrad débâcle and beyond were Kurt Rick, the Staffelkapitän of 2./St.G 77, 'Stutz' Stüdemann, since 17 August Gruppenadjutant of the I./St.G.77, Werner 'Piepel' Weihrauch, Heinrich Zwipf, Staffelkapitän of the 3./St.G.77 from September onward. Helmet Leicht, Staffelkapitän of the 2./St.G.77 and deputy Kommandeur of the I./St.G.77 (on 11 January he was to leave the unit to join the Stab of Fliegerkorps IV), and Paul Langkopf fought through all the Stalingrad period with 1. Staffel. They were the lucky ones. But lucky or not, all were totally exhausted by the almost unceasing action of the previous six months which had taken them from the great 'highs' of Sevastopol and Rostov, to the bitter depths of another Russian winter and another German collapse. As the battle ebbed and flowed in the snow and the ice St.G.77 once more returned home to Germany for a period of rest and recreation.

X
The Kuban, Kharkov and Kursk

During the bitter winter fighting of 1942/43 St.G.77 had been led by Major Walter Ennecerus, who had taken over as Kommodore on 13 October 1942, after the tragic death of Major Alfons Orthofer. 'Ennec' as he was known, was one of the most outstanding of the Stuka leaders, but a very different person to 'Ali', who preceded him, being much more in the style of reserved, formal but caring 'old guard' as represented by von Schönborn-Wiesentheid or Günter Schwartzkopff. Like both these older men, 'Ennec' was strictly honest and forthright in his dealings and always put his aircrew first. This was to be his undoing. Perhaps his most famous deeds had been the devastatingly accurate dive bombing of the British aircraft carriers *Illustrious* (off Malta in January 1941), and *Formidable* (in May of the same year), but he had seved with the II./St.G.77 throughout the earlier war months within Poland before transferring to II./St.G2. Now he was back, having taken command on 13 October.

I. Gruppe was led by Helmet Bruck, II. Gruppe by Major Kurt Huhn until 1 April, and III. Gruppe's Kommandeur between 26 August and 1 December was Hauptmann Georg Jakob. Other familiar faces included Leutnant 'Quax' Piske who joined 5./St.G.77 in December and Franz Kieslich, who became the Staffelkapitän of the 7./St.G.77 soon after flying his 500th combat sortie, near Stalingrad, on 20 December 1942. Heinz Welzel, flying with 4./St.G.77, had fought successively at the Crimea, in the Caucasus, on the drive across the Kuban, at Voronesh, Stalingrad and was to feature at the battles of Orel, Minsk and Kharkov.

Helmut Leicht had recuperated from his earlier injuries and was serving as Staffelkapitän of 2./St.G.77 and deputy Kommandeur of the I./St.G.77 at the turn of the year and Heinrich Zwipf was still flying as Staffelkapitän of the 3./St.G.77. Paul Haidle was flying with the 8. Staffel in III./St.G.77. Osmar Griebel survived a crash-landing behind enemy lines early in 1943, but somehow managed to reach German lines after eight days adrift.

Leutnant Ernst Orzegowski was one of those awarded the Honorary Cup which he received on 3 February. Kurt Huhn, Gruppenkommandeur since 1 July, had completed 400 missions in the Stuka by March, most of them on the Eastern Front. On 17 March he was awarded the Ritterkreuz. Oberleutnant 'Alex' Gläser, leader of the 4./St.G.77 received the Ritterkreuz on 19 February after 500 missions.

As always, old comrades left them for good. Their one former surviving leader, Clemens Graf von Schönborn-Wiesentheid, was now commanding the Stukaschule at Wertheim/Main. Much later in the war he was to become the Air

A Junkers Ju87 D of 3./St.G.77 seen over the Russian Black Sea port of Nikolayev in March 1943. (Sellhorn Archiv)

Attaché at the German Embassy in Sofia and was chief of the German Air mission in Bulgaria. He died on 30 August 1944, when his Fieseler 'Storch' aircraft crashed at Sofia airfield. Hauptmann Heinz Niehuus, who had served so diligently with I./St.G.77, left early in 1943 to take up his new post as Chief of Inspection and Supervision of the LKS 1 at Dresden. Another veteran of 1. Staffel's battles this winter was Oberfeldwebel Paul Langkopf. When the Gruppe returned to the front again from Germany following its all too brief period of rest and recreation after Stalingrad, Paul had thrown himself into combat with fresh zest. On 19 February he was awarded the Knight's Cross on completion of 550 missions. During the following month, however, he was badly injured in a flying accident and was hospitalised for the rest of the spring and summer. He never rejoined St.G.77 for, on 1 August, he was appointed Flying Instructor at the Stuka school at St Raphael in southern France, moving later to Metz and then to Fassberg in the same capacity. Unteroffizier Horst Gortler transferred to the 8./St.G.2.

The period subsequent to Stalingrad, from 5 September to 29 December 1942, had marked a distinct turning point in the air war for the Luftwaffe. Fighting on many fronts and far outnumbered on all of them both in the air, on land and at sea, only the excellence of Germany's men and material remained to offset the huge Allied preponderance.

More, the Allies' potential was growing by leaps and bounds, whereas Germany's aircraft production was little changed from 1940.

Both Hitler and Göring were reluctant to face such stark facts at the beginning of 1943 and new offensives for the coming summer months were planned in which the Stukas, again for want of any effective replacement, were to be the spearhead, just as in 1939, 1940, 1941 and 1942. The battle against the Communist hordes was still of course the principal fight, a crusade to save Europe from being overrun, but the British and American victories in North Africa, and then in Sicily and Italy, could not be completely ignored. The possibility of yet another front, in France itself, also occupied German minds more and more as the months passed. To help fill the enormous gaps in the Army's divisions, almost a quarter of a million of the Luftwaffe's ground personnel had been transferred to the new 'Field Divisions' which were to fight as infantry.

This necessarily had a grave effect on the operational efficiency of the front-line air units like St.G.77. Another critical factor was fuel, which, in turn, effected air-crew training. The hours young Stuka pilots spent in learning their highly skilled trade before being thrown into the cauldron were steadily reduced. Finally, Field Marshal Milch had to take over from the chaos left by poor Ernst Udet's suicide and inject some rationalisation and urgency into aircraft production itself. The output of the Ju87D-3 was 100 per month in 1942, but, with the lack of any replacement and severe losses in the East, this had to be urgently increased.

We have already seen the failure of the Stuka's replacement types. The remedy finally adopted was the fitting of the Focke-Wulf FW190 fighter aircraft, with bomb racks fitted to enable it to operate as a makeshift dive bomber and close support machine. Known to its pilots as 'long-nose', the FW190 was hardly the most suitable aircraft for the job. It proved that it could dive, after a fashion, but of course visibility was abysmal and its high speed, so outstanding in its de-signed role, was of no use in precision targeting or lingering over the target, the things for which the Junkers Ju87 was loved by the troops on the ground. There was also the overlooked fact that piloting such a different type of aircraft required the re-training of all the skilled dive bomber pilots, with the resultant hiatus this produced at the front line, as it had to be phased in slowly and carefully.

There was also the fact that dive bombing, so accurate and necessary for most close support missions, was not the ideal way to stop tanks. Conventional bomb-ing could blow their tracks off but it was the Stukas machine guns that proved the most effective means in scoring vital hits on vulnerable sections of the T-34's armoured skin. What was required was a new weapon to punch its way through such a thick hide. The answer was found in the Ju87G.

The Luftwaffe had early on started experiments with heavy cannon as anti-tank weapons. In December 1942 the Ju87D-1 became one of the first close-support aircraft to be tested at the Rechlin centre as a flying tank-buster. It was equipped with two of the powerful Flak 18 antil-tank guns of 37 mm calibre, (*Bord Kannon* 3.7 cm), one under each of the outer wings. Each 16 ft long gun had a muzzle velocity of 2,820 feet per second and each cannon was supplied with twelve rounds of the 3 lb shells. The armour-piercing shells themselves were cored with Wolfram, which enabled them to penetrate the T-34's tough hide before exploding inside.

Tests showed that such weapons were effective, but the aircraft was made far more unmanoeuvrable carrying such weapons. Speed was also reduced and the landing speed increased, all of which made the new aircraft a very tender mount and even more of a specialised machine to fly and handle. Accurate shooting was also considered problematical save in the hands of very experienced pilots. Several veterans were sent home from the front to test the new aircraft out and a special combat unit equipped with the new Ju87G-1 (converted from D-3s), the Panzerjagdkommando Weiss, was set up in February 1943 for actual combat testing. They proved their worth at Kursk that summer, and a total of 208 Ju87 G-2s (*Gustav*) were produced up to October 1944. These new Stukas did not reach St.G.77, however, until later in the year. Their aircrew which used them found that the best way of employing them in combat was with a protective screen of conventional Ju87Ds which suppressed the enemy flak guns thus enabling the limited numbers of the new *Kanonvogel* to operate with impunity. Soon *Panzerknacker* aces began to appear in each unit, although none equalled the famous Rudel, St.G.77 was to throw up its own aces in this field.

With St.G.77, the conventional dive bomber still predominated in 1943. A new variant, the *Dora-3*, was introduced into the Gruppe as the year progressed. This had improved wing loading qualities with the lengthening of the wingtips, which were tapered rather than squared-off. The MG-17 machine-guns in each wing were replaced by the much more lethal Mauser MG 151 20 mm cannon, and the siren mountings were finally done away with completely on this model of Stuka. Because of the mud problems a jettisonable undercarriage was fitted as standard and there were minor modifications to the bomb-release and lubrication systems. The basic fuselage and engine remained as before, but some alterations were made to the pilot's cockpit. Well over a thousand of this model of Stuka were to be built at the Tempelhof and Bremen-Lemwerder plants before all Ju87 production ceased in 1944.

Both the D-3 and D-5 were given added striking power for their new missions as the dams against which the flood of the Soviet high-tide now pressed for the last three years of the war. The versatility of the Stuka, over and above the two principal roles of dive bombing and tank busting, are reflected in the many types of underwing pods carried from this time onward. In addition to the mixed bomb loads of SC 50 and SC 250 light bombs, Stukas could now carry the WB 81 'watering can' weapons pods, with the three MG 81Z machine guns for infantry strafing, the AB 250 light weapons dispenser, the 500 litre all-purpose container for transport purposes and flare and smoke discharging units, all of which were transferable. Some Stukas were fitted out as glider tugs for towing cargo gliders, others with wing mounted gondolas, for evacuating wounded personnel.

Meanwhile the grim holding operations in the aftermath of Stalingrad had to carry on with what they had. The Russian advance had become general, and Voronezh on the upper Don fell to them, but it was the general abandonment of the hard-won cities of Kharkov, which fell on 16 February, Rostov-on-Don and Voroshilovgrad, during February, that involved St.G.77 in some of the grimmest fighting of its career so far.

The Russian advances also forced the abandonment of all the land so painstakingly won in the Kuban the previous autumn, with Krasnodar falling in February. For I./St.G.77, January saw them operating briefly from the airfield at Signat in the Kuban. On 6 January their targets were armoured vehicles and tanks south of Stvropol in the central foothills. Six days later they flew against positions in the village of Krapnyi-Skotowod. As the enemy pressed hard on the retreat heels of 17 Armee so the importance of these holding actions increased. Two missions were flown on 13 January, against tanks and troops at Krassi-Oktjadz. This mission was in fact the last combat sortie led by Helmut Leicht as Kommandeur of the Gruppe. Sellhorn was flying as rear-seat man to Feldwebel Rabben in S2 + BB. It was Sellhorn's 565th flight and 319th combat sortie in the Stuka. The same afternoon they hit Soviet tanks and infantry at Vikobyowsky.

During the course of 15 January the weather in the Kuban cleared enough for I./St.G.77 to launch three sorties, at 1054, 1225 and 1400, their targets being the same in each case, troops and armoured units in the region of Krassi-Oktjadz and at Manytsih some 40 kilometres south of Ssatsk. Next day two more sorties hit the enemy in and around the same strategic village at 0600 and 0730. They were then forced to shift base back again, via Stenograd, to Rostov-North and from here they flew five missions on 25 January against Soviet spearheads, which had reached the town of Manychstraja. They dive-bombed advance enemy columns at this town and also those located at the villages of Arpatschimca and Fedir-toffca, only 25 and 55 kilometres respectively from the outskirts of Rostov itself. Apart from the little cover offered by these hamlets, the Kuban plain was a featureless steppe. Only the broken clefts, the *Balkas*, which split the bare earth, could offer the T-34 hordes any concealment from the ranging Stukas. These were always scrutinised and often revealed worthwhile targets. It was much the same story the following day, with dive bombing missions against the same villages and also Alitub and Bagajewskaja, 30 and 50 kilometres respectively from Rostov. The enemy was getting very close now and on 1 February, yet another withdrawal was forced upon them, Rostov being given up for the airfield at Rowenki, between Rostov and Voroshilovgrad.

Most of the fighting centred on the lower Don but whenever one of the many-headed advances of T-34s threatened German positions during those grim months, the gallant little Stukas were often the only thing between a crisis and absolute annihilation. Between October and mid-January the Don-Donetz area of front doubled its number of aircraft at the expense of all the other battlefields in the east. Most of the Stukas now operated under the newly set up Fliegerdivision Donetz to hold the line.

From their new base at Rowenki I./St.G.77 flew two missions on 1 February, at 1040 and 1317 against the village of Wowsihilosgrad re-conquer the Caucasus again one-day and the maintenance of a strong position east of the Kerch Straits was deemed essential for this strategy, which was to be so much pie-in-the-sky in fact. The Soviets were equally as determined to pinch this position out and fre-quent amphibious landings were made across the Black Sea, supported by their Black Sea fleet, in the rear of the German defenders both east and south-east of Novorossiysk.

Further north the retreat continued unabated at this time, although von Man-stein was preparing for a masterly counter-stroke as he gave ground. The bulk of the Stuka Geschwader, meanwhile moved to Stalino, itself under threat and soon to fall. Here II./St.G.1 and I./St.G.77 worked together, although with greatly reduced numbers, to stem the flood.

In addition to being swamped and having their landing grounds and supply bases overrun, the weather, as always, worked against the Luftwaffe at this period. Thus, by 5 February, the enemy was across the Donetz and a week later all von Manstein's forces in the Stalino-Rostov area had been virtually cut off. A disaster on a scale even larger than Stalingrad threatened for a time. Nonetheless, the dive bombers stuck to their tasks and their bases.

Operating from Kuteimkowa on 9 February missions were flown against hordes of troops advancing through the Don delta. Soviet tanks forces of the Front Mobile Group had broken out through Slavyansk and were wheeling south behind Stalino (now Makeyevka) in an enveloping movement. At Krasnoarmeyskoye 1 Panzer launched its counter-attack to stop this attack in its tracks and I./St.G.77 was heavily engaged in the region of this town throughout the next vital days. Attacks were made on 11 February against armoured vehicles and T-34s by Grisihino, 50 kilometres north-west of Stalino itself and missions in this area continued to be flown throughout the next two days, five sorties, being flown by Sellhorn's unit on 12 February alone.

Thus it was that the high-tide of the Soviet flood was reached and passed and once again Stuka-led German dominance began to redress the situation. A special task force was set up under Fliegerkorps IV commanded by General Kurt Pflugbeil. The 80 Ju87s of the re-strengthened St.G.77 were added to those of St.G.1, so that Oberstleutnant Paul-Werner Hozzel had some 125 Stukas concentrated under his control to act as mobile flying artillery with which to throw against any further Russian breakthroughs. The enemy thrusts were also allowed to make ground westward along the coast from Rostov across the river Mius as 4 Panzer Armee disengaged rapidly. Thus I./St.G.77 was hitting at Soviet troops at Matnajekinja, 50 kilometres north of Taganrog on 19 February.

In this period of high crisis, the date of 19 February 1943 was the significant one for the St.G.77. This was the day that Major Walter Ennecerus was summarily dismissed from command for his steadfast refusal to despatch his young Stuka crews on what he considered to be a suicidal mission. As his daughter later told me, there was considerable embarrassment at his forthright decision and many senior Luftwaffe officers secretly agreed with his stand. Some others felt that the Stukas had a reputation to maintain of flying to the aid of their comrades no matter what the dangers or the risks. Of course it was the Kommandeur's final decision on the balance of each operation. With 'Ennec's' reputation and record of fearlessness there of course could be no questioning of his integrity, but nonetheless his removal was insisted upon. His decision was blamed on stress brought on by over-work and the death of his father. He was not therefore either court-martialled or charged but merely sent back to Germany on extended leave, going on holiday with his family at Kitzbühel. His place was taken by the Kommandeur of I. Gruppe, Hauptmann Helmut Bruck. He had been awarded the Oak Leaves to his Ritterkreuz for his outstanding work, having completed 300 combat missions. On 1 March he was promoted to Major for his new responsibility and he was to continue to lead the Gruppe until February 1945.

This led to further re-organisation. Karl Henze had enhanced his already formidable reputation when he had rescued a wounded downed aircrew of his Gruppe west of Taganrog under heavy enemy fire. In March he became Gruppenkommandeur, a position he was to hold until 15 November 1944. Major Werner Roell became I. Gruppe's Kommandeur which he led to the end of 1943. 'Alex' Gläser was promoted to Hauptmann on 1 April and became the new Gruppenkommandeur of II./St.G.77.

After this re-organisation St.G.77 was once more, under overall command of the revitalised Luftflotte IV, able to apply itself to the tasks in hand, the reoccupation of the Donetz front. This called for the re-capture of Kharkov, Voroshilovgrad, Taganrog and Rostov-on-Don, before the enemy could consolidate his recent gains. Finally the last remaining bridgehead in the Kuban had to be held to allow the orderly withdrawal of the extended troops at risk of isolation in the Caucasus. A period of rest and refurbishment followed in readiness for the new offensive. The proof that the Stuka forces were neither cowed nor overawed despite the months of intensive operations was conceded even by the RAF historian who was forced to admit that:

...the reorganisation and re-establishment of fighting efficiency within the space of 2-3 weeks under continued Russian pressure was a remarkable feat, revealing the resilience of the Luftwaffe. Not the least notable feature was that the reorganisation was carried through without having to draw appreciably on forces from other fronts or from other sectors of the Russian front.

The next move I./St.G.77 made was to the main airfield of the city of Dnepropetrovsk on the Dnieper river in readiness for von Manstein's brilliant counter-stroke which was initiated on the 20th. Next day Sellhorn was flying four missions a day against troop concentrations 40 kilometres south of that base and against T-34s at both Makeyevka and at Bogisslaw six kilometres south of Pavlograd. On 22 February it was much the same story with strikes being put in against tracked vehicles at the village of Zyganowka south of Pavlograd, and the villages of Nichailowka and Romanowka north of Dnepropetrovsk. The two corps of the German 4 Panzer Armee joined hands at Pavlograd next day, cutting off the head of the Soviet General Nicholas Vatutin's 6 Armee and other forces, trapping them. It was another German pocket battle and in the subsequent fighting the Russians lost 615 tanks, 400 guns and 32,000 men.

The Stukas were heavily committed in this round-up. 24 February saw Sellhorn's team flying anti-tank and strafing missions against enemy formations caught at Wabki and Pavlograd and against others trapped in a laager at the village of Bogdanowka, 15 kilometres to the south of the village. The following day brought four sorties, the first at 0555 the last at 1450. Targets included the village of Barwenkowa, 50 kilometres west of Islaijansk and Losowaja, 50 kilometres north of Pavlograd, as well as at Krassnopawlowka, 30 kilometres north of Losowaja. Similar targets were hit on the last day of the month.

The second stage of von Manstein's counter-blow saw the re-taking of Kharkov. On 4,5,6,9 and 11 March I./St.G.77 flew twelve further strikes against these disintegrating armies at Balakleya, south-east of Kharkov, Tamowka, Barki-Persvomayskiy, 30 miles south of Kharkov, and other locations as the German pinchers closed in on that city, which Stalin had ordered to be defended to the last. These were just the preliminary moves and there was much bitter fighting in the town itself between 11 and 15 March before it was cleared.

The Stab Staffel of St.G./77 returning to base after a sortie over southern Russia in the spring of 1943. Note the empty bomb-release forks, the removal of the wheel spats, and the new wing and rear machine-guns. (Sellhorn Archiv)

Above *Celebrating the 500th combat sortie of Unteroffizier Alois Wosnitza, 6./St.G.77 Kalinowka, Russia, in April 1943. Note the prancing horse unit crest of the Gruppenstab of the II./St.G.77 painted on the side-car, while the standard with the Buffalo motif is that of 6. Staffel itself. Wosnitza is in the sidecar and on the pillion seat is Oberleutnant Theodor Haker, Staffelkapitän. Alois went on to fly 1,217 missions in all, including about 150 as an FW190 pilot with SG.10 in the East. (Maahs via Sellhorn Archiv)*

Left *At Kharkov-Rogan airfield, May 1943. Heinz Sellhorn poses with hand on undercarriage siren of his machine. Note the modified wheel spat, the short stubby MG–17 wing-mounted machine-gun and the large diameter of the Stuka's propeller. (Sellhorn Archiv)*

Still based at Dnepropetrovsk airfield, with occasional forays to the forward airstrip at Pavlograd, I./St.G.77 was fully employed supporting all these attacks with nine more combat sorties between the 11th and 13th of the month. On 15 March they twice dive bombed the tractor works in Kharkov itself, still held in a last-ditch stand by fanatical Communist defenders, as well as the rail station at Genijewka-Sheludowka. These accurate blows ended the last enemy resistance in the city.

This victory was followed by an advance on Belgorod to the north by Operational Group Kempf. In three days of heavy fighting the Stukas of I./St.G.77 led this punch with three attacks on 16 March (at Moilanatschi, against the airfield of

Mikoyanovka, 15 kilometres south-west of Belgorod and soon to be the new base of Fliegerkorps VIII, and in support of German armoured spearheads operating 20 kilometres north of Kharkov), three more on 17 March (against Malinowska, Krossnoja-Sarja and Udy, 60 kilometres north of Kharkov) and two on 28 March

Below *Chow time with the Stabkompanie of the St.G.77 at Kharkov in 1943 with Kitchen Feldwebel Hacker in the centre.* (Hacker via Sellhorn Archiv)

Bottom *Unteroffizier Maahs, a long-serving rear-seat man with the Geschwader, garlanded for his 500th combat sortie, in front of his Junkers Ju87 D at Kharkov airfield with his pilot and commander, Oberleutnant Theodor 'Bubi' Haker (with walking stick), the flight leader and Staffelführer of the 6. Staffel St.G.77. On 25 July 1944 their Stuka was set aflame by P–51 Mustang fighters. Haker got his stricken machine down in the Russian zone but it ground-looped. Both men were badly injured and Haker was blinded. Rescued by National Polish forces, who sent for German troops to bring them out, they were ambushed by partisans and shot. Haker was killed and Maahs badly injured, but was miraculously rescued by Waffen SS soldiers who brought him to safety.* (Niermann via Sellhorn Archiv)

(against Tamaravka north-west of Belgorod). This was the day that Belgorod finally fell to the Grossdeutschland Panzer Division, but there was no immediate cessation of work for the Junkers Ju87s. They flew five combat missions on 19 March and were continually in action for the remainder of the month, working also from Kharkov-North and Stalino airfields keeping up constant pressure on the southern bulge of the Soviet salient around the city of Kursk, with 15 sorties between 23 and 30 March.

There was, 'no disputing the skill with which Richthofen handled the forces under his command', records the RAF historian.

In the actual employment of those close-support forces, he had the benefit of the advice of Oberstleutnant Weiss, Inspector of Ground-Attack Forces, who had been detached from Berlin to Luftflotte 4 with the express object of directing the anti-tank units.

The main factor behind Richthofen's success, however, was extreme flexibility, co-ordination and concentration. In this offensive, in which the forces of Luftflotte 4 under Field Marshal von Richthofen played an important – perhaps a decisive – part, the Germans had achieved their main objectives. The energy with which the air operations were directed and executed showed that, even after the disasters of the previous two months, the Luftwaffe was still a factor to be reckoned with.

The coming of the spring thaw and the resultant mud brought most ground movement on the battlefields to an abrupt halt. The German armies and aircraft now readied themselves for the renewal of the battle task. Not until 1 May did I./St.G.77 resume action. Sellhorn was again flying with Zwipf from Kharkov-North airfield and during May they clocked up twenty-one combat sorties from here and Nikolayev-East, Sellhorn achieving his 426th combat flight on the last day of that month.

Although Fliegerkorps VIII had returned to Mikoyanovka after further attacks in the Kuban, the famous leader, von Richthofen was not with them. Despite his outstanding achievements with this famous striking force he had been sent south to the Mediterranean front at the request of Kesselring and his place was taken by General Otto Dessloch. It was the end of an era. Planning now began in earnest for the major German summer offensive in the east, the pinching out of the Kursk salient, Operation 'Citadel'.

'Citadel' was due to be launched on 5 July at 0330 and General Hans Seidemann had some 1,000 aircraft packed into the five main airfields around Kharkov, including the bulk of the Stuka dive bombers, with which to support the southern pincher of the German attack by 4 Panzer Army under Colonel-General Hoth.

'Citadel' was to be the last great air offensive that St.G.77 was to participate in and many of the old hands were there at the outset. Among those standing ready were Herbert Dawedeit flying with 8./St.G.77. He had fought on the Mius front where he had broken up an attack by an enemy infantry regiment with bombing and machine-guns attacks at very low level. In another outstanding episode, it was recorded that near Bogodukhov, a dangerous penetration by T-34's tank units had got to within 15 kilometres of his operational airfield, but that he had led his flight in continual sorties which firstly halted then routed the enemy. At the Kharkov battle also he had personally destroyed two anti-aircraft guns, 11 trucks, 16 horse-drawn carriages and two field-guns when he wiped out a gun emplacement in the Akhtyrka area.

This was the sort of Stuka flyer that success in the Kursk operation was to require. St.G.77 was rich in them by now. They included Herbert Piske, Staffelführer of 5./St.G.77, Leutnant Fritz Neumüller, Gruppenadjutant of the II./St.G.77 who had been awarded the German Cross in Gold on 17 May. Ernst Orzegowski had been awarded the same high honour the week before. Also ready stood Hauptmann Günther Ludigkeit, Staffelkapitän of the 5./St.G.77, and Gerhard Stüdemann, who was to be appointed Staffelkapitän of the 9./St.G.77 on 14 July.

Oberfeldwebel 'Sepp' Huber was serving with 8./St.G.77 after several months away as a flying instructor at Stukaschule at St. Raphael in the south of France. There too was Alex Gläser who had flown his 800th mission near Kharkov earlier, Hauptmann 'Cherry' Bran with 6./St.G.77, and Oberleutnant Werner Weihrauch. 'Piepel' had achieved his 500th mission in June and was to fly another 300 combat missions between then and September, which gives some indication of the intensity of Stuka operations as late as the summer of 1943. He notched up his 600th mission in July during 'Citadel'.

Among the grizzled veterans a few new faces stood out. One of these was Berliner Günter Kilian, a 22-year-old who had not joined the Luftwaffe until November 1939. He had served the Luftwaffe's Auxiliary Regiment 71 until May 1940 and then had served as a motorcycle messenger with a supply unit in Western France until October. Finding this rather tame, Günter had applied for pilot training and been accepted. He went through various schools until December 1942, including the LKS 1 in Dresden. Between January and May 1943 he underwent Stuka pilot training at the Stuka school at St Raphael and came to 6./St.G.77 on the eve of the battle. The Eastern Front soon made or broke men and Günter was later to fly with 5./St.G.77 as Kettenführer.

After a delay due to bad weather, 'Citadel' jumped off on 5 July. This last *Blitzkrieg* saw the southern pincher of the German attack operating out of Belgorod, slice deep into the Soviet defence lines. Forewarned by traitors of the German plans, the Soviets had constructed the most powerful system of defence works ever devised and it was through this maze of tank traps, trenches, fortifications, block-house, machine-gun posts, miles of concrete and wire and huge numbers of dug-in troops backed by thousands of the latest tanks, that the Junkers Ju87 Stukas, aided by small numbers of the new FW 190 fighter-bombers and Hs129 anti-tank aircraft, for the last time showed their worth. Attack after attack went in with the dive bombers braving both heavy concentrations of enemy flak and the

Through the smoke and explosions of battle, a Kette from 3. Staffel St.G.77 flies over the blazing tractor works of Kharkov during the operations leading to the recapture of the city in 1943. (Niermann via Sellhorn Archiv)

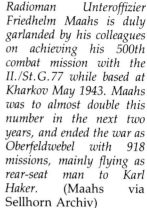

Radioman Unteroffizier Friedhelm Maahs is duly garlanded by his colleagues on achieving his 500th combat mission with the II./St.G.77 while based at Kharkov May 1943. Maahs was to almost double this number in the next two years, and ended the war as Oberfeldwebel with 918 missions, mainly flying as rear-seat man to Karl Haker. (Maahs via Sellhorn Archiv)

A Kette of the I./St.G.77's Doras returning to base at Kharkov in the summer of 1943. The crew of this machine was Unteroffizier Rabben and Obergruppenführer Ostermeyer. (Maahs via Sellhorn Archiv)

duelling artillery of both sides to deliver their pile-driver blows to force pathways through the minefields for the magnificent new 'Panther' and 'Tiger' tanks of 4 Panzer Army. The experimental *Kanovogel* and Hs129 B-2's aided the Junkers Ju87 D-3's in blasting the counter-attacks launched again and again by untold hordes of T-34s, of which the Soviets seemed to have unlimited numbers. The Stukas alone destroyed 64 Soviet tanks in just one day's operations on 7 July. Up to six sorties a day were flown by the dive bombers over the first three day period, during which the German tanks smashed 25 miles northward.

I./St.G.77 operated mainly from Bogodukhov, Khotmyzhsk and Krement-schug airfields, all to the north of Kharkov, during the early part of the battle. The targets were always the same, tanks, trenches, fortifications and yet more tanks. Despite all their efforts, the German pinchers failed to close. Vast tank battles took place with slaughter of the armoured giants taking place on an unprecedented scale. Then, with all the German reserves fully committed, on 11 July came the Russian counter-attacks. At the village of Prokhorovka, Hoth's magnificent Tigers thrusting north met the T-34s of General Pavel Rotmistrov's 5 Guards Tank Army head on. Aided by the wheeling Stukas, the Soviets had 300 tanks smashed to scrap and withdrew.

This massive tank battle was still underway when waves of fresh Soviet men and tanks burst out north of the Orel salient and soon the Germans had to go over onto the defensive once more. They were never again to regain the initiative save in a few local battles. From now on the Stukas were to fight a defensive war.

By 19 July, the enemy had reached Khotinez far to the rear of Orel. The Stuka dive bombers had to be hastily switched from the successful attack in the south to aid their comrades in the north. The Russian armoured brigade which had steamrollered its way through was tackled by every flyable Stuka of Oberst Dr Ernst Kupfer's dive bomber force working from Karachev airfield. Over the next three days, every Junkers Ju87 that could fly was thrown in continuously against this steel mass. The result was a massacre with T-34s burning all over the vast Russian plains. The attack was stopped dead in its tracks from the air and a vast catastrophe was averted. Karachev was the Stukas' biggest and last victory over the Soviet tank forces.

None of this was achieved without loss to the Stuka flyers, of course. Lost at Kursk was Hauptmann Rudolf Blumental, Staffelkapitän of 9/St.G.77. Another casualty was Hauptmann Karl Fitzner, killed at Ssyrtsevo, 40 kilometres north-

Gruppenadjutant Karl Henze of the I.St.G.77 celebrates his 800th Stuka mission with the usual bouquet of flowers from his comrades at Tolokonoje airfield, north of Kharkov in July 1943. Wounded during the attack on Ford airfield near Portsmouth during the Battle of Britain. Henze went on to survive several crash-landings and finally made a grand total of 1,098 missions, most of them with the Stuka. He ended the war as a Major and Kommodore of the Luftwaffe's Auxiliary Geschwader. (Henze via Sellhorn Archiv)

Members of 3. Staffel relax in Russia, 1943. From left to right: Flugzeugführer Oberst Sirrenberg, Flugzeugführer Feldwebel Honnefeller; Bordfunker Oberfeldwebel Brink; Flugzeugführer Stabfeldwebel Jauernick; and Flugzeugführer Oberfeldwebel Wosnitza. (Niermann via Sellhorn Archiv)

west of Belgorod, on 8 July. His Ju87 was hit during his final attack dive; the Stuka exploded in mid-air with the instant demise of both Fitzner and his radio operator, Feldwebel Ernst Meyer. Karl had completed almost 700 Stuka flights.

Even as this enemy attack was thwarted, a fresh offensive commenced to the south, with Russian armour again bursting through the Rumanian divisions holding the line of the Lower Donetz and causing yet further dispersal of the dive bomber forces to cover this new threat. I./St.G 77 was now attacking targets to the south to try and stem the rot; on 20 July, for example they flew six combat sorties, the first at 0405 and the last at 1730, against Soviet columns in the vicinity of the village of Stepanowka, 80 kilometres north-west of Taganrog, and against others pushing west of the river Mius.

By 21 July, the Germans were being forced to pull out of their gains at the Kursk salient by these outflanking attacks and, on 4 August, both Orel and Belgorod fell to the enemy. The enemy now launched a major offensive designed to take them through to the River Dnieper and beyond. Kharkov fell on 23 August and with it went the strategic airfields there. The Stukas were forced back again to Dnepropetrovsk, Krementschug and Mirgorod. Four days later the Soviet steamroller had bludgeoned its way west between Stalino and Taganarog and Fliegerkorps VIII, covering the Poltava, had to switch aircraft to this threatened sector. The record of Sellhorn's diary shows I./St.G.77 hitting tanks and enemy columns between 21 and 25 August near the villages of Grgarjewka, Gerany, Kalinowka, Stepanowka and Telisawertiskij. Even so, Taganrog fell on 30 August.

These defensive battles saw the men of St.G.77 achieve even greater totals in their combat sorties, exceeding even the Crimea operations in their intensity. Men literally flew until they dropped. Leutnant Fritz Neumüller clocked up his 400th mission on 21 July and completed his 500th flight on 25 August. Franz Kieslich flew his 600th flight on 25 July, and undertook his 700th attack only a month later on 29 August. Gerhard Stüdemann flew his 500th mission on 17 August, Oberfeldwebel Hans Meier also acheived his 500th mission on 25 August, while Oberstleutnant Georg Jakob, promoted to Gruppenkommandeur of the III./St.G.77 on 26 August, had reached his 600th milestone on 25 July and his 700th on 29 August. Werner Piepel had been awarded the Knight's Cross on 19 February after 480 sorties but that total was doubled in the next six months' operations. He flew his 700th mission that August, and his 800th was made against Vasilkov near Kiev a month later. Leutnant 'Jony' Jauernik was to reach 800 sorties by September.

Hans-Joachim Brand flew his 500th mission on 3 August. Hauptmann Manfred Goetze had become Staffelkapitän of 5./St.G.77 on 13 July and the following month achieved his 400th combat flight. Paul Haidle had carried out some 600 missions, flown with his Ju87, when he was wounded on 25 August. Likewise, Oberfeldwebel Josef Grewe was wounded on both 10 and 11 July at Kursk. After recuperation in hospital at Halle-Dohlau he re-joined his former unit that same autumn and was back in the flight. Feldwebel Ignaz Schweizer with II./St.G.77 won the German Cross in Gold on 12 July. Hauptmann Anton Andorfer became Staffelkapitän on 16 July. Alex Gläser had also fought well at Kursk, with St.G.77 operating under Helmut Bruck flying Ju87 D's.

Thus passed, in carnage and slaughter, the fatal and fateful battle of Kursk.

XI
Re-organisation and the Long Retreat

The latter part of July 1943 saw I./St.G.77 engaged in bitter and fierce fighting again. Flying from Tolokonoje airfield between the 22nd and 24th of that month eleven sorties were made and the targets included the villages of Grgarjewka, two strikes against tanks in laager to the west of Germany; attacks on Teliswetuiskij and Kalinowka villages, and against batteries south of Stepanowka. Tanks and anti-aircraft guns were the targets on Hill 2020, five kilometres south-west of Mawnowka, and tanks again, a kilometre west of Kalinowka. The enemy was everywhere.

The end part of July saw 1./St.G.77 moving base rapidly via Bawenkowo to Tolokonoje which remained their airstrip for four days. Thus, from the 25th of the month, they were back in action in earnest with five strikes, the first at 0627 against a wooded area east of Kisselewo. Still flying with Hauptmann Zwipf in S2+NL, Sellhorn accompanied his unit in many further strikes that day, against transport in position on the open steppe some two kilometres south-west of Gostishtschevo; on infantry in woods two kilometres south-west of Glushcin-skij; and yet more enemy columns and infantry near Trivetschwje. Two sorties were made on 27 July in the same area, against transport and troops three kilometres north-east of the same village, but a second attack had to be aborted due to strong enemy fighter and flak defences. The Soviets were now easily able to outnumber the Germans in the air as well as on the ground, and, increasingly, their superior numbers in all arms was compensating for their comparative lack of skill. But they were learning all the time, especially at the highest level, and the Germans were now given no time to settle or plan. Thrust followed thrust up and down the front and what forces were available had to be continually switched to meet each one.

And so the battle continued. On 28 July, two sorties, the first aborted due to thunderstorms and torrential rain, the second in the late afternoon, hitting Soviet tanks on the steppe north of Kriwoiy-Rog. Two more attacks were made the following afternoon, against infantry in woods a kilometre west of Kishini village and once more against Trivetschwnje. The Stukas moved again next morning, to Kirteimkowo-South airfield, and from here bombed the village of Marinowka.

August brought no respite, only continued pressure. Six attacks were made by I./St.G.77 on the first day of the month – their targets were, as ever, troops and transport two kilometres south-west of Marinowka and on Hill 2020; pin-point dive-bombing; attacks on bunkers and trenches south-west of Hill 2139, three kilometres from Stehanowka and positions 1.5 kilometres south of Marinowka;

Above *How to deal with the masses of Russian infantry. The AB (Abwurfbehalter) 500 All-Purpose Light Weapons Container containing a package of 180 BZW–360, 2 kilo, bomblets.* (Gohmann via Sellhorn Archiv)

Below *A Staffel of St.G.77's Doras in 1943 fitted with the underwing 500 Litre All Purpose Container (derisively known as the Kleiderbomben, 'Clothes Bomb', by the aircrews) under each wing.* (Sellhorn Archiv)

Bottom *The funeral of Stuka aircrew at Kharkov.* (Dr Armbrust via Sellhorn Archiv)

and two strikes against emplacements and dug-in T-34s in the same area. Anti-tank guns two kilometres north-west of Marinowka were hit the next day and again Russian positions south-west of the Mius, eight kilometres south-west of that village. Then they shifted base back to Tolokonoje once more on 3 August. Orel fell to the enemy on the following day as did Belgorod. Engine failure aborted one mission that day by S2+N1 but they switched aircraft and with, S2+AL, they struck transport and tanks columns at Stepnoje; tanks two kilometres north of Nowaja-Devewije; at Kareitschew; and south and east of Kemenki in seven sorties on 4 August. There were seven missions the following day also, the first at 0504 and the last at 1830. Targets were armoured track vehicles and tanks near Kasytschev; tanks near Nowaja-Derewija; the village of Nowaja-Ghinka; tanks and tracked vehicles at Kemewky but the last flight that day was a quick retreat from their forward base, now under immediate threat, to Kharkov-North airfield.

From Kharkov on 6 August I./St.G.77 flew six missions, on 8 August six more and on 10 August a further five. That evening they pulled back yet again, via Kharkov-South to Poltava airfield once more and, on 12 August, were conduct-ing dive-bombing strikes against the villages of Krysino, Moskaleuki, Alexan-drowka and Krjushchki – all in the Bogadinoff area. It was the same story on 13 August, with five sorties and 14 August, five sorties. Bitter fighting here served to delay, but not stop, the relentless Russian onslaught. This day too Sellhorn completed his 800th Stuka flight, which was also his 506th combat sortie. On 16 August they flew four missions, four more next day, one on 18 August and four more on the following day. Aircraft and men were wearing out in this relentless action. Among Sellhorn's mounts during this period were S2+KL, S2+NL and S2+JL (this latter machine being the first of the D5 variants to operate with the Staffel). Of all the pilots that Sellhorn had flown with no less than three, Decker, Fitzner and Knauer, fell in action on the Eastern Front at this time.

The remorseless enemy advance continued. Kharkov fell on 23 August as related. Still flying from Poltava from 23 to 27 August, Sellhorn took part in 12 more combat flights, the catalogue of targets reflecting the progress of the enemy attacks as they thrust ever deeper westward. Tanks and troops north west of Moika; infantry on the march east of Oleschuja; troops in woods eight kilometres south-west of Tschupackowka; tanks twelve kilometres west of Kharkov; the village of Wssadky; Karolowka; many attacks around Katewa. In the retreat from Kharkov I./St.G.77 found themselves based at Krima, 15 kilometres west of Krasnograd, from 30 August onward. The first missions were not flown from this field until 8 September, when five sorties were made; the targets were the village of Schiloff, 12 kilometres north-west of Walki; the western end of the village of Batki; Schilowka, and Borki, eight kilometres north-west of Taranowika. On 10 September they flew a further three sorties from this base, then moved back to Poltava from where their targets included infantry and tanks both north and west of Batki.

One strike was made next day, against Luka village, ten kilometres west of Lochiviza, but the 13 and 14 September saw four and five missions each day. The Stukas targets never varied, troop concentrations in woods three kilometres west of Linka; infantry in the woods north of Milowidroje, six kilometres north-east of Rublewka; the southern part of the village of Galijka, 12 kilometres north-west

15 September 1943. In the retreat from Kharkov, St.G.77 was based at the airfield of Poltava, about 30 km south-west of Kiev. From here innumerable sorties were flown over the crumbling southern front to try to stem the flood of Soviet forces westwards towards the Dnieper river line. Here I./St/G/77 returns across that vital river after another 'Fire Brigade' mission to the east. (Sellhorn Archiv)

This quartet of Doras of the 3. Staffel St.G.77 is preparing to land with empty bomb racks. The wheel spats are in position as this is September 1943, and the airfields are good ones, while the weather has not yet turned the Russian summer dust into late autumn quagmires. Kursk has failed, and St.G.77 is flying desperate missions to stem the tide of the Soviet advance. (Sellhorn Archiv)

of Oposchuja; batteries in the open near Alexojewka, 20 kilometres north-west of Walki; the village of Iserdnjaki, 20 kilometres west of Gadjatsch; tanks and infantry at Konowaloff, 20 kilometres west of Gadjatsck, and free-ranging sorties over the steppe where the enemy was bound to be found in ravines or sheltering in the debris of shattered homesteads.

By the middle of September the retreat had brought them as far west of Kiev on the Dnieper river, such was the pace of the enemy advance. Flying from Poltava via Kiev-West airfield, I./St.G.77 found itself based at Wassilkolf, an airstrip 30 kilometres south-west of the city. This was to be their airfield for the rest of the month. Between 18 and 27 September they flew daily missions against Soviet spearheads, pressing in on Krivoi-Rog west of the Dnieper and on the road to Nikolayev and Odessa. On the 18th, 19th and 21st there were many strikes at Kozelets and to the north-west of Oster on the river Desna; on 23 against Pereyaskavl on the eastern bank of the Dnieper, to the south-west of Kiev; and by 26 of the month they were strafing troops in woods north of Balyka and columns of troops on the roads leading from Rohischthev. Some 1,200 sorties a day were being mounted by all the Luftwaffe units in this sector and they played a substantial part in stemming the Soviet advance on Krivoi Rog to the south, but this left the northern approach to Kiev dangerously exposed.

Meanwhile, in the aftermath of the Kursk tragedy and subsequent withdrawals, there came drastic and far-reaching changes in the Luftwaffe command and organisation, which affected St.G.77 and thereby brings our story to its last chapter. Changes would have come about in any event but the failure of 'Citadel' brought matters prematurely to a head. The first event was the suicide of Chief of the Luftwaffe General Staff, Generaloberst Hans Jeschonnek. Like Udet he could not continue working with Göring, with whom he had many arguments. He had worn himself out tirelessly battling the Reichsmarshall's indifference to many vital matters and when, Hitler ignored a memorandum listing Göring's many failings, Jeschonnek felt he had no way left but to take his own life, which he did on 18 August.

Jeschonnek's place was taken by Generaloberst Günther Korten. On 5 October he issued Oberkommando der Luftwaffe 2. Abteilung Order 11125/43 which set up the new Schlachtflieger force. This now combined, under a single overall controller, *all* close-support forces (dive bombers, ground-attack and fighter-bombers) in order to rationalise them into an effective whole. The new title reflected nothing more than a general grouping of all the army support units, but has been presumed by many since to mark the demise of dive bombers and dive bombing in the Luftwaffe. In fact it meant nothing of the sort; the Stukas were certainly due to be replaced eventually – their design was after all now seven years old – but they continued to dive bomb, as did the new FW190s. That did not stop Stukas from carrying out low-level strafing, as indeed they always had done, in common with the FW190s, Hs129s and Henschel 123 biplanes.

One of Korten's first changes had been to appoint a specialist to take command of this new force and, if proof was needed that dive-bombing experience was still the most valid requirement for this new post, Korten appointed an ex-Stuka man for the post of General der Schlachtflieger, the former Kommodore of St.G.2, Oberst Dr Ernst Kupfer. However, before Kupfer could get a grip on his new command he was killed in a flying accident on 6 November and his place was

Unteroffizier Ostermeier makes the most of a brief break at Kharkov-North airfield in 1943. The primitive log cabins are typical of air and ground crew accommodation at even the most permanent of Russian air bases. (Sellhorn Archiv)

taken by another former Stuka pilot, Oberst Hubertus Hitschold.

Following the establishment of the Schlachtflieger force on 6 October 1943, there was a degree of re-naming and re-numbering of the Stuka units. All the Stukagruppen were now termed Schlachtgruppen. Thus I. Gruppe was re-designated the I./SG.77 on 18 October; the III. Gruppe was likewise renamed on 18 October as III./SG 77. With II. Gruppe, which had been commanded by Haupt-mann Helmut Leicht since 1 April, it was not so simple a transition. Initially it became the II./SG.77 but, between 1943 and 1944, it became the Gruppe III./SG.10, and it was the renamed I./SG.1 which then became the new II./SG.77.

All continued to operate the standard Junkers Ju87D5 in both dive bombing and strafing attacks, but, beginning that winter, pilots were progressively sent back to the Reich for conversion training to the FW190 bomb carriers before re-joining their units. This all took time, because of shortages of fuel for training which spread a normal two-month course over five months. There were other factors which further delayed the conversions, like shortages of the 20 mm ammunition, the predominant need to train fighter pilots to oppose Western firestorm raids on German civilian targets and the like, and it was not until November that the first of SG.77 units began combat flying the new machines. II./SG.77 was sent 20 FW190's that month but the other units had to wait until March 1944 for their new aircraft to arrive.

Each crew that changed meant that a rear-seat man became excess to re-quirements and could either also apply to re-train (not likely) or was moved to another post. Some remained almost to the end of hostilities because, despite some post-war historians' comments to the contrary, the Junkers Ju87 kept flying and fighting right to the very last day of the war. The loss of a rear-seat man to identify the target and note the result of attacks, coupled with the loss of accuracy when converting from Stuka to FW190, meant that the extra speed was only bought by a loss of accuracy and efficiency by the close-support units. In addition the usual nightmare conditions of the Eastern Front in winter meant that often the more lightly-built and narrow-tyred Focke-Wulfs were completely unable to operate at all while the broad-tyred and rugged Stukas continued to get airborn. Having *regular* close-support from an *old* aircraft was infinitely more valuable to the soldier on the ground than having *no* support at all from a technically *superior* machine. The Western Allies had found this at Tunisia and the German soldier, hitherto always assured of the friendly sight of the inverted-gullwing Junkers over his head in any situation, became more and more disillusioned at lack of reliable and lingering air cover.

In addition to the conventional dive bombers, each *Sch* was allocated a number of the tank-busting Ju98 Gs and these were identified as II./SG.77 (Pz). Each of these Panzerstaffel was equipped with twelve *Gustavs* plus four conventional *Doras* for flak suppression. Thus from October 1943 to September, the SG.77 units flew a mixture of Ju87 D-3s, Ju97 Gs and FW190s. By September 1944, FW190s had completely re-equipped the units, except for 10. Staffel which still flew the Kanonvogels, and these were joined by rocket-firing FW190 F-8s with 5. 'Panzerschreck' and 9 'Panzerblitz' Staffeln by 20 April 1945.

While the paper and technical changes proceeded, the actual fighting showed no let-up and the men of SC.77 continued to fly and fight without pause or hin-

The presentation of the Ritterkreuz to the Staffelkapitän of the 2. Staffel St.G.77, Hauptmann Günter Hitz, awarded on 22 November 1943. The senior officer on the left is General Seidemann. Hitz completed 832 Stuka sorties and became deputy Kommandeur of I./SG.77 in 1944. He was shot down by flak when attacking Soviet columns at Khodackov on 11 April 1944. (Conradt via Sellhorn Archiv)

drance throughout the grim winter of 1943/44. Kommandeur Helmut Liecht was promoted to Major on 1 October after his sterling work at Sevastopol and Kharkov.

Franz Kieslich now led the 7. Staffel from September onward, and Leutnant Werner Haugk 6./St.G.77, but in the autumn the latter was transferred to Me110 'Destroyer' type twin-engined fighter-bombers and joined the 4./ZG.76. Osmar Griebel was flying with the 2. Staffel, and Herbert Piske had flown his 500th mission from Poltava that autumn.

Georg Jakob was promoted to Major on 1 September, and by the end of the following month had achieved his 800th war sortie. Ernst Orzegowski continued to lead his Staffel until March, while Franz Neumüller flew his 600th mission on 29 September. Paul Haidle was now serving with the re-named 8./SG.77 and Werner Weihrauch on 30 October clocked up his 886th mission (the highest count of any SG.77 pilot up to that time), but his Stuka was hit and shot down by Russian fighters. Werner himself was wounded but managed to get out and parachuted to safety.

Less fortunate was Feldwebel Karl Zellner of 1./St.G.77. On 13 September his Ju87 was accidentally rammed by another aircraft when climbing through a layer of cloud. The Stuka crashed to the north-east of Poltava, killing Karl outright. His radio operator, Unteroffizier Josef Lobert, managed to bale out. Unfortunately his parachute got entangled in the diving aircraft's tailplane and he plummeted to earth, dying of his injuries the following day in Poltava field hospital. He had conducted 505 Ju87 missions and, on 29 February, was posthumously awarded the Ritterkreuz.

Others they lost through the Focke-Wulf re-training programmes, including Ignaz Schweizer and Heinz Welzel. Both spent the period October to March at the FW190 transition training camp at Neudorf-Oppeln, the II./St.G.77 being renamed III./SG.10. Heinrich Zwipf, Sellhorn's old pilot and companion, had achieved his 600th mission on 6 October, during a sortie from Beresovka. This was also Heinz's 600th mission. Heinrich was promoted to Hauptmann and awarded the Knight's Cross, but ten days later he was sent back to commence FW190 conversion. He never returned, losing his life on 1 December leading the

I./SG.4 in Italy. Another loss was Kurt Huhn who from August to October had been the Flying and Tactics Instructor at the LKS 9. More losses to transition training to the FW190 included Ernst Orzegowski, who flew with the 7. Staffel. He joined III./SG.10 with which he remained until 1945. Franz Neumüller's training also took place between October and March after which he joined the II./St.G.77 which returned to action from May 1944 as the III./SG.10 in Bessarabia. Manfred Goetze transferred to transition training over the same period and with the re-equipment of the FW190 as well as the renaming of II./St.G.77 as III./SG.10 again took up the struggle.

Among the newcomers who began to make names for themselves flying the tank-smashing *Gustav* was Ulrich 'Tex' Mundt, a 28-year-old Berliner. Another veteran he, like so many others, had been a keen glider pilot pre-war and on 1 October 1934 had volunteered for Luftwaffe, but first been temporarily inducted into the Army switching a year later. He had started his pilot training on 1 April 1938, completing the course at the Kitzingen Stukaschule on 3 September 1939. Next day he had joined the 5./St.G.1 as Unteroffizier seeing war service in Poland, France, 18 sorties against England, in the Mediterranean and against Malta. He had severely damaged a British cruiser off Benghazi. From 22 June he had fought in Russia and following his training on the *Gustav* had joined the 10.(Pz)/SG.77, with whom he undertook 55 combat missions up to the end of November, before returning home to become an anti-tank instructor after personally destroying 40 Soviet tanks in the field.

As we have already seen, the defence of the Donetz was the main preoccupation of the stretched Luftwaffe forces in the East, but, with no reserves, the same handful of close-support aircraft now had to be switched from one reeling front to another as the Russian masses punched through time and time again.

We left I./SG.77 at the end of September when they were working from Wassilkoff. On the 30th, they moved base to Beresowka, 12 kilometres from Alexandrovka, east of Krivoy Rog and north of Nikopol. Here they resumed their work at 1328 with an attack against infantry advancing across open steppe two kilometres north-east of Dnepropetrovsk itself. Next day they flew at 0830, 1135, and 1430, the targets being the village of Isokolowka four kilometres east of Taranzolf. On 3 October they hit the enemy east of the village of Barodajewka in the morning and troops on the steppe two kilometres east of Isokolowo and four kilometres south of Borodajewka. Four attacks were made the following day, against Mischurim-Rog; one to the south-east of Isokolowo and one against Kuzewolkowka village. Exactly the same targets were struck again on 5 October. After a day's respite they were flying again at 0600 on 8 October against the same targets and same area, three missions in all, with an attack on another Soviet bridgehead across the Dnieper at Novo Georgievsky due west of the main enemy concentrations at Kremenchug. Here the Soviets were busy pouring in fresh forces across the river barrier in readiness for a renewal of their attack south and west. Despite frequent attacks, the Germans failed to dislodge them from these positions.

Fresh pressure against Kiev necessitated another hasty shift. Back to Wassilkoff the unit flew at first light on 12 October and, at midday, they were taking off from that base to strike at infantry on the steppe south of the village of Ljuts, 15 kilometres north of Kiev itself. Missions from here between 13 and 16

Here is one of those rare occasions when fighter escort was provided for 3.SG.77 by a pair of Me109s. The aircraft are seen returning to their base at Vinnitsa, on the river Bug, south-west of Kiev, after a strike against Soviet columns in January 1944. (O. Sorrenberg via Sellhorn Archiv)

October were mainly at thrusts coming in through the villages of Lyntesh, Iswaromije and Petrnosk. I./SG.77 was now played out and its personnel exhausted. On this day they received orders to move back west for another period of rest and recuperation by men and machines. The whole of the flying personnel flew back to Lemberg (now Lv'ov) and did not rejoin the fighting on the Eastern front until the last day of November.

Almost as if they had been waiting for the I. Gruppe's Stukas to depart, from 20 October onward the Soviets pushed forward from their bridgehead at Kremenchug into the Dnieper Basin with the aim of taking Krivoi Rog. All the remaining available German Junker Ju87s and other close-support aircraft (along with long-range bombers as well), were thrown in against this thrust which led to the weakening of those units defending Kiev further north. A fresh enemy offensive in this area and that strategic city fell to the Russians on 6 November despite much hard fighting.

Nor was this all, for the enemy now drove hard for Zhitomir. Once again machines had to be switched from the 'weathered-out' southern flank to tackle this new menace. Here a German counter-attack from Zhitomire, launched on 15 November, was initially partially successful. Thus, yet again, on two occasions the Stukas had halted dangerous Russian breakthroughs, but it was mainly the closing in of the weather that saved the completed collapse of the German position in the central and southern sectors. The Germans clung on grimly to the Crimea but the garrison there looked more and more isolated once the Russians had once more overrun the Perekop Isthmus the preceding month.

Helmut Liecht became another of the unit's casualties, being wounded on 9 November. He was sent home to heal and kept on training duties until May. He was sorely missed at the front. Helmut Bruck was promoted to Oberstleutnant on first of the month and completed his 500th mission, while Franz Kieslich flew his 800th mission on 30 November. Hauptmann Günter Hitz, Staffelkapitän of the 2. Staffel, received a well-merited Ritterkreuz on 22 November after completing 700 Stuka missions.

Herbert Dawedeit was among those engaged in the struggle for Kiev. He also flew sorties against the Soviet bridgehead near Rshishchev. His accuracy in the face of the very heavy flak positions, now such a regular feature of the Russian

'Jolanthe' joins the celebrations for the 1,000th combat flight of the Gruppenkommandeur of the I./St.G./77, Major Karl Henze, on 26 February 1944 at Uman airfield. This outstanding achievement also earned him the award of the Oak Leaves. The 'Swine-holder' is the Gruppe's pay officer, Oberzahlmeister Sagan. (Henze via Sellhorn Archiv)

advances, was phenomenal. Herbert scored several direct hits on these bridges, as well as being credited with the destruction of many small landing craft. He also attacked a landed Soviet infantry regiment with bombs and guns at the Kremenchug actions. By 1 November 1943 his personal tally was legendary and in 627 missions, (two of which had been over the English Channel) he was officially credited with the destruction of a destroyer, five freighters, (with damage to three others), and eight landing craft. He had also wiped out a coastal battery, a radio station, two armoured trains, seven bridges, 11 trains, 34 tanks, 45 gun battery emplacements, two mobile AA guns, 67 trucks, and 74 horse-drawn carriages.

Herbert's outstanding list of targets hit up to this time also included three major fortifications, an ammunition dump, twelve rail links, 26 AA guns and 32 enemy positions effectively attacked. On 1 November 1943 he was commended for the Ritterkreuz. Soon after this, in January 1944, this outstanding pilot was lost to SG.77 when he was appointed to the Blindflugschule at Stubbendorf. Feldwebel Osmar Griebel also received the award of the Knight's Cross on 5 December, after more than 700 combat fights, all on the Stuka.

At least the Stukas had achieved some victories against the Russian land forces, the adoption of western-type 'strategic' bombing by Korten was, by contrast, a complete flop. The enemy resumed the offensive from Kiev in December and once more every effort was diverted to holding this blow until the weather again closed down operations. I./SG.77 was now back in the fight after their brief respite. Their first mission was flown on 15 December from the threatened airstrip at Zhitomir due west of Kiev. The railway bridge at the town of Malin, midway along the Kiev to Koroston rail link, was their target, and it was duly demolished. A second attack that day by the Stukas hit Malin itself which was packed with enemy units moving east to escape from the German counterattack.

Bad weather caused a twelve-day lull in operations here and Stuka attacks from Zhitomir did not resume until 27 December but targets were few and well dug in. Kiev stayed in Soviet hands. The Soviets were becoming increasingly sophisticated in the approach and defence tactics against the marauding Stukas. After the first snowfall during the Kiev operations, reconnaissance seemed to indicate heavy concentrations of enemy tanks and artillery in the area. The giveaway was that there were no track marks on the snow-clad steppe. A few of SG.77's aircraft were accordingly dispatched to confirm these suspicions and dropped several cluster bombs on these 'tanks'. The resultant devastation revealed them for what they were, merely ply-wood dummies to draw German fire while the real T-34s probed elsewhere in the line.

The attrition continued. Staffelführer Jürgen Harang was wounded in the eye on 20 December while flying a mission in the Nikopol region. However, other faces seemed to go on forever despite the hazards. Oberleutnant 'Cherry' Brand, Staffelkapitän of 1./SG.77 received the Ritterkreuz on 5 December after 500 missions. Oberfeldwebel Werner Honsberg with I./SG.77 continued to lead his Staffel into battle until late 1944.

I./SG.77 had meantime moved down to Uman, south-west of Cherkassy for a new field of operation, arriving there on the last day of January. Hydra-like, the Russian armies had pushed out a new head against Nikopol during January 1944. The consequences of this continued shifting of emphasis was spelled out clearly in this manner: '...the Germans were thrown back in the main on their close-support forces at the very time when, in view of improvement in the quality and quantity of the Soviet fighter force, they had planned to withdraw Ju87 dive-bomber units for re-equipment with the FW.190...' Working from Uman, Sellhorn, now flying with Unteroffizier Happe in the white distemper-dappled S2+MH, was soon in heavy action amid the snowdrifts to stop this new assault. On 31 January and 1 February the weather permitted the maximum number of missions to be flown in the hours of daylight and four attacks were made on each of those days. The villages of Kirtschkowka, 30 kilometres from Shaschkoff; Ryshanowka, Cholkowka; Tazkowizkaja, five kilometres north of Zybilew; and Wapilkow, three kilometres west of Shpola were all dive bombed. The last place was only a few kilometres north-west of the Stukas' own base itself for the enemy was thrusting down from Cherkassy. Nikopol on the coast was cut off and kept supplied from the air.

Pilot's view of his rear-seat man! An aerial in-cockpit shot of Heinz Sellhorn taken by his pilot, Herbert Rabben, flying their Dora–5 with the Stab of I./Gruppe St.G.77 in 1944. He is wearing his oxygen mask and flying goggles indicating a high-altitude flight, as well as a throat microphone for internal communication. (Rabben via Sellhorn Archiv)

The lean and mean profile of the Ju87 D belonging to the Geschwaderstab of SG.77 at Lemberg airfield which is still under snow in March 1944. The move back this far west showed the seriousness of the situation on the Eastern front following the third winter campaign. (Grunwald via Sellhorn Archiv)

The snow closed down operations again until 9 February when again I./SG.77 was airborne at 0830 and 1350. Their targets were enemy troops at the villages of Autowka, 15 kilometres north-west of Bessowka and at Bessowka itself, which was 25 kilometres north-west of Zventgorodka and even closer to their airfield. Masses of Russian infantry were again hit on 11 February in a bombing attack on woods at Bessowka and a strafing attack at Tschessnowka, when the 'watering can' was liberally used to some good effect, and it was a similar story during the next two days later when Tschessnowka, Winograd and Chishinzy were all repeatedly hit.

Fresh Soviet tanks now reinforced the enemy, whose advance had been stalled south-west of Cherkassy, and T-34/76s and the new T34/85s, supported by the super-heavy KVs, were found rolling south past Oktjabr at midday on 16 February and routed. Sorties continued intermidantly in this area for the rest of the month with the Stukas operating alternately from Uman and Baschtanka against targets which included Isusslowa, 15 kilometres from Kirovograd; Warwarowka; Petrovo, 40 kilometres north of Krivoy Rog itself; Isitajewka; and Wassiltkowa. A particularly noteworthy mission was one of the 'Stuka Specials', a pin-point dive-bombing of a Soviet Army Staff HQ at Warwarowka village, carried out on 26 February with excellent results.

Krivoy Rog was temporarily saved by such efforts. However, this fresh commitment of the Junkers Ju87s yet further delayed the replacement programme as they were required almost daily to stem the Soviet onrush towards the vital Rumanian oilfields. I./SG.77 made their last flight from Uman on 1 March and then shifted base north-west to Kamionka Strumitowa, north-east of Lemberg, in response to yet another Soviet thrust.

While the Russian probing had continued in the northern sectors of the vast Eastern front, the southern sectors had enjoyed a small period of relative calm until March, 1944, when again the massed ranks of the T-34's moved forward towards the Rumanian oil fields. Close-support units, including I./SG.77, were concentrated in the defence of the Ukraine around Yampol. On 6 March the Stukas were attacking targets in the Yampol region, just 15 kilometres north of Staro Konststantinov. Unfortunately this switch of the Junkers Ju87s north left a

corresponding gap in the German defences along the northern shoreline of the
Black Sea. Nikolayev fell to the Soviet advance there on 28 March, followed by
Odessa itself on 10 April where the rest of SG.77 was bitterly contending the
ground when they could get airborne. Muddy weather during the Russian
attacks around Odessa meant that only the Ju87s, with their wide tyres, could
take off and they were in constant action.

Yet another notable achievement was recorded in April 1944. I./SG.77 was
now flying from Lemberg itself as the Russians thrust towards the Carpathians to
outflank Germany's wavering Hungarian and Rumanian allies. It was nothing
less than the 100,000 combat mission, which was flown by a Stuka of 8./SG.77.
This unique event was celebrated in due style, with the actual aircraft being
decorated and a visit being made to the unit by Generalleutnant Hans
Seidemann, the commander of Fliegerkorps VIII, with whose exploits St.G.77
will be forever linked. He was welcomed to the party by Helmut Bruck and a

Right *The Geschwader Kommodore of
SG.77 Oberstleutnant Helmut Bruck, in
conversation with the Gruppenkommandeur
of III./SG.77, Hauptmann Franz Kieslich at
Lemberg airfield, 4 April 1944, on the return
of the latter from his 900th combat mission.
Kieslich had become Kommandeur that
February and went on to make a total of 1,078
combat sorties, all but 40 in Stukas. He
survived the war despite being shot down 21
times, and baling out once! Wounded in
action, he continued combat flying with vision
slightly impaired by his dressing, as can be
seen in this photo.* (Gohmann via Sellhorn
Archiv)

Below *Lemberg airfield, 14 April 1944.
Slush turns to mud, but for SG.77 flying
continues as before. The Kommodore,
Oberstleutnant Bruck, is briefing his aircrew
after return from the 900th mission.*
(Gohmann via Sellhorn Archiv)

I./SG.77's Ritterkreuz holders in the summer of 1944. From the left: Ofw. Alois Wosnitza; Oblt Theodor Haker (killed in action 25 July 1944), Staffelkapitän, 3. Staffel; Hptm. Hans-Joachim Brand, Staffelkapitän, 1. Staffel (killed in action 18 April 1945); Offw Otto Weiss; Offw Herbert Rabben; in the background Oblt Stratomeyer (killed in action July 1944, Poland). (Rabben via Sellhorn Archiv)

Hungary, July 1944: expecting the main thrust of the Russian offensive from the south, Luftwaffe close support units contended with unstable Hungarian allies. This demonstration was both a warning and a steadying exercise, involving dive bombers from the newly formed NSG.151 and those of the Stuka training school, recognised by the large white numerals on their tail rudders. (Sellhorn Archiv)

An outdoor meal with their ladies for SG.77 pilots undergoing the conversion programme from Ju87 Ds to the FW190 at Sifersdort, Schlesien, in August 1944. The two officers are Oberst Helmut Bruck, Gruppen-kommandeur SG.77, and Major Karl Henze of I./SG.77. (Dittewig via Sellhorn Archiv)

Russian prisoners of war hauling bombs on makeshift sleds to the Stukas of Stab SG.77 at a snow-girted Lemberg (Lv'ov) airfield in April 1944. (Gohmann via Sellhorn Archiv)

November 1944. Oberst Bruck clambers from his Stuka at Seifertsdorf in Silesia. Now Kommodore of SG.77, Bruck became Kommodore of the newly formed SG.151 in January 1945 which he led in Hungary and elsewhere on the Eastern Front until April when he was appointed the last General der Schlachtflieger-North. (Berzlmaier via Sellhorn Archiv)

special salute was taken by both aircrew and the ground personnel.

Sellhorn himself flew his last two missions as rear-seat man to Feldwebel Herbert Rabben, flying with the Stab of I./SG.77. Rabben had been awarded the German Cross in Gold on 8 March for his outstanding work with the unit which stretched back to the Balkan campaign of 1941. On 4 May he was awarded the Knight's Cross after achieving more than 600 missions and was promoted to Oberfeldwebel. Heinz himself flew three sorties with this pilot, all from Lemberg on 5 May. Flying Stuka S2+EH, their targets were enemy formations near Khovackow and Potapinice west of Ternopol. For Sellhorn himself these last Stuka missions were his 957th, 958th and 959th flights, and his 643rd, 644th and 645th (and last) combat mission. If we are amazed at such numbers, it must be remembered that such sortie rates were the norm for German dive bomber crews and they saw nothing too exceptional in them. It is also a pertinent reminder that the endless wartime and post-war propaganda about the Junkers Ju87 being a death-trap and fighter bait never mentions the scores of aircrew, just like Sellhorn, who fought from 1 September 1939 until the middle of 1944 exclusively

'Blackmen' servicing the new Focke-Wulf FW190 ground attack variant of the famous single-seat fighter, various marks of which equipped the Schlacht units from the middle of 1944 onwards. The D indicates that this machine belongs to SG.77, and the date is early 1945. (Berzlmaier via Sellhorn Archiv)

in Stukas and survived the war. Such facts don't fit the accepted Allied view that speed was all, and so are usually omitted, but they are still facts.

There was not much else to celebrate at that period of SG.77's history. Far away to the south the Crimea, scene of one of their greatest victories, was by that time completely isolated by the enemy. By 8 May the last German airfield on the peninsula had been made untenable. It was a period of endless reverses for the Germans and it left a huge Soviet salient south of the Pripet Marshes, taking in parts of Rumania and the whole of Bessarabia save for a German toe-hold west of the Dniester river. Yet this was but the prelude to an even more immense disaster for the following month, in the aftermath of the Allied invasion of Normandy, the Russian summer offensive commenced.

But by the time SG.77 became involved in that débâcle, in which the whole of the German 'Army Group Centre' was shattered and smashed to the four winds and the enemy reached the borders of the Reich, the Stuka dive bomber had almost disappeared from the unit's active strength. Almost all the final years missions were flown with the FW190 although a few Junkers Ju87s did fly isolated combat sorties during that ghastly period. They were but as pebbles on a seashore against the incoming tide.

One such incident is recorded on 5 July 1944 in the German 4 Army sector of the disintegrating front. XXXIX Panzer Corps made a fighting withdrawal to a line five kilometres east of Molodechno and east of Khozevo under heavy enemy pressure. However, the vital rail link from Vilnius to Smorgon' remained intact to the enemy. Therefore 221 Infantry Division was sent in against the River Vilnya bridge, to the north-east of Smorgon', with Junkers Ju87 Stuka support.

Thus the Stukas fought to the last in the crash of the 'Thousand-Year Reich'. In defeat, as in their many victories, the men of SG.77 were proud of the fact that, 'Where the infantry went, so did the Stukas'. In good days and bad, they did not fail their comrades on the ground.

Appendix I
The Junkers Ju87 'Stuka': layout and equipment

Variants

1: Prototype
V-1 – 1935. Twin tail fins, powered by 640 hp Kestrel V engine.

V-2 – 1935. Single tail fin, powered by 610 hp Jumo 210 Aa engine.

V-3 – 1936. Added endplate fins for stability, engine mounting lowered.

V-4 – 1936. Increased tail surfaces, engine lowered more, MG17 fitted in starboard wing mounting.

V-5 – Not proceeded with.

V-6 – 1938. Experimental testbed for Jumo 211 A engine.

V-7 – 1938. Modified cockpit canopy, enlarged rudder and fins, wheel 'Spats' replaced 'Trousers', extra MG17 in port wing mounting.

V-21 – 1940. Prototype of Dora with 1,400 hp Jumo 211 J

V-22 – 1941. Prototype of Dora, 1,800 kg bomb capacity.

V-23 – 1941. Prototype of Dora, strengthened undercarriage.

V-24 – 1941. Tropical trials testbed for Dora.

Anton
A-0 – 1937. Pre-production run of ten machines, wing leading edges modified.

A-1 – 1937. Initial production run with 635 Jumo 210 Da engine.

A-2 – 1937. Broader-bladed propeller fitted.

Bertha
B-0 – 1938. Pre-production run of ten machines following V-7, fitted with Jumo 210Da engine.

B-1 – 1938. Production run with 1,210 hp Jumo 211 Da engine.

B-1/U1 – 1939. Retrospective identity for B-1 on variants

B-1/U2 – 1939. Revised radio equipment.

B-1/U3 – 1941. Additional armour protection fitted.

B-1/U4 – 1941. Experimental ski undercarriage fitted.

B/Trop – 1941. Tropicalised B-1 for Mediterranean ops.

B-2 – 1940. Modified undercarriage, 1,210 Jumo 211 Da engine.

B-2/U1 – 1941. Retrospective identity for B-2 variants.

B-2/U2 – 1941. Revised radio equipment.

B-2/U3 – 1941. Additional armour protection.

B-2/U4 – 1941. Experimental ski undercarriage fitted.

Caesar
C-0 – 1939. Navalised version with arrestor hook, carrier catapult stressing.
C-1 – 1940. Navalised version with folding wings for carrier stowage and jettisonable undercarriage.

Dora
D-1 – 1941. Production run, fitted with VS11 airscrew.
D-1/Trop – 1942. Tropicalised D-1
D-2 – 1942. Glider towing hook added, tailwheel strengthened.
D-3 – 1942. Increased armour protection.
D-4 – 1941. Experimental torpedo bomber variant.
D-5 – 1943. Increased wingspan, jettisonable undercarriage.
D-6 – Not proceeded with.
D-7 – 1942. D-3 with two 20 mm MG151/20 cal guns.
D-8 – 1942. D-5 with two 20 mm MG151/20

Gustav
G-0 – 1942. Pre-production Ju87 D equipped with tank busting 37, Flak 18 cannon
G-1 – 1943. Tank busting model. Initial production run, based on D-3 as above.
G-2 – 1943. Tank busting model. Production run, based on D-5

Richard
R-1 – 1940. Long-range B with wing drop tanks and extra radio gear.
R-2 – 1941. Additional fuel stowage and strengthening.
R-2/Trop – 1941. Tropicalised R-2
R-3 – 1941. Minor equipment alterations. R-4 – 1942.
R-2/Trop production version.

Other variants

E – 1943. Not proceeded with.
F – 1943. Enlarged tyres for Russian winters. Not proceeded with.
H – 1943. Dual-control trainer
H-1 – 1943. Dual control, no armament
H-2 – 1944. Trainer version of H-1
H-3 – 1944. Unarmed trainer based on D-1
H-4 – 1944. Trainer
H-5 – 1944. Unarmed trainer based on D-3
H-6 – Not proceeded with
H-7 – Unarmed versions of D-7
H-8 – Unarmed version of D-8

'Super' Stuka
Ju187. Jumo 213 engine, retractable undercarriage etc, etc. Project only, not proceeded with.

Appendix II
Personnel and Equipment of a
St.G.77 Staffel, Summer 1942

A Staffel (Squadron) consisted on nine aircraft divided into three Ketten, each Kette (flight) having three aircraft.

There were nine Staffeln, totalling 81 aircraft, to a Stukagruppe (dive bomber group); with three Stukagruppen having a Stab (Staff) Flight on three aircraft; with three Gruppen to a Stukageschwader, St.G.77, and with the Stukageschwader each having its own Stab of three machines, St.G.77 would have had a total establishment aircraft strength of 94 aircraft.

The identification markings changed from code 52+ on 1 May 1939 when I. and II./St.G.165 became I. and II./St.G.77 instead. The new code for St.G.77 was S2+. Typically codes on each side of a Stuka's fuselage would read S2+AL. The letters S2 designated St.G.77; the + is the black Balkenkreuz nationality markings carried on fuselage and both surfaces of the wings, a Black Cross picked out in a white outline; A indicates the 1st aircraft of the Staffel (A = 1st, B = 2nd, C = 3rd etc) and L indicates the 3rd Squadron. The swastika symbol would be similarly painted and carried either side of the tail fin.

Staffel Ground Personnel

Establishment	Ranks
1 Staffel commander	Hauptmann
1 Officer for special purposes (Ia)	Oberleutnant
11 Pilots	3 Leutnants, 8 Oberfeldwebel
12 Radio Operator/Rear Gunners	12 Oberfeldwebel
1 Flying personnel Flight Sergeant	Oberfeldwebel
12 Flying personnel attendants	4 Feldwebel, 8 Unteroffiziere
18 Aircraft mechanics	8 Unteroffiziere, 10 Flieger
6 Aircraft engine fitters	4 Unteroffiziere, 2 Flieger
2 Aircraft electricians	2 Flieger
1 Aircraft precision engineer	1 Flieger
1 Air weapons Flight Sergeant	1 Oberfeldwebel
14 Air weapons armourers	1 Feldwebel, 4 Unteroffiziere, 9 Flieger
1 Radio Flight Sergeant	1 Oberfeldwebel
3 Radio mechanics	1 Unteroffiziere, 2 Flieger
1 Flying equipment administrator	Oberfeldwebel
2 Parachute and Safety-harness Personnel	2 Unteroffiziere
1 General Disciplinary Officer	Oberfeldwebel

1 Flight Sergeant	Oberfeldwebel
1 Accountant	Feldwebel
1 Equipment Store Administrator (Armaments and Undercarriage)	Unteroffizier
1 Issue Clerk (Clothing and Uniforms)	Unteroffizier
1 Issue Clerk (Weapons and Radio spares)	Unteroffizier
1 Cook	Unteroffizier
1 Secretary/Writer	Unteroffizier
2 Assistant Cooks	1 Unteroffizier, 1 Flieger
11 General Duties Personnel	2 Unteroffiziere, 9 Flieger
1 Sanitary Duties Sergeant	Feldwebel
1 Equipment Stores duty.	Oberfeldwebel
1 Transport Driver	Flieger
2 Armoured Radio Car Drivers	2 Flieger
24 Truck drivers	5 Unteroffiziere, 19 Flieger
2 Fuel-tanker drivers	2 Flieger

Total: 139 Officers, NCOs and men.

Spare equipment stocked for a St.G.77 Staffel, Summer 1942

9 Flimo-Tool Cases
1 Electricians' Case
1 Motor fitters' Case
1 Mechanics' workchest, large
1 Precision engineers case
36 Spades
1 Weapons' box
1 T 1 Cabin equipment spares set for Ju87 D
1 T 1 Spares set for Jumo 211 engine
1 T 2 spares set for Jumo 211 engine
1 Special toolset
1 Set equipment and ordnance (II) Regulation airframe equipment
1 Set Equipment and ordnance (II) Regulation Motor equipment
5 Fire extinguishers
10 Storm lanterns
1 Electromechanical set
1 Mixing can
2 Service chests for Airscrews
1 Medical chest
1 Large folding tent
3 Round tents
2 Rotors complete with fittings
2 Refrigerators

1 Protective shelter
1 Weapons testing case for MG17 machine guns
1 Large Workcase for Bomb-release equipment
1 Weapons Master Works case
4 Small Works cases for Weapons equipment
1 Spares case for MG17 machine guns
1 Spares case for MG81 machine guns
1 Cleaning case 38
3 Sets Command accessories
1 Barrel case for MG81 machine gun
1 Bullet-belt case for MG81 machine gun
1 Starting handle 37
1 Safe
3 Engine-changing Block and Tackles
12 Machine-gun Sights MG17
2 Quick-release gears
1 Revi Supply case (Reflex visors)
4 Revi equipments
1 Chest for Parachute and Harness Equipment

1 Workcase for Parachute and Harness equipment
1 Packing bag for Parachutes
30 Parachutes
3 Chests for Medical Equipment
2 Chests Small hand cameras (6 Stocked)
1 Fu.G. VIIc
2 Small Radio sets
1 Quartz Lens
1 Small wireless battery
1 Small Cleaning material set for Weapons
3 Stick grenades
4 Fast fuel pumps

Appendix III
Comparative ranks and equivalents of Luftwaffe and RAF personnel and units

Luftflotte: (Air Fleet – 1, 2, 3, 4, 5)
Fliegerkorps: (Flying Corps I, II, III, IV, V, VII, etc)
Geschwader: (Wing)
Gruppe: (Group)
Staffel: (Squadron) – Nine Operational and three reserve aircraft each
Kette: (Flight) – Three aircraft
Rotte: (Pair) – Two aircraft

Rank Translation and nearest British equivalent:

Flieger	=	Aircraftman
Bundfunker	=	Radio operator
Obergefreiter	=	Leading Aircraftman
Hauptgefreiter	=	Aircraftman 1st class
Unteroffizier	=	Corporal
Feldwebel	=	Sergeant
Oberfeldwebel	=	Flight Sergeant
Fahrenjunker	=	Officer Cadet
Leutnant	=	Pilot Officer
Oberleutnant	=	Flying Officer
Hauptmann	=	Flight Lieutenant
Major	=	Squadron Leader
Oberstleutnant	=	Wing Commander
Oberst	=	Group Captain
Generalmajor	=	Air Commodore
Generalleutnant	=	Air Vice Marshal
Generaloberst	=	Air Chief Marshal
Reichsmarschall	=	Marshal of the Royal Air Force

Appendix IV
The highest decorated personnel of St.G.77

RK – Ritterkreuz (Iron Cross)
KC – Knight's Cross of the Iron Cross

Amelung, Major Heinz-Günter (9-4-17, Magdeburg)
  15-7-42 RK
Andorfer, Hauptmann Acton (23-12-19, Linz, Austria)
  26-3-44 RK
Axthammer, Oberfeldwebel Erich (3-12-20, Pichlschloss, Gemeinde Mariahof-bei-Neumark, Steiermark/Austria)
  28-4-45 RK
Bauer, Oberfeldwebel Gerhardt (26-8-16, Jena/Thuringen)
  29-2-44 RK
Bauhaus, Hauptmann Gerhard (22-12-08, Brunen-bei-Wesel/Niederrh)
  25-5-42 RK
Blasig, Major Arnulf (30-12-13, Berlin). Nickname 'Blasmich'
  4-9-41 RK
Bode, Major Helmuth (15-10-07, Metz/Lothringen)
  10-10-41 RK
Brand, Hauptmann Hans-Joachim (16-5-16, Lüneburg). Nickname 'Cherry'
  5-12-43 RK
Bruck, Oberst Helmut (16-12-13, Kittlitztreben/Krs. Bunzlau)
  4-9-41 KC. 19-2-43 Oak Leaves
Bumen, Feldwebel Robert (12-10-18, Freiburg/Brsg.)
  29-10-44 RK
Burr, Oberfeldwebel Leonhard (13-3-13, Zindorf-bei-Nurnberg). Nickname 'Leo'
  30-11-41 RK
Dawedeit, Oberfeldwebel Herbert (20-5-14, Essen)
  1-11-43 KC
Dalwigk zu Lichtenfels. Major Friedrich-Karl Frhr. von (1-4-07, Torgau/Elbe). Nickname 'Kuken' (Chicken)
  21-7-40 RK posthumously
Diepold, Oberleutnant Max (1-2-21, Amberg/Opf.)
  28-3-45 RK
Fechner, Oberfeldwebel Konrad (1-11-18, Hofmeteln-bei-Schwerin)
  4-5-44 RK

Fitzner, Oberleutnant Karl (4-7-15, Düsseldorf)
    27-11-42 RK

Fritzsche, Oberleutnant Immo (16-12-18, Docklitz/Krs. Querfurt (Sachsen)
    16-4-43 RK

Gläser, Oberleutnant Alexander (4-1-14, Budingen/Hessen). Nickname 'Alex'
    7-4-45 Oak Leaves awarded personally by Göring

Goetze, Oberleutnant Manfred (5-11-20, Dresden). Nickname 'Lion of Banya
    Luka'
    19-8-44 RK

Görtler, Oberfeldwebel Horst (18-2-21, Wallroda/Krs. Dresden). Nickname
    'Macki'
    28-3-45 RK

Grewe, Oberfeldwebel Josef (9-9-08, Schuren-bei-Meschede/Westf.)
    20-7-44 RK

Griebel, Fahrerjunker-Feldwebel Osmar (21-11-19, Nurnburg)
    5-12-43 RK

Gschwendtner, Leutnant Karl-Georg (26-6-18, Wollomos-bei-Aichach/Obb.).
    Nickname 'Schorschl'
    5-2-44 RK

Günther, Fahrerjunker-Feldwebel Paul (15-7-16, Bischke/Krs. Kolmar (Posen)
    2-2-45 RK

Haidle, Oberleutnant Paul (25-8-19, Stuttgart)
    16-2-45 KC

Haker, Oberleutnant Theodor (29-12-20). Nickname 'Bubi'
    29-2-44 RK

Harang, Oberleutnant Jürgen (30-8-18, Halle/Saale)
    2-2-45 RK posthumously

Haugk, Pilot Officer Werner (29-4-12, Gelsenkirchen)
    8-8-44 RK

Heinrich, Oberfeldwebel Otto (12-9-20, Alt-Valm-bei-Neustettin)
    20-7-44 RK posthumously

Henze, Major Karl (20-1-16, Holzminden/Weser)
    15-7-42 RK. 20-5-44 Oak Leaves

Hettinger, Oberfeldwebel Franz (28-7-13, Stuttgart)
    27-7-44 KC

Hitz, Hauptmann Gunter (17-7-16, Kohlfurt-bei-Gorlitz/Schl.)
    22-11-43 RK

Honsberg, Oberfeldwebel Werner (15-2-14, Eberswalde/Mark Brandenburg).
    Nickname 'Blackberry'
    20-7-44 RK

Honnefeller, Leutnant Gunter (29-5-23, Niederbieber B. Neuwied)
    17-10-44 KC

Hüber, Oberleutnant Josef (18-7-15, Kempten/Allgau). Nickname 'Sepp'
    20-7-44 KC

Huhn, Major Kurt (1-8-12, Paaren/Osthavelland)
    17-3-43 RK

Jakob, Oberstleutnant Georg (27-3-15, Furth/Bayern)
    27-4-42 RK

30-9-44 Oak Leaves

Jauernik, Leutnant Georg. (23-11-15, Leiswitz/Oberschlesien). Nickname 'Jonny'
   27-11-42 RK

Joswig, Oberleutnant Wilhelm. (2-2-12, Klein-Zechen/Krs, Johannesburg, South Africa)
   29-2-44 KC

Kaubisch, Major Horst (2-2-12, Freital-Zaucherode/Sachsen)
   16-11-42 KC. 24-6-44 Oak Leaves.

Kieslich, Major Franz (17-3-13, Bochum) 5-1-43 KC. 10-10-44 Oak Leaves

Kilian, Oberleutnant Günter (2-4-21, Berlin)
   2-4-45 RK

Langhart, Oberleutnant Theodor (21-9-19, Graz, Austria)
   22-1-43 KC posthumously

Langkopf, Oberleutnant Paul (7-7-15, Sarstedt-bei-Hildesheim)
   19-2-43 KC

Lau, Major Lothar (30-1-13, Konigsberg, East Prussia)
   24-6-41 KC

Leicht, Major Helmut (2-11-16, Ludwigsburg/Wurtt)
   3-9-42 KC. 24-10-44 Oak Leaves posthumously

Lehmann, Hauptmann Hans-Joachim (18-8-12, Treuenbritzen/Mark Brandenburg)
   23-11-41 RK

Loymeyer, Leutnant Hans-Georg (25-3-19, Brilon/Westf.) Nickname 'Schorsch'
   6-10-44 RK

Ludigkeit, Hauptmann Günther (22-9-19, Berlin)
   26-3-44 RK

Luhr, Oberfeldwebel Hans (25-8-16, Nieder Kasbach-am-Rhein)
   29-2-44 RK

Meier, Oberfeldwebel Hans (29-3-15, Hamburg-Wandsbeck)
   9-6-44 RK posthumously

Mundt, Oberfeldwebel Ulrich (24-10-15, Berlin-Lichtenberg) Nickname 'Tex'
   25-11-44 RK

Neumüller, Leutnant Fritz (14-3-16, Herford/Westfalen)
   4-5-44 RK

Niehuus, Hauptmann Heinz (26-4-13, Hamburg)
   17-4-45 KC

Orzegowski, Leutnant Ernst (19-10-19, Hamburg)
   14-1-45 KC

Orthofer, Oberstleutnant Alfons (7-12-09, Neustadt/Donau) Nickname 'Ali'
   23-11-41 KC

Piske, Oberleutnant Herbert (22-11-21, Hamburg-Osdorf) Nickname 'Quax'
   15-3-45 RK

Plewig, Major Waldemar (6-1-11, Ostrowo, Poland)
   14-12-40 Knight's Cross was sent to him and awarded with all military honours by the commander of POW camp Shap Wells Hotel between Carlisle and Kendall.

Pressler, Oberstleutnant Gustav (13-10-12, Hamburg)

4-2-42 KC. 26-1-43 Oak Leaves.
Rabben, Oberfeldwebel Herbert (26-8-18, Oldenburg i.Oldg.)
   4-5-44 KC
Reussner, Oberfeldwebel Rudi (10-1-18, Bergen, Norway)
   29-2-44 RK
Rick, Hauptmann Kurt (26-6-18, Ebersteinburg-bei-Baden-Baden)
   3-4-43 KC posthumously
Roell, Major Werner (8-2-14, Ailly-sur-Noye, France)
   25-5-43 KC
Ruppert, Oberleutnant Hermann (8-8-15, Irbit, Siberia, Russia)
   23-11-41 KC
Sattler, Oberleutnant Hans-Karl (13-3-17, Herbstein/Oberhessen)
   16-2-42 KC
Schmidt, Leutnant Herbert (31-1-09, Nautzken/Krs. Labiau, East Prussia)
   9-6-44 RK
Schmidt, Hauptmann Otto (23-2-17, Bruhlhof/Gemeinde Wehbach/Sieg.)
   3.9.42 RK
Schönborn-Wiesentheid, Oberst Clemens Graf von (3-4-05 Munich)
   21-7-40 KC
Schutt, Oberfeldwebel Christian (3-2-17, Terkelsbull/Sudtondern)
   18-11-44 KC
Schwartzkopff, Generalmajor Günter (5-8-98, Forbach-bei-Posen) Nickname
   'Father of the Stukas'
   24-11-40 KC posthumously
Schweizer, Feldwebel Ignaz (13-6-19, Rosswangen/Wurtt) Nickname 'Natz'
   30-9-44 KC
Stifter, Leutnant Kurt (19-4-18, Vienna, Austria)
   22-1-43 KC posthumously
Stüdemann, Hauptmann Gerhard (19-6-20, Rom-bei-Parchim in Mecklenburg)
   Nickname 'Stutz'
   26-3-44 RK
   28-3-45 Oak Leaves
Trenn, Hauptmann Rudolph (22-11-17, Altefahr auf Rugen)
   25-5-43 RK posthumously
Waldhauser, Oberleutnant Johann (1-3-13, Freising/Obb)
   24-1-42 KC
Weigel, Hauptmann Rudolf (10-5-13, Ludwigshafen/Rhein)
   27-4-42 KC
Weihrauch, Oberleutnant Werner (22-8-16, Kreuzburg/Schlesien) Nickname
   'Piepel'
   19-2-43 KC
Weiss, Oberfeldwebel Adolf (15-2-17, Munich)
   29-2-44 KC
Welzel, Oberfeldwebel Heinz (28-8-16, Breslau)
   5-9-44 RK
Wosnitza, Oberfeldwebel Alois (17-11-14, Gleiwitz/Oberschlesien)
   26-3-44 KC
Zellner, Feldwebel Karl (28-9-18, Hangalzesberg/Bayr. Wald)

29-2-44 RK posthumously
Zwipf, Hauptmann Heinrich (13-1-14, Pirmasens)
  31-12-43 KC

Appendix V
Organisation and principal Commanders of Sturzkampfgeschwader 77 (St.G.77)

The Sturzkampfgeschwader 77 was the first of the Stukageschwader of the Luftwaffe, to be ready for use against Poland having the Stab and two Gruppen in action. On 18 October 1943 the Geschwader was renamed Schlachtgeschwader 77. At the same time came the previous I./Schlachtgeschwader I. and II. Gruppen of SG 77, of this Geschwader combined and became the III./SG.10. On 18 October 1943 also the Panzerjagerstaffel St.G. was formed. 1. and 10.(Pz)/SG.77 in the Geschwader combined, and, on 27 January 1944 retired after the Geschwader had been reduced. On 7 March 1944 the two 6./SG.2 were replaced. By 15 July 1942 the Geschwader had registered 30,000 (and by 1 May 1944 100,000) combat sorties. Finally, about June 1944, the Stukaschulen for training and the operational Geschwader alike converted to the FW190 and flew these fighter-bombers until the end of the war.

Commanders

1-6-39 to 14-5-40   Oberst Günter Schwartzkopff
15-5-40 to 20-7-42   Major Graf Clemens von Schönborn-Wiesentheid
25-7-42 to 12-10-42   Major Alfons Orthofer
13-10-42 to 20-2-43   Major Walter Ennecerus
20-2-43 to 15-2-45   Major Helmut Bruck
16-2-45 to 8-5-45   Oberstleutnant Manfred Mossinger

I. Gruppe:

The I. Gruppe was formed in 1936 as I./162 at Kitzingen airfield, renumbered in June 1936 as I./165; on 1-5-39 as I./St.G.77, and on 18-10-43 as I./SG.77

Commanding Officers:
1-6-39 to 13-7-40 Hauptmann Friedrich-Karl Freiherr von Dalwigk zu Lichtenfels
14-7-40 to 18-8-40   Hauptmann Meisel
28-8-40 to 19-2-43   Hauptmann Helmut Bruck
20-2-43 to 1-12-43   Major Werner Roell
1-12-43 to 1-2-45   Major Karl Henze
1-2-45 to 16-4-45   Hauptmann Hans-Joachim Brand

II. Gruppe:

The II. Gruppe was formed in 1937 at Schweinfurt as II./165, and on 1 May 1939 renamed as II./St.G.77; in 1943/44 was the Gruppe of III./SG.10, and I./SG.1 the new II./SG.77

Commanding Officers
1-6-39 to 15-5-40   Hauptmann Graf Clemens von Schönborn-Wiesentheid
15-5-40 to 8-8-40   Hauptmann Waldemar Plewig
1-7-42 to 1-4-43   Major Kurt Huhn
1-4-43 to 18-10-43   Hauptmann Helmut Leicht
2/44 to 8-5-45   Hauptmann Alexander Gläser

III. Gruppe:

At the end of the campaign in France the III. Gruppe was formed on 9 July 1940 from the II./St.G.76, renamed on 18 October as III./SG.77

Commanding Officers
9-7-40 to 25-8-42   Hauptmann Helmut Bode
26-8-42 to 1-12-42   Hauptmann Georg Jakob
1-1-43 to 19-2-45   Hauptmann Franze Kieslich
20-2-45 to 8-5-45   Hauptmann Gerhard Stüdemann

Index